His Divine Grace A. C. Bhaktivedanta Swami Prabhupāda
The Founder-Ācārya of ISKCON and greatest exponent of Kṛṣṇa consciousness in the Western world.

nama oṁ viṣṇu-pādāya kṛṣṇa-preṣṭhāya bhū-tale
śrīmate bhaktisiddhānta-sarasvatīti nāmine

Śrīla Bhaktisiddhānta Sarasvatī Gosvāmī Mahārāja
The spiritual master of
His Divine Grace A. C. Bhaktivedanta Swami Prabhupāda
and foremost scholar and devotee in the recent age.

Śrīla Gaurakiśora dāsa Bābājī Mahārāja
The spiritual master of
Śrīla Bhaktisiddhānta Sarasvatī Gosvāmī
and intimate student of
Śrīla Bhaktivinoda Ṭhākura.

Śrīla Bhaktivinoda Ṭhākura

The pioneer of the program to inundate the entire world with Kṛṣṇa consciousness.

Śrī Pañca-tattva

Lord Śrī Kṛṣṇa Caitanya,

The ideal preacher of Śrīmad Bhagavad-gītā,

surrounded by His principal associates.

Plate 1 Dhṛtarāṣṭra inquires from Sañjaya about the events of the battle. *(p.1)*

Plate 2 "O my teacher, behold the great army of the sons of Pāṇḍu."
(p.3)

Plate 3 Kṛṣṇa and Arjuna sounded their transcendental conchshells.
(p.5)

Plate 4 Kṛṣṇa and Arjuna in the midst of the two armies. *(p.9)*

Plate 5 When Arjuna saw all different grades of friends and relatives, he becam overwhelmed with compassion. *(pp.9–10)*

Plate 6 The insulting of Draupadī.

Plate 7 Bhagavān Śrī Kṛṣṇa is the Supreme Personality of Godhead. He is the Supreme Person, and His body is eternal, full of knowledge and bliss. He is the primeval Lord Govinda, the cause of all causes. *(pp.17–18)*

Plate 8 The Blessed Lord said: "The wise lament neither for the living nor the dead." *(p.21)*

Plate 9 As the embodied soul continually passes, in this body, from boyhood to youth to old age, the soul similarly passes into another body at death. Just as a person puts on new garments, giving up old ones, similarly, the soul accepts new material bodies, giving up the old and useless ones. *(p.28)*

Plate 10 The body changes, but the soul remains the same. Although there are many movie frames, when seen consecutively they appear as one picture. Similarly, although one's body is changing at every second, it appears to be the same body. *(pp.24–25)*

Plate 11 Kṛṣṇa and the living entity are seated within the same body just as two friendly birds are seated on the same tree. *(pp.28–29)*

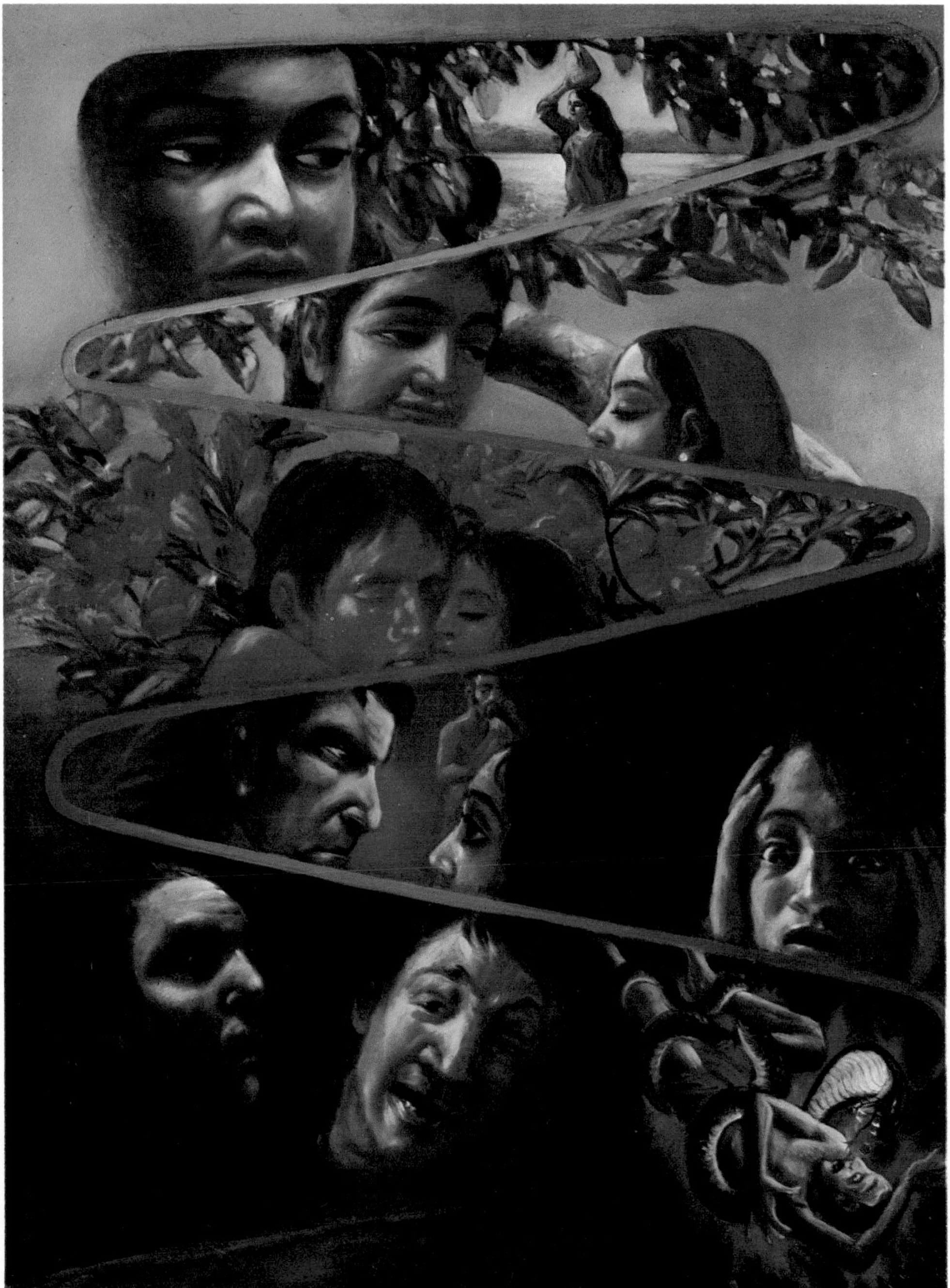

Plate 12 While contemplating the objects of the senses, a person develops attachment for them. From such attachment comes lust, then anger, illusion, bewilderment of memory and loss of intelligence, and then one falls down into the material cycle of birth and death. *(pp.39–40)*

Plate 13 In this age of Kali, people endowed with sufficient intelligence will worship Lord Śrī Caitanya Mahāprabhu, who is accompanied by His associates, by performance of the *saṅkīrtana-yajña*. (pp.48–49)

Plate 14 The demigods, being satisfied by the performance of sacrifice, supply all needs to man. *(pp.48–50)*

Plate 15 As fire is covered by smoke, as a mirror is covered by dust, or as the embryo is covered by the womb, the living entity is covered by different degrees of lust. *(p.60)*

Plate 16 The Blessed Lord first instructed this imperishable science of *yoga* to the sun-god, Vivasvān. Vivasvān instructed it to Manu, the father of mankind, and Manu in turn instructed it to Ikṣvāku. *(p.63)*

Plate 17 The Lord descends whenever there is a decline in religious principles. Although there are many transcendental forms of the Lord, they are still one and the same Supreme Personality of Godhead. *(pp.68–69)*

Plate 18 To deliver the pious and to annihilate the miscreants, as well as to re-establish the principles of religion, Lord Kṛṣṇa advents Himself millennium after millennium. *(p.69)*

Plate 19 Kṛṣṇa awards the desires of the fruitive workers, mystic *yogīs*, impersonalists, devotees in the material world, and His most fortunate, pure, unalloyed devotees who reside eternally in the spiritual world. *(pp. 73–74)*

BHAGAVAD-GĪTĀ
AS IT IS

BOOKS by
His Divine Grace A. C. Bhaktivedanta Swami Prabhupāda

Bhagavad-gītā As It Is
Śrīmad-Bhāgavatam, Cantos 1–8 (24 Vols.)
Śrī Caitanya-caritāmṛta (17 Vols.)
Teachings of Lord Caitanya
The Nectar of Devotion
The Nectar of Instruction
Śrī Īśopaniṣad
Easy Journey to Other Planets
Kṛṣṇa Consciousness: The Topmost Yoga System
Kṛṣṇa, the Supreme Personality of Godhead (3 Vols.)
Perfect Questions, Perfect Answers
Dialectic Spiritualism—A Vedic View of Western Philosophy (3 Vols.)
Transcendental Teachings of Prāhlad Mahārāja
Kṛṣṇa, the Reservoir of Pleasure
Life Comes from Life
The Perfection of Yoga
Beyond Birth and Death
On the Way to Kṛṣṇa
Rāja-vidyā: The King of Knowledge
Elevation to Kṛṣṇa Consciousness
Kṛṣṇa Consciousness: The Matchless Gift
Back to Godhead Magazine (Founder)

A complete catalog is available upon request

International Society for Krishna Consciousness
3764 Watseka Avenue
Los Angeles, California 90034

All Glory to Śrī Guru and Gaurāṅga

BHAGAVAD-GĪTĀ AS IT IS

Abridged Edition

with translations and elaborate purports

by

His Divine Grace
A.C. Bhaktivedanta Swami Prabhupāda
Founder-Ācārya of the International Society for Krishna Consciousness

THE BHAKTIVEDANTA BOOK TRUST
New York · Los Angeles · London · Bombay

Readers interested in the subject matter of this book
are invited by the International Society for Krishna Consciousness
to correspond with its Secretary.

International Society for Krishna Consciousness
3764 Watseka Avenue
Los Angeles, California 90034

Library of Congress Catalog Card Number: 75-34536
International Standard Book Number: 0-912776-80-3

First Bhaktivedanta Book Trust Printing, 1975: 350,000 copies
Second Bhaktivedanta Book Trust Printing, 1976: 500,000 copies

Printed in the United States of America

To
Śrīla Baladeva Vidyābhūṣaṇa
who presented so nicely
the "*Govinda-bhāṣya*" commentary
on
Vedānta philosophy

CONTENTS

Illustrations

The illustrations of *Bhagavad-gītā As It Is* were painted by members of the International Society for Krishna Consciousness working under the personal direction of the author, their spiritual master. In the following descriptive index, the numbers in boldface type which follow each plate number refer to the chapter and verse of the *Gītā* that the picture illustrates.

Chapter 1

Plate 1 **1.1** Dhṛtarāṣṭra is on the throne, and Sañjaya is describing what is taking place on the Battlefield of Kurukṣetra. Because of Sañjaya's mystic powers, the battlefield discourse between Kṛṣṇa and Arjuna is revealed in his heart.

Plate 2 **1.3** Droṇācārya is seated in his tent, and Duryodhana is pointing to the two armies.

Plate 3 **1.14** Kṛṣṇa blows His transcendental conchshell to herald the battle. Arjuna is in the background.

Plate 4 **1.24** The chariot of Kṛṣṇa and Arjuna is in the midst of the two armies on the Battlefield of Kurukṣetra.

Plate 5 **1.26–29** Arjuna laments upon seeing his relatives ready to oppose him in battle. Kṛṣṇa, smiling, is ready to console His friend with His transcendental teachings.

Plate 6 **1.33–35** Draupadī, the wife of the Pāṇḍava brothers (Mahārāja Yudhiṣṭhira, Arjuna, Bhīma, Sahadeva and Nakula), is being disrobed by Duryodhana and Duḥśāsana, two sons of Dhṛtarāṣṭra, after being lost to them in a gambling match. Dhṛtarāṣṭra is sitting on the throne. Kṛṣṇa is becoming Draupadī's infinite robe to save her from being seen naked by the assembly. Because of this incident and other offenses to the Pāṇḍavas, Kṛṣṇa wanted the battle to take place and the miscreants killed.

Chapter 2

Plate 7 **2.2** Śrī Kṛṣṇa, Govinda, is in the blooming beauty of youth. His two hands are adorned with a flute and jeweled ornaments, His head is bedecked with peacock feathers, His figure of beauty is tinged with the hue of blue clouds, and His unique loveliness is charming millions of Cupids.

Plate 8 **2.11** A devotee of the Lord comes upon a dead man and two other men in conditions of bodily misery. Although the body is destined to be vanquished today or tomorrow, the soul is eternal; thus the devotee understands that there is no cause for lamentation.

Plate 9 **2.13** The conditioned spirit soul is seen changing bodies from childhood to youth to old age to death and then into the womb of another mother. Verse 22 is also illustrated by this same picture. Above, a man is changing garments; below, the soul is changing bodies.

Plate 10 **2.13** When seen consecutively, the many frames on a reel of movie film appear as one picture on the screen although there are actually many different pictures. Similarly, we see a man as localized (above), but actually his body is changing at every second. All this is happening without the notice of the viewer. However, the soul within the heart (seen as a sparkling star) does not change; he remains eternally the same.

Plate 11 **2.22** The bird on the left is captivated by the fruits of the tree, while the friendly bird on the right acts as witness. Similarly, the embodied living entity enjoys or suffers the fruits of his material activities, while the friendly Supersoul acts as witness and waits for His friend to turn to Him.

Plate 12 **2.62–63** The path of the destruction of the conditioned soul's intelligence due to the dictation of the senses and mind is portrayed.

Chapter 3

Plate 13 **3.10** Lord Caitanya, wearing yellow robes, leads thousands of followers in the congregational chanting of the holy names of Śrī Kṛṣṇa. His four associates are:

a) Nityānanda Prabhu, wearing purple robes, at Lord Caitanya's immediate right.

b) Advaita Prabhu, wearing white robes, at Nityānanda's immediate right.

c) Gadādhara Paṇḍita, at Lord Caitanya's immediate left.

d) Śrīvāsa Paṇḍita, at Gadādhara's immediate left.

Plate 14 **3.12** Devotees are engaging in *saṅkīrtana-yajña.* Above the clouds are the demigods, and above them the Lord, who is pleased by the singing of His holy names. The demigods are, left to right, Candra (the moon-god), Indra (the god of rain), Vivasvān (the sun-god) and Vāyu (the god of air). At the far right is Lakṣmī, the goddess of fortune.

Plate 15 **3.38** The living entity in the center is being enveloped by fiery lust. The analogy in verse 38 is illustrated here. At the top is fire covered by smoke, symbolizing human life. At the bottom left is a mirror covered by dust, symbolizing animal life. At the bottom right is an embryo covered by the womb, symbolizing tree and plant life.

Chapter 4

Plate 16 **4.1** At the top, Kṛṣṇa teaches the science of *Bhagavad-gītā* to Vivasvān, the sun-god. Below, Vivasvān teaches his son, Manu, and in the circle at the right, Manu teaches his son, Ikṣvāku.

Plate 17 **4.7** In the center square, Kṛṣṇa is shown in His original two-handed form, holding a flute. Surrounding Him are ten of His eternal incarnations, pictured in the order in which they appear in the material world, beginning clockwise from the lower left-hand corner.

a) Matsya, the fish incarnation, is saving the *Vedas.*

b) Kūrma, the tortoise incarnation, is holding the Mandara hill on His back.

c) Varāha, the boar incarnation, is fighting with the demon Hiraṇyākṣa.

d) Nṛsiṁhadeva, the lion incarnation, is killing the demon Hiraṇyakaśipu.

e) Vāmanadeva, the dwarf incarnation, is begging some land from King Bali.

f) Paraśurāma is killing the demoniac *kṣatriyas.*

g) Lord Rāmacandra is going off into exile with His wife, Sītā, and brother, Lakṣmaṇa.

h) Kṛṣṇa is lifting Govardhana Hill, and beside Him is His brother, Balarāma.

i) Lord Buddha.

j) Lord Kalki is riding on His horse, killing all the demons and thus liberating them.

Plate 18 4.8 Kṛṣṇa's demoniac uncle, Kaṁsa, is being killed by the Lord. Balarāma, Kṛṣṇa's brother, is standing on Kṛṣṇa's right. Behind Kṛṣṇa are His parents, Devakī and Vasudeva, who were imprisoned by Kaṁsa but are now being freed by their son. This scene takes place in Kaṁsa's wrestling arena in Mathurā province.

Plate 19 4.11 At the top, Kṛṣṇa is dancing with His purest devotees as a lover. On the lotus petals the Lord is reciprocating with His devotees as a son, as a friend and as a master. Below left, a devotee in the material world is associating with Kṛṣṇa personally by painting His transcendental form. Next, an impersonalist, by his meditation, is merging with the *brahmajyoti,* the spiritual effulgence emanating from the Lord's body. On the right, a mystic *yogī* is walking on the water. On the far right, a fruitive worker is receiving the fruits of his labor.

Chapter 5

Plate 20 5.4–6 Above, a devotee is engaged in various devotional activities for the Deities (authorized incarnations of the Lord, who come in this form to accept our service). Below, a *sāṅkhya-yogī* engages in the analytical study of matter and spirit. After some time he realizes the Lord (the forms of Rādhā and Kṛṣṇa include all other forms of the Lord) within his heart, and then engages in devotional service. The end is the same—devotional service.

Plate 21 **5.18** A sage sees the Supersoul accompanying the sparklike individual soul in each body.

Chapter 6

Plate 22 **6.11–14** The goal of *yoga* is Viṣṇu, residing in the *yogī's* heart.

Plate 23 **6.24** The little sparrow is trying to drink up the ocean in order to retrieve her eggs. Because of her determination, Lord Viṣṇu has sent Garuḍa, who is standing behind her, to threaten the ocean into giving up the eggs.

Plate 24 **6.34** The chariot of the body. The five horses represent the five senses (tongue, eyes, ears, nose and skin). The reins, the driving instrument, symbolize the mind, the driver is the intelligence, and the passenger is the spirit soul.

Plate 25 **6.47** Śyāmasundara, the object of the ideal *yogī's* meditation.

Chapter 7

Plate 26 **7.4–5** The material universe of earth, water, fire, air, and ether is represented by the body. The subtle body—mind, intelligence and false ego—is represented by the red dot on the forehead. The soul, accompanied by the Supersoul, is seated in the heart of the gross body. The material universe is sustained by spirit soul.

Plate 27 **7.4** While Mahā-Viṣṇu, an expansion of Kṛṣṇa, sleeps within the Causal Ocean, He breathes out innumerable universes, and a further expansion, Garbhodakaśāyī Viṣṇu, enters into each universe.

Plate 28 **7.15–16** At the top, Lakṣmī-Nārāyaṇa are shown in the Lord's transcendental abode. Below are four kinds of miscreants who do not surrender to God and four kinds of pious men who turn to Him in devotional service.

Plate 29 **7.22–23** Above is Lord Viṣṇu, who empowers the demigods to bestow their benedictions on their worshipers. Below left, a worshiper of goddess Umā, the wife of Lord Śiva, is receiving the benediction of a wife. In the middle, the worshiper of Sūrya, the sun-god, is receiving the benediction of good health, and on the right, the worshiper of goddess Sarasvatī, the mother of learning, is receiving the benediction of advancement of material knowledge.

Chapter 8

Plate 30 **8.21** Kṛṣṇa brings His thousands of *surabhi* cows back home from the fields at the end of the day.

Chapter 9

Plate 31 **9.11** The fools mock the humanlike form of Lord Kṛṣṇa, but the devotee offers his obeisances. Behind Kṛṣṇa are Mahā-Viṣṇu, Garbhodakaśāyī Viṣṇu and the entire cosmic manifestation—all working under Kṛṣṇa's direction.

Plate 32 **9.26** The devotee is offering fruits and flowers to the *arcā-vigraha* Deity incarnation of the Lord.

Chapter 10

Plate 33 **10.12–13** Arjuna offers prayers to Kṛṣṇa.

Plate 34 **10.41** A sampling of Kṛṣṇa's infinite manifestations, both in the spiritual and material worlds. Outer cirlce, clockwise (beginning from the upper left-hand corner): Indra carrying the thunderbolt, the Himalayas, Lord Śiva with the Ganges River in his hair, the moon, the horse Ucchaiḥśravā, the transcendental *om*, Kapila, Rāma, flower-bearing Spring, *kāmadhuk*, Arjuna, Vyāsadeva, Prahlāda, the shark, Vāsuki, Skanda, Varuṇa, Yamarāja, the lion, Kuvera, Agni and Airāvata. Inner circle, clockwise (beginning from four-headed Lord Brahmā sitting on the lotus flower): Brahmā, Nārada, Garuḍa, the sun, the ocean, Lord Viṣṇu, Ananta, and the chanting of the holy names—Hare Kṛṣṇa, Hare Kṛṣṇa, Kṛṣṇa Kṛṣṇa, Hare Hare/ Hare Rāma, Hare Rāma, Rāma Rāma, Hare Hare.

Chapter 11

Plate 35 **11.8** Kṛṣṇa is running on the bank of the Yamunā River in Vṛndāvana, along with His elder brother Balarāma, His cowherd boyfriends and His *surabhi* cows.

Plate 36 **11.9–13** Kṛṣṇa's universal form is displayed to Arjuna. The Lord, however, does not lose His original eternal identity. He remains seated on the chariot with Arjuna.

Plate 37 **11.50** After showing Arjuna His universal form, Kṛṣṇa shows him His four-handed Nārāyaṇa form in which He presides over all the spiritual planets. Then He changes to His two-handed form to demonstrate that He is the source of the universe and the source of Nārāyaṇa.

Chapter 12

Plate 38 **12.6–7** Kṛṣṇa is riding on His feathered carrier. Garuḍa, toward His devotee to lift him out of the ocean of birth and death.

Plate 39 **13.15** The Supreme Lord is situated in the heart of every living being as the four-handed Supersoul. He is shown here holding the four symbols of Godhead—the lotus, wheel, conch and club.

Chapter 14

Plate 40 **14.14;15,18** Life in the higher planetary system. the society of human beings and the animal kindgom are portrayed.

Chapter 15

Plate 41 **15.1–3** Śrī Kṛṣṇa and His eternal consort, Śrīmatī Rādhārāṇī, are shown in Their eternal abode, Goloka Vṛndāvana. The upside-down tree below Them is the banyan tree, representing the material world, which is a perverted reflection of the spiritual world. The demigods are on the top branches, the human beings are on the middle branches, and the animals are on the lower branches. On the right, a man is disentangling himself from the tree by cutting it with the weapon of detachment.

Plate 42 **15.6** The huge lotus is the original spiritual planet, Goloka Vṛndāvana, the abode of Śrī Śrī Rādhā-Kṛṣṇa. The spiritual effulgence around this planet is the *brahmajyoti,* which is the ultimate goal of the impersonalists. Within the unlimited *brahmajyoti* are innumerable spiritual planets which are dominated by plenary expansions of Lord Kṛṣṇa and inhabited by ever-liberated living beings. Sometimes a spiritual cloud overtakes a corner of the spiritual sky, and the covered portion is called *mahat-tattva,* or the material sky. The Lord, as Mahā-Viṣṇu, lies down in the water, called the Causal Ocean, within the *mahat-tattva.* While Lord Viṣṇu sleeps, innumerable universes generate from His breathing and float in the Causal Ocean. Mahā-Viṣṇu enters each universe as Garbhodakaśāyī Viṣṇu and lies in the Garbha Ocean on the serpentine Śeṣa incarnation. From His navel a lotus stem sprouts, and on the lotus, Brahmā, the lord of the universe, is born. Brahmā creates all the living beings in different shapes, in terms of their desires, within the universe. He also creates the sun, moon and other demigods.

Plate 43 **15.8** Top section: On the left, a boy is dancing before the Deities of Śrī Śrī Rādhā-Kṛṣṇa; the result of such devotional consciousness is shown on the right, where he is dancing with Kṛṣṇa as a playmate in the Lord's spiritual abode. Second section: On the left a man is offering charity to a *brāhmaṇa;* on the right he has taken the body of a demigod and is enjoying heavenly delights. Third section: A man is eating meat and other abominable foods; in his next life he is seen in the body of a hog who eats anything and everything. Bottom section: A man is approaching a woman with lust; this bestial consciousness carries him to a dog's body.

Chapter 16

Plate 44 **16.5** Two men (standing where the stairway makes its turn) are being offered both liberation and bondage. One man looks upward, following the spiritual master, who points toward Śrī Śrī Rādhā-Kṛṣṇa. The other man embraces the demoniac qualities by accepting the garland offered by Māyā, Kṛṣṇa's illusory energy. Drawn by ropes which are held by the personifications of lust, greed and anger, he follows her down the steps. At the bottom he is reaching for *māyā,* and gliding toward hell.

Plate 45 **16.10–18** A sample of the demoniac qualities is illustrated here.

Chapter 17

Plate 46 **17.4** On the top, three demigods, Vivasvān, Lord Brahmā and Lord Śiva, are being worshiped by their devotees. Just below, a man is worshiping a famous mundane personality. At the bottom, women are worshiping a tree which is inhabited by a ghost, and another person is worshiping the tomb of a dead man.

Plate 47 **17.8–10** Above: A devotee takes foods in the mode of goodness, after offering them to the Supreme Personality of Godhead. Lower left: Foods in the mode of passion, which cause pain, distress, and disease, are shown. Lower right: Food cooked more than three hours before being eaten, which is tasteless, stale, putrid, decomposed and unclean, is food liked by people in the mode of ignorance.

Chapter 18

Plate 48 **18.13–14** For anything one does there must be some activity; that is the endeavor, the energy employed. The place must be favorable, the activities must be authorized, the doer (the man who is acting) must be expert, the instruments must be fit, and the help from the Supersoul must be adequate. These are the five factors for action.

Here a man is conducting business. If he goes to the marketplace it will be very nice, since there are so many customers. Similarly, one looking for spiritual life goes to where there are devotees to associate with them. One must go to a particular type of place for a particular type of activity, and the person acting must be well versed, or expert, just like an expert salesman whose method of business is bona fide. The senses must be in order, to guard against cheating, hear offers, etc. Above all is the help from Supersoul, who dictates in such a way that everything is successful, spiritually or materially. Among the five factors portrayed here, the endeavor is the business which is being conducted.

Plate 49 **18.41–46** While engaged in their prescribed duties, a *brāhmaṇa* (above left), a *kṣatriya* (above right), a *vaiśya* (below left) and a *śūdra* (below right), representatives of the four social orders (*varṇas*) are thinking of Lord Kṛṣṇa and offering Him the results of their work.

Plate 50 **18.65** Gopāla Kṛṣṇa, the beautiful original form of the Lord.

Plate 51 **18.78** Arjuna's illusion is now gone, and he is acting according to Kṛṣṇa's instructions. Kṛṣṇa, the Lord of countless universes, is driving the chariot of Arjuna.

Introduction

Bhagavad-gītā is also known as *Gītopaniṣad.* It is the essence of Vedic knowledge and one of the most important *Upaniṣads* in Vedic literature.

There are many commentaries on *Bhagavad-gītā,* and the necessity for another should be explained in the following way. An American lady asked me to recommend an English edition of *Bhagavad-gītā* which she could read. I was unable to do so in good conscience. Of course, there are many translations, but of those I have seen—not only in America, but also in India—none can be said to be authoritative because in almost every one of them the author has expressed his personal opinion through the commentaries, without touching the spirit of *Bhagavad-gītā* as it is.

The spirit of *Bhagavad-gītā* is mentioned in the *Gītā* itself. It is like this: if we want to take a particular medicine, then we have to follow the directions written on the label of the bottle. We cannot take the medicine according to our own directions or the directions of a friend not in knowledge of this medicine. We must follow the directions on the label or the directions of our physician. *Bhagavad-gītā* also should be accepted as it is directed by the speaker himself. The speaker is Lord Śrī Kṛṣṇa. He is mentioned on every page as the Supreme Personality of Godhead, or Bhagavān. Bhagavān sometimes means any powerful person or demigod, but here it means Kṛṣṇa. This is confirmed by all the great teachers, including Śaṅkarācārya and Śrī Caitanya Mahāprabhu. In India there are many authorities on Vedic knowledge, and they have virtually all accepted Śrī Kṛṣṇa as the Supreme Personality of Godhead. We should therefore accept *Bhagavad-gītā* as it is directed by the Supreme Personality of Godhead Himself.

Now, in the Fourth Chapter, the Lord tells Arjuna that the *yoga* system of *Bhagavad-gītā* was first spoken to the sun-god:

> The Blessed Lord said: I instructed this imperishable science of *yoga* to the sun-god, Vivasvān, and Vivasvān instructed it to Manu, the father of mankind, and Manu in turn instructed it to Ikṣvāku. This supreme science was thus received through the chain of disciplic succession, and the saintly kings understood it in that way. But in the course of time the succession was broken, and therefore the science, as it is, appears to be lost.

Arjuna was neither a great scholar nor a Vedāntist, but a great soldier. A soldier is not supposed to be scholarly, and so Arjuna was selected to understand *Bhagavad-gītā* because of one qualification only: he was a devotee of the Lord. This indicates that *Bhagavad-gītā* is especially meant for the devotee of the Lord.

There are three kinds of transcendentalists: the *yogī*, the impersonalist, and the *bhakta*, or devotee. Kṛṣṇa says to Arjuna, "I am making you the first man of the disciplic succession. The old succession has been broken. I wish to reestablish the line of teaching which was passed down from the sun-god. So you become the authority of *Bhagavad-gītā.*" *Bhagavad-gītā* is directed to the devotee of the Lord, who is directly in touch with the Lord as a friend. To learn *Bhagavad-gītā*, one should be, like Arjuna, a devotee having a direct relationship with the Lord. This is more helpful than *yoga* or impersonal philosophical speculation.

A devotee can be in relationship with the Lord in five different ways:

1. He may have a passive relationship;
2. He may have an active relationship;
3. He may be in friendship;
4. He may have the relationship of a parent;
5. He may have the relationship of a conjugal lover of the Lord.

Arjuna was a devotee in relationship with the Lord as a friend. This friendship is different from friendship in the mundane world. This kind of friendship is transcendental. Everyone has some relationship with the Lord. Unfortunately, in our present status, we have forgotten that eternal tie. Yet each of the millions upon millions of living beings has its particular relationship. By the process of service one can revive one's original status with the Lord.

Now, Arjuna was a devotee and he was in touch with the Supreme Lord in friendship. Thus, *Bhagavad-gītā* was explained to him. How he accepted it should be noted. This is mentioned in the Tenth Chapter. After hearing *Bhagavad-gītā* from the Lord, Arjuna accepted Kṛṣṇa as the Supreme Brahman. Every living being is Brahman, or spirit, but the supreme living being is the Supreme Brahman. Arjuna accepted Kṛṣṇa as pure, free from all material contamination, as the supreme enjoyer, the foremost person, the Supreme Personality of Godhead, who is unborn and is the greatest. Now, one may say that since Kṛṣṇa and Arjuna were friends, Arjuna was only saying these things to his friend. But Arjuna mentions that Kṛṣṇa is accepted as the Supreme Personality of Godhead not only by him but by Nārada, Vyāsa, and numerous other great persons.

Therefore, Arjuna says, "Whatever You have spoken to me, I accept as perfect. Your personality is very difficult to understand. You cannot be known even by the demigods." This means that even persons greater than human beings cannot know Kṛṣṇa. How, then, can a human being know Kṛṣṇa unless he is a devotee?

In studying *Bhagavad-gītā*, one should not think that he is the equal of Kṛṣṇa. Kṛṣṇa is the Supreme Personality of Godhead. One who wants to understand *Bhagavad-gītā* should accept Kṛṣṇa as the Supreme Personality of Godhead. Otherwise it is very hard to understand, and it becomes a great mystery.

Bhagavad-gītā is meant to deliver one from the nescience of material entanglement. Everyone is in difficulty, just as Arjuna was on the Battlefield of Kurukṣetra. Not only Arjuna, but each of us is full of anxieties because of this material entanglement. Our existence is eternal, but somehow we are put into this position which is *asat. Asat* means unreal.

Unless one is inquiring as to why he is suffering, he is not a perfect human being. Humanity begins when this inquiry is awakened in the mind. Every activity of the human being is said to be a failure unless this inquiry is present. One should ask, "Where am I from? Where am I going? Why am I here?" When these inquiries are awakened in the mind of a sane human being, then he can understand *Bhagavad-gītā*. He must also have respect for the Supreme Personality of Godhead. Kṛṣṇa comes here just to establish the real work of life, which man forgets. Out of many, many human beings, *Bhagavad-gītā* is directed to the one who seeks to understand his position. The Lord has great mercy for human beings. Therefore, He spoke *Bhagavad-gītā* to Arjuna to enlighten him. Arjuna was actually above all such ignorance, but he was put into ignorance on the Battlefield of Kurukṣetra just to ask what life was all about, so that our mission of human life could be perfected.

It is the preliminary study of the science of God which is explained here. The first question is: What is the cause? Next: What is the constitutional position of the living entities in respect to the controller? Living entities are not controllers. If I say, "I am not controlled, I am free," I do not speak well for my sanity. In this conditioned state of life, at any rate, we are all controlled. Next we may consider *prakṛti*, or nature. Then time—the duration of the existence or manifestation of this created universe. Then *karma*, or activity. The living beings are all engaged in different activities. All cosmic manifestation is engaged in activity.

So, we have to learn from *Bhagavad-gītā* what God is. What is the nature of the living entity? Its relationship with the supreme controller? What is *prakṛti*, the cosmic manifestation? What is the control of time? And what are the activities of the living entities?

In *Bhagavad-gītā* it is established that the Supreme, or Kṛṣṇa, or Brahman, the supreme controller—whatever name you like—is greatest of all. The living beings are controlled. The Lord has control over universal affairs—the material nature. Material nature is not independent. It is working under the direction of the Supreme Lord. When we see wonderful things happening, we should know that behind these manifestations is a controller. Matter belongs to the inferior nature, or *prakṛti;* and the living entities are explained as being of the superior nature. *Prakṛti* means "who is controlled." *Prakṛti* is female. A husband controls the activities of his wife. *Prakṛti* is also subordinate, predominated. The Lord, the Supreme Personality of Godhead, is the predominator, and *prakṛti*, the living entities and material nature, is predominated over. So according to *Bhagavad-gītā*, the living entities, although part and parcel of the Supreme, are taken as *prakṛti.* It is clearly mentioned in the Seventh Chapter of *Bhagavad-gītā* that material nature is *prakṛti* and that the living entities are also *prakṛti.* The constitution of the material, or inferior, *prakṛti* is divided into three modes: the mode of goodness, the mode of passion, and the mode of ignorance. Above these modes is eternal time. By the combinations of these modes and the control of eternal time, the activities, called *karma*, come into being. These activities have been going on from time immemorial, and we are suffering from—or enjoying—the fruits of these activities, just as in the present life we enjoy the fruits of our activities. It is as though I am a businessman who has worked very hard and intelligently and has amassed a large bank balance. I am the enjoyer of the fruits of my activities. Again, if I open a business with a large amount of money and lose it all, I am the sufferer. Similarly, in the field of life, we enjoy the different fruits of our work. Now, these things—the Supreme, the living entities, *prakṛti* (nature), time and *karma*—are explained in *Bhagavad-gītā.*

Of these five, the Lord, time, *prakṛti* and the living entity are permanent and eternal. The manifestations of *prakṛti* are temporary, but not false, as some philosophers say. According to the philosophy of Kṛṣṇa consciousness, the manifestations are quite real, but temporary. They are like the clouds which appear during the rainy season but disappear during the dry season. These manifestations occur at certain intervals, and then they disappear, and the vegetation dries up. Nevertheless, this process of nature is working eternally.

Material nature is separated energy of the Supreme Lord. The living entities are also energy of the Lord, but they are not separated. They are eternally related to the Lord. So, the Lord, nature, the entity and time are all eternal. *Karma* is not eternal. The effects of *karma* may be old, and we may be suffering from the results of activity performed in time immemorial, but we are able to change our activities. We simply do not know which activities will give us release from these material entanglements. This is explained in *Bhagavad-gītā.*

The position of God is that of supreme consciousness. The entities, being parts and parcels, are also consciousness. The entity is *prakṛti,* or nature, and so also is material energy; but the living entities are conscious, and matter is not. Therefore, the entity is called the higher energy. But the living being is never supremely conscious at any stage. The supreme consciousness, explained in *Bhagavad-gītā* as the Lord, is conscious, and the living beings are conscious: the entity of his limited body, and the Lord infinitely. The Lord lives in the heart of every being. Therefore, He has the consciousness of all living entities.

The Supersoul is living in each heart as the controller. He is giving directions to act as He desires. The living entity, however, forgets what to do. He determines to act in one way, then becomes entangled in his own actions and reactions, and achieves only frustration. When he gives up one body for another, as one changes a dress, the reactions of his past activities remain with him, determining his next birth. Actions can be changed when a living being is in goodness and, in that state of sanity, chooses to end his entanglement.

So of the five items, all are eternal except *karma*. Now, the entity's consciousness and the Lord's consciousness are both transcendental. They are not generated by association with matter. The theory that some material combination can generate consciousness is rejected in *Bhagavad-gītā*. Just as light may be reflected according to the color of glass, consciousness is reflected in the material world. But it does not depend upon matter for its existence.

The supreme consciousness is different from the consciousness of the living entity in this way: the Supreme Lord says that when He descends into the material world, His consciousness is not materially affected. If He had been contaminated by contact with matter, He could not have spoken *Bhagavad-gītā*. However, we living entities are contaminated by the material world. *Bhagavad-gītā* teaches that we must purify our activities in order to draw our consciousness back from that material entanglement. This purification of activity is called *bhakti*, or devotional service. This means that although devotees' activities appear to be ordinary, they are actually purified. One may appear to work like an ordinary man, but the activities of a devotee of the Lord are not contaminated by the three modes.

When our consciousness is contaminated by matter, this is called our conditioned state. The false ego is the belief that one is the product of matter. One who is absorbed in this bodily conception, as Arjuna was, must get free from it. This is preliminary for one who wants liberation. Freedom from material consciousness is called *mukti*. In *Śrīmad-Bhāgavatam*, also, *mukti* is used to mean liberation from material concepts, and a return to pure consciousness. The whole aim of *Bhagavad-gītā* is to teach us to reach this state of pure consciousness. On the last page of *Bhagavad-gītā*, Kṛṣṇa asks Arjuna if he is now in purified consciousness. And this implies action in accordance with the directions of the Lord.

So, consciousness is there, but because we are only parts, we tend to be affected by the modes of nature. That is the difference between the individual living entities and the Supreme Lord. In contamination, consciousness says, "I am the Lord. I am the enjoyer." Every material being thinks this. Consciousness has two psychic divisions: One says, "I am the creator," and the other says, "I am the enjoyer." Actually, the Lord is the creator and the enjoyer. The entity cooperates like a part in a machine. In the body, for example, there are hands, legs, eyes, etc. But these parts are not the enjoyers. The stomach is the enjoyer. All the parts of the body are engaged in satisfying the stomach. All food should be given to the stomach. You can become healthy throughout your entire body when the parts of the body cooperate with the stomach. Similarly, the Lord is the enjoyer, and we living beings have only to cooperate with Him. If the fingers try to enjoy the food, they are unable. They must give the food to the stomach in order to receive the benefit of it.

The central figure in existence is the Supreme Lord. The entities, by cooperation, can enjoy. If a master is satisfied, his servants are also satisfied, of course. The entities have this tendency to create and enjoy because the Lord has it, and the entities are His parts and parcels.

We find in *Bhagavad-gītā* that the Lord, the entities, manifestation, time and action are completely explained. Taken together, this complete whole is called the Absolute Truth, Śrī Kṛṣṇa. The impersonal Brahman is also subordinate to the Complete Person. It is explicitly explained in the *Brahma-sūtra* as being like the rays of the sun emanating from the sun disc. Brahman realization of the Absolute Truth is therefore incomplete. The Supreme Personality is above Brahman. The Supreme Personality of Godhead is called *sat-cit-ānanda.*

Brahman realization is realization of His *sat,* or eternal, feature. Supersoul realization is realization of His *sat-cit* aspect—eternity and knowledge. But realization of the Personality of Godhead, Śrī Kṛṣṇa, is realization of all features—*sat-cit-ānanda* (eternity, knowledge and bliss)—in full *vigraha,* or form. The Lord has form. He is a transcendental person. This is confirmed in all Vedic literature. Just as we are persons, so is the ultimate truth. Realization of the Supreme Personality of Godhead is realization of all features of the Absolute Truth. The complete whole personality must have all that we see and all that we do not see.

This phenomenal world is complete by itself. The twenty-four elements of which this manifestation is comprised are complete in this universe. No outside energy is needed. When the time comes, the universe will be annihilated by the complete arrangement of the complete. Small completes exist in the whole complete. Incomplete knowledge results from misunderstanding of the complete Absolute Truth.

Bhagavad-gītā is complete. The Vedic knowledge is infallible. Here is an example of how the Hindus accept Vedic knowledge as complete. Cow dung is sacred, according to Vedic scripture. If one touches the dung of an animal, he must bathe his whole body, and yet cow dung can purify an impure place or person, according to Vedic scripture. This seems contradictory, but because it is a Vedic injunction, we accept it, and by that acceptance we make no mistake. It has been found by modern chemists that cow dung is a composition of antiseptic properties.

Vedic knowledge is complete, for it is above all doubts or errors. And *Bhagavad-gītā* is the essence of all Vedic knowledge. Vedic knowledge comes down from higher sources. It is not like our material independent research work, which is imperfect. We must receive this knowledge from the spiritual master, through the disciplic succession, which began with the Lord Himself.

Just as Arjuna accepted *Bhagavad-gītā* without any cutting, so we too must accept *Bhagavad-gītā* without any cutting, interpretation or whimsy. We should accept it as perfect knowledge, spoken by the Lord Himself. Only the Lord could have given this infallible knowledge. A living entity would not be able to.

A living being in the mundane world has four defects:

1. He is sure to commit mistakes;
2. He is sure to be illusioned;
3. He has a tendency to cheat;
4. His senses are imperfect.

With these four defects, one cannot offer perfect information. But Vedic knowledge was imparted by God in the heart of Brahmā, the first living being in our universe, who passed it down through his sons and disciples.

Except for the Lord, no one is the proprietor of anything. The Lord is the original creator. He is the creator of Brahmā, the original being in our universe. Therefore, we should accept things given to us by the Lord as our allotment. Arjuna had decided not to fight. He told the Lord that he could not enjoy the kingdom if he killed his relatives to obtain it. This was due to his bodily concept of himself, and thus to his relationships with uncles, brothers, nephews, and so forth, all of which pertain to the body. But, finally, Arjuna agreed to work for the Lord's enjoyment. We should not act like ordinary animals. Human life is meant for something else. Vedic literature is meant for human beings, not for animals. An animal can kill without sin because he is bound by the modes of nature. But if a man kills, he is responsible. He has a choice in his actions.

In *Bhagavad-gītā* activities are explained as determined by the three modes of nature. Thus there are actions performed in ignorance, actions performed in passion, and actions performed in goodness. There are also three kinds of eatables: food eaten in ignorance, in passion, and in goodness. These are clearly described.

Therefore, if we properly follow the instructions in *Bhagavad-gītā*, our lives will be purified, and we will reach our ultimate destination. This destination is also explained in *Bhagavad-gītā:*

Beyond this material sky is a spiritual sky. The material sky is temporary, and at the end of this universe it will be annihilated. That is the law of material nature. But there is another nature, which is eternal. The soul is eternal just as the Lord is eternal. We have an intimate relationship with the Lord, and we are qualitatively equal to the Lord. The transcendental abode is also eternal. And the association of the Lord and the living entities in the transcendental abode is the ultimate aim of human life.

The Lord is so kind to the living entities because the living entities all have a claim to being sons of the Lord. The Lord says that of every type of living being, whatever it may be, He is the father. The Lord wishes to reclaim all these souls, to have them back in the eternal sky. The entities can be restored to the eternal sky once they are free of illusion. So He comes Himself, in different incarnations, or else He sends His confidential servants as son or as teachers, to reclaim the conditioned souls. This reclaiming is no sectarian religious process. It is the eternal function of the eternal living entities in relationship with the eternal Lord.

Sanātana-dharma means the eternal religion. This word "eternal" is explained as meaning something without beginning and without end. We must accept it like this. The word "religion" is somewhat different from the idea of *sanātana-dharma.* It means faith, and faith may change from one object to another. But *sanātana-dharma* means "that which cannot be changed." Liquidity cannot be taken from water. Heat cannot be taken from fire. Similarly, *sanātana-dharma* cannot be taken from the living entities. We must find out the eternal function of the eternal living entities in order to know what *sanātana-dharma* is. Rāmānujācārya says this has no beginning and no end. Some may feel that this is a somewhat sectarian concept, but if we look deeper, we will see that *sanātana-dharma* is the business of all the people of the world—nay, of all the living entities in the universe.

Now a particular religious faith may have some beginning in the history of human society, but *sanātana-dharma* lies outside of history, for it belongs to the living beings, who have no birth and who never die, who continue to live after the destruction of the material body, just as they lived before its formation.

Let us try to understand this eternal religion from the Sanskrit word root for *dharma*. This word root, *dhṛ*, means "to sustain." Therefore, *dharma* is that quality which remains always and which cannot be taken away. When we speak of fire, it is concluded that light and heat will be there. Otherwise we cannot call it fire. In a similar way, we must find the constant companion of the living being. That eternal part or quality is his religion.

When Sanātana Gosvāmī asked Lord Caitanya Mahāprabhu about *svarūpa*, or the real constitution of the living being, the Lord replied that the real constitution of the entity is to render service to the Lord. Extending this, we see that one being serves another living being in some capacity and thus enjoys its life. An animal serves a man, a friend serves his friend, mother serves child, husband serves wife, Mr. A serves Mr. B, Mr. B serves Mr. C, and so on. There is no exception to service in the society of living beings. The politician convinces the voter of his capacity for service and thus gets his job. The artisan serves the merchant; the store owner serves his customer. In fact, no living being is exempted from rendering service to others. Service, then, is a constant companion of the living being, and so we may conclude that rendering service is the eternal religion of the eternal living entity.

When a man claims allegiance to some designated faith or sect, such as Hinduism, Buddhism, Islam or Christianity, this is not eternal. Such faiths can be changed. The Muslim may become a Christian, or the Christian may become a Hindu. Such changeable faith, therefore, is not religion. However, if one be Hindu, Muslim, or Christian, one is always a servant. So the particular faith is not the religion; service is the religion.

We are in a relationship of service to the Supreme Lord. He is the enjoyer, and we are His servants. We are created for His enjoyment, and if we accept that position, it makes us happy. Going back to our earlier example, fingers cannot be independently happy without the cooperation of the stomach. Similarly, the living entity cannot be happy without rendering service to the Supreme Lord.

Worship of demigods is not approved in *Bhagavad-gītā* because in the Seventh Chapter, twenty-eighth verse, the Lord says, "Only those who are cast adrift by lust worship the demigods and not the Lord."

Now, when we speak of Kṛṣṇa, we should remember that this is not a sectarian name. Kṛṣṇa means "all pleasure." Kṛṣṇa, the Supreme Lord, is the reservoir of pleasure. Our consciousness seeks happiness because we are part and parcel of the Lord. The Lord is always happy, and if we dovetail our activities with His, we will partake of His happiness.

The Lord incarnates in order to show us His joyous nature and pastimes. When Kṛṣṇa was at Vṛndāvana, His activities with His friends the cowherd boys and His girl friends, and all His other pastimes, were full of happiness. The whole population of Vṛndāvana was mad after Him. At this time, He even restricted His father from worshiping the demigods, to show us that no one need worship any god but Him.

The purpose of human life is to return to the abode of the Lord. This eternal sky is described in *Bhagavad-gītā*, in the Eighth Chapter, verses nineteen and twenty. We have a material concept of the sky, with the sun, stars, moon, etc. But the Lord says that in the eternal sky there is no need of sun or moon, nor of fire or electricity, because the spiritual sky is already illuminated by the *brahmajyoti*, the rays of the Supreme Lord. The *brahmajyoti* is in the spiritual sky, wherein the planets are named the Vaikuṇṭhas and Goloka. The Lord resides eternally in His supreme abode, but He can be approached from here also.

The Lord comes to manifest His real form, *sat-cid-ānanda-vigraha*, so that we don't have to imagine what He is like. However, although the Lord comes among us and plays with us like a human being, we should not think that He is one of us. It is because of His omnipotence that He can come among us and show us His pastimes.

There are innumerable planets in the *brahmajyoti*, just as there are in the material sky, but all these planets are spiritual, not material. The Lord says that anyone who can approach the spiritual sky need not return to this material sky. In the material sky, even if we live on the highest planet, which is called Brahmaloka, we must still suffer the miseries of material existence. These miseries are four: birth, death, disease and old age. No material being is free of them.

The Lord says that the living entities are traveling from one planet to another. We need not rely upon mechanical arrangements to go to other planets. For anyone who wants to go to another planet, such as the moon, *Bhagavad-gītā* instructs that there is a simple formula—even to go to the highest planet. If we practice the process of worshiping the particular demigod of the particular planet, we can go there.

> Those whose minds are distorted by material desires surrender unto demigods and follow the particular rules and regulations of worship according to their own natures. I [Kṛṣṇa] am seated in everyone's heart as the Supersoul. As soon as one desires to worship demigods, I make his faith steady so that he can devote himself to that particular deity. Endowed with such a faith, he seeks favors of that demigod and obtains his desires—but in actuality these benefits are bestowed by Me alone. Men of small intelligence worship the demigods, and their fruits are limited and temporary. Those who worship the demigods go to the planets of the demigods, but My devotees reach My supreme abode.

In this way, we can go to the sun, the moon, or any other planet. However, *Bhagavad-gītā* advises us not to go to any of these material planets, not even the Brahmaloka, which can only be reached by mechanical means after forty thousand years. In the spiritual sky there are innumerable planets, which are never annihilated, but there is one called Kṛṣṇaloka, or Goloka Vṛndāvana, which is the supreme planet. *Bhagavad-gītā* gives us the opportunity to leave this material world and to go to that eternal existence in the eternal abode of the Lord.

The description of the material world is given in the Fifteenth Chapter of *Bhagavad-gītā*. The material world is described as an *aśvattha* (*pippala*), a tree which has its roots upward. Do you know of a tree which has its roots upward? We have experience of this if we stand on the bank of a river or reservoir. We can see in the reflection that the tree's roots are upward and its branches downward. So this material world is a reflection of the spiritual world, just as the reflection of the tree from the bank is seen to be upside down. This material world is like a shadow. In a shadow there cannot be any substance, yet we can understand from the shadow that there is a substance. In the reflection of the spiritual world there is no happiness, but in the spiritual world itself there is real happiness.

The Lord suggests that the eternal spiritual world can be reached by one who is *nirmāna-moha.* Let us examine this phrase. We are all after designations. Artificially, we seek designations. Someone wants to become sir, lord, president or king. These designations belong to the body, but we do not. We are not the body; we are pure spirit soul. As long as we are attached to such designations, we are associated with the three modes or qualities of material nature. The Lord says that these attachments are due to our lust. We want to be lords over the material nature, and, as long as we want to lord it over material nature, there is no chance of going back to the spiritual kingdom of God. That eternal kingdom, which is not destructible like this material world, can be approached only by one who is not bewildered or attracted by this material nature. One who is attracted by devotional service to the Lord can go to that eternal kingdom.

Our senses are so imperfect that we cannot see even all the planets that exist in the material sky. Vedic literature gives us information of many worlds that exist there. But one should hanker after the spiritual sky and the supreme kingdom. When one reaches the supreme kingdom, he doesn't have to return to the material world.

Now, a question may be raised: How do we approach the abode of the Supreme Lord? In the Eighth Chapter, verses five through eight, the means for approaching the Lord's supreme abode are given: At the time of death, if one thinks of Kṛṣṇa and remembers the form of Kṛṣṇa and then quits the present body, he surely approaches the spiritual kingdom. Just as the transcendental nature of the Lord is *sat-cid-ānanda-vigraha,* so the Lord has His form, but this form is eternal. This present body of ours is not *sat-cid-ānanda.* This body is *asat,* or perishable, full of ignorance, and not happy.

The Lord says that when one quits this material body remembering the form of Śrī Kṛṣṇa, he at once achieves his *sat-cid-ānanda-vigraha*—the spiritual existence. The acts of this life are a preparation ground for the next life. A man dies when his next birth has been decided by higher authorities. Thus we are preparing for the next life by the activities of this life. So if we make preparations to go to the abode of the Lord, we get a spiritual body, or spiritual nature, like the Lord's.

Now, there are different kinds of transcendentalists, as we have already explained. There is the *brahmavādī,* the *paramātmāvādī,* and the devotee. In the spiritual sky, or *brahmajyoti*, there are innumerable spiritual planets. These planets are far more numerous than all the universes of the material world. The spiritual world represents three-fourths of the creation. One-fourth of the creation consists of innumerable material universes like this one. Each material universe has millions and millions of planets, but all of these universes together comprise only one-fourth of the whole creation.

Now, one who wishes to go to the spiritual abode and wishes to enjoy the association of the Supreme Lord enters into a planet of the spiritual sky. There are many names for these planets. Any transcendentalist who at the time of death thinks of the *brahmajyoti*, the Supersoul or Śrī Kṛṣṇa enters the spiritual sky, but only the devotees may go to the Lord. The Lord further says that there is no doubt of this. One should not disbelieve it. When the Lord speaks, we should not reject any part of what He says. Arjuna, whom we should emulate, says, "I believe everything that You have said." The Lord tells us that at the time of death, whoever thinks of Him will enter into the spiritual sky. There should be no doubt of this.

Bhagavad-gītā also describes how one should act in order to enter into the spiritual kingdom. Material nature is a display of one of the energies of the Supreme Lord. In the *Viṣṇu Purāṇa*, the energies of the Supreme Lord have been summarized. The Lord has diverse, innumerable energies, of which we cannot conceive. But great, learned souls have summarized all of these energies into three categories. The first is the superior, or internal, potency of the Lord. That energy is transcendental. Next is the marginal energy, which lies between the spiritual and the material. The third energy, matter, is in the mode of ignorance. Material energy is also from God. At death, we can either leave this material world or remain here. Therefore, we are called marginal.

We are accustomed to think in terms of material energy. How can we transfer our thinking of material energy into thinking of spiritual energy? There is so much literature of the material world, like novels, newspapers, etc. We must transfer our reading from these to the spiritual Vedic literature. The learned sages wrote a great deal of literature, like the *Purāṇas*. In the *Caitanya-caritāmṛta* there is a verse which reads: "The conditioned souls have forgotten their eternal relationship with the Lord and are engrossed in thinking of material things.

They should just transfer their thinking to the Lord. He has created so many *Vedas* for this purpose."

At first, there were four *Vedas*. Then, Vyāsadeva explained them by the *Purāṇas*. Then, for those incapable of understanding these, he gave the *Mahābhārata*, in which there is *Bhagavad-gītā*. Then the *Vedānta-sūtra*, which summarizes all Vedic knowledge. Last, the *Vedānta-sūtra* was explained in *Śrīmad-Bhāgavatam*.

Just as the materialist is always engaged in reading materialistic literature, so the devotee centers his reading capacity in this literature, so kindly presented by Vyāsadeva, so that at the time of death the devotee may think of the Lord and go to Him.

Kṛṣṇa advises Arjuna not simply to go on remembering Him and give up his material duty. The Lord never suggests anything impractical. To maintain the material body, one has to work. The working world is divided into four parts: *brāhmaṇa*, *kṣatriya*, *vaiśya* and *śūdra*. Each one works in a different way, as a learned man, administrator, mercantile man or laborer. The Lord advises us not to give up work, but to remember Him always, along with the struggle for existence. This is Kṛṣṇa consciousness. Unless one does this, it is not possible to go to the Lord.

Lord Caitanya Mahāprabhu practiced *kīrtana*, or chanting. One should always chant the name of the Lord because the name of the Lord and the Lord are not different. Lord Caitanya's instructions to always chant the name of Kṛṣṇa and Kṛṣṇa's injunction to remember Him always are not different. The Lord and His name are not different from each other. In the absolute status, there is no difference between one thing and another. Since the Lord is absolute, there is no difference between His name and Himself. He is omnipresent. We should know Him always, twenty-four hours a day.

How is this possible? A crude example is given by the great teachers. If a married woman is in love with another man, such an attachment is necessarily very strong. Now, the woman always wants to show her husband that she is busy in family affairs, so that he won't suspect her of having a lover. However, she is always thinking of her lover, although she carries on her household duties well—in fact, with greater care than she might if she had no lover. In the same way, we must establish our love for the Lord, and carry out our duties well.

Kṛṣṇa did not advise Arjuna to go off to the Himalayas to practice *yoga.* When the Lord described the system of *yoga* to him, Arjuna declined, saying that it was too difficult for him. But then the Lord said that one who thinks always of Him is the greatest *yogī*, the supermost seer and the best devotee. The Lord said, "As a warrior, you cannot give up your fighting; but devote all your actions to Me." He also says that if one is completely surrendered to Him, there is no doubting.

One has to learn this process of Kṛṣṇa consciousness. To do so, one should approach a person who is fixed firmly in this consciousness. The mind is always flying from this thing to that, serving no real benefit. One must learn to fix the mind always on the Supreme Lord. The mind is very restless and difficult to manage, but one can concentrate the ear on the sound of Kṛṣṇa. The Supreme Personality of Godhead can be approached by one who is constantly thinking of Him in this way.

These processes are given in *Bhagavad-gītā*. No one is barred from them. Hearing of Lord Kṛṣṇa is possible for everyone, even a human being in the lowest status of life. Laborer, tradesman, or woman—these are counted in the category of less fully developed intelligence. But the Lord says that even one lower than this—anyone, in fact, who accepts this principle of devotional service and accepts the Supreme Lord as the highest goal of life—can approach the perfection of human existence. This is the one permanent solution of life.

This is the sum and substance of *Bhagavad-gītā*.

The conclusion is that *Bhagavad-gītā* is a transcendental literature that should be read very carefully. If one follows the instructions, he can be freed of all fears and sufferings in this life and attain a spiritual birth in the next life.

Another result is that if one reads *Bhagavad-gītā* seriously and reverently, the reactions of his past deeds will no longer affect him. The Lord says, in the end, that He Himself takes the responsibility to indemnify all the reactions of sins for one who comes to Him. One cleanses himself daily by bathing in water, but for one who once bathes in the sacred Ganges water of *Bhagavad-gītā*, the dirt of past sins is washed away for all time. If one reads *Bhagavad-gītā* regularly and attentively, no other literature is needed.

In the present age, people are engaged by so many things that they have no time to devote their energy to other topics. However, one who simply reads *Bhagavad-gītā* need not read any other Vedic literature.

Bhagavad-gītā is the essence of all Vedic knowledge. It is said that one who drinks the water of the Ganges will be freed from sin. Similarly, one who studies *Bhagavad-gītā* has no need of any other literature whatever. Lord Kṛṣṇa is the original Viṣṇu, the ultimate end of all knowledge and of all seeking after knowledge.

THE DISCIPLIC SUCCESSION
(Brahma-Mādhva-Gauḍīya Sampradāya)

In the Fourth Chapter of *Bhagavad-gītā*, Lord Kṛṣṇa says, *evaṁ paramparā-prāptam imaṁ rājarṣayo viduḥ:* "This supreme science was thus received through the chain of disciplic succession, and the saintly kings understood it in that way." Lord Śrī Kṛṣṇa, the Supreme Personality of Godhead, is the original teacher of a chain of spiritual masters which continues to the present day. Just as an unbroken wire delivers electricity, so, for the benefit of all mankind, this unbroken disciplic succession delivers the spiritual knowledge of *Bhagavad-gītā:*

(1) **Lord Śrī Kṛṣṇa**
(2) Lord Brahmā
(3) Nārada Muni
(4) Śrīla Kṛṣṇa Dvaipāyana Vyāsadeva
(5) Śrīla Madhvācārya
(6) Śrīla Padmanābha Tīrtha
(7) Śrīla Narahari Tīrtha
(8) Śrīla Mādhavācārya
(9) Śrīla Akṣobhya Tīrtha
(10) Śrīla Jaya Tīrtha
(11) Śrīla Jñānasindhu
(12) Śrīla Dayānidhi
(13) Śrīla Vidyānidhi
(14) Śrīla Rājendra
(15) Śrīla Jayadharma
(16) Śrīla Puruṣottama
(17) Śrīla Brahmaṇya Tīrtha
(18) Śrīla Vyāsa Tīrtha
(19) Śrīla Lakṣmīpati
(20) Śrīla Mādhavendra Purī
(21) Śrīla Īśvara Purī, Śrī Nityānanda Prabhu, Śrī Advaitācārya
(22) **Śrī Kṛṣṇa Caitanya Mahāprabhu**
(23) Śrīla Rūpa Gosvāmī, Śrīla Sanātana Gosvāmī, Śrīla Svarūpa Dāmodara Gosvāmī
(24) Śrīla Jīva Gosvāmī, Śrīla Raghunātha dāsa Gosvāmī, Śrīla Gopāla Bhaṭṭa Gosvāmī, Śrīla Raghunātha Bhaṭṭa Gosvāmī
(25) Śrīla Kṛṣṇadāsa Kavirāja Gosvāmī
(26) Śrīla Narottama dāsa Ṭhākura
(27) Śrīla Viśvanātha Cakravartī Ṭhākura
(28) Śrīla Baladeva Vidyābhūṣaṇa
(29) Śrīla Sārvabhauma Jagannātha dāsa Bābājī Mahārāja
(30) Śrīla Bhaktivinoda Ṭhākura
(31) Śrīla Gaurakiśora dāsa Bābājī Mahārāja
(32) Śrīla Bhaktisiddhānta Sarasvatī Gosvāmī Mahārāja Prabhupāda
(33) His Divine Grace A. C. Bhaktivedanta Swami Prabhupāda

CHAPTER ONE

Observing the Armies on the Battlefield of Kurukṣetra

1. Dhṛtarāṣṭra said: O Sañjaya, after assembling in the place of pilgrimage at Kurukṣetra, what did my sons and the sons of Pāṇḍu do, being desirous to fight?

PURPORT

Bhagavad-gītā is the widely read theistic science summarized in the *Gītā-māhātmya* (*Glorification of the Gītā*). There it says that one should read *Bhagavad-gītā* very scrutinizingly, with the help of a person who is a devotee of Śrī Kṛṣṇa, and try to understand it without personally-motivated interpretations. The example of clear understanding is in *Bhagavad-gītā* itself, in the way the teaching is understood by Arjuna, who heard the *Gītā* directly from the Lord. If somebody is fortunate enough to understand *Bhagavad-gītā* in that line of disciplic succession, without motivated interpretation, then he surpasses all studies of Vedic wisdom and all scriptures of the world. One will find in *Bhagavad-gītā* all that is contained in other scriptures, but the reader will also find things which are not to be found elsewhere. That is the specific standard of the *Gītā*. It is the perfect theistic science because it is directly spoken by the Supreme Personality of Godhead, Lord Śrī Kṛṣṇa.

The topics discussed by Dhṛtarāṣṭra and Sañjaya, as described in the *Mahābhārata*, form the basic principle of this great philosophy. It is understood that this philosophy evolved on the Battlefield of Kurukṣetra, which is a sacred place of pilgrimage from the immemorial time of the Vedic age. It was spoken by the Lord when He was present personally on this planet for the guidance of mankind.

The word *dharmakṣetre* (a place where religious rituals are performed) is significant because on the Battlefield of Kurukṣetra the Supreme Personality of Godhead was present on the side of Arjuna. Dhṛtarāṣṭra, the father of Arjuna's enemies, the Kurus, was highly doubtful about the ultimate victory of his sons. In his doubt, he inquired from his secretary Sañjaya, "What did my sons and the sons of Pāṇḍu do?" He was confident that both his sons and the sons of his younger brother Pāṇḍu were assembled in that field of Kurukṣetra for a determined engagement of the war. Still, his inquiry is very significant. He did not want a compromise between the cousin-brothers, and he wanted to be sure of the fate of his sons on the battlefield. Because it was arranged to be fought in the place of pilgrimage, Kurukṣetra, which is mentioned elsewhere in the *Vedas* as a place of worship, even for the denizens of heaven, Dhṛtarāṣṭra became very fearful about the influence of the holy ground on the outcome of the battle. Dhṛtarāṣṭra knew very well that this would influence Arjuna and the sons of Pāṇḍu favorably because by nature they were all virtuous. Sañjaya was a student of the sage Vyāsa, and therefore, by the mercy of Vyāsa, Sañjaya was able to envision the Battlefield of Kurukṣetra even while he was in the room of Dhṛtarāṣṭra.

Both the Pāṇḍavas and the sons of Dhṛtarāṣṭra belong to the same family, but Dhṛtarāṣṭra's mind is disclosed herein. He deliberately claimed only his sons as Kurus, and he separated the sons of Pāṇḍu from the family heritage. One can thus understand the specific position of Dhṛtarāṣṭra in relationship with his nephews, the sons of Pāṇḍu. As in the paddy field the unnecessary plants are taken out and real paddy plants are shoved in, so it is expected from the very beginning of these topics that in the religious field of Kurukṣetra, where the father of religion, Śrī Kṛṣṇa, was present, the unwanted plants, Dhṛtarāṣṭra's son Duryodhana and others, would be wiped out and the thoroughly religious persons, headed by Yudhiṣṭhira, would be established by the Lord. That is the significance of the Sanskrit words *dharmakṣetre* and *kurukṣetre*, apart from their usual historical and Vedic importance.

2. Sañjaya said: O King, after looking over the military phalanx arranged by the sons of Pāṇḍu, King Duryodhana went to his teacher and began to speak the following words.

PURPORT

Dhṛtarāṣṭra was blind from his very birth. Unfortunately, he was also bereft of spiritual vision. He knew very well that his sons were equally blind in the matter of religion, and he was sure that they could never reach an understanding with the Pāṇḍavas, who were all pious since birth. Still he was doubtful about the influence of the place of pilgrimage. Sañjaya could understand the motive of his asking about the situation on the battlefield. He therefore wanted to encourage the King in his despondency, and thus he assured him that his sons were not going to make any sort of compromise under the influence of the holy field. He therefore informed the King that his son, after seeing the military force of the Pāṇḍavas, at once went to the commander in chief, Droṇācārya, to inform him of the real position. Although Duryodhana is mentioned as the king, he still had to go to the commander on account of the seriousness of the situation. He was therefore quite fit to be a politician. But his diplomatic behavior could not disguise his fearful mind when he saw the military arrangement of the Pāṇḍavas.

3. O my teacher, behold the great military phalanx of the sons of Pāṇḍu, so expertly arranged by your disciple, the son of Drupada.

PURPORT

Duryodhana, a great diplomat, wanted to point out the defects in Droṇācārya, the great *brāhmaṇa* commander in chief. Droṇācārya had had some political quarrel with King Drupada, the father of Draupadī, who was Arjuna's wife. As a result of this quarrel Drupada had performed a great sacrifice, by which he received the benediction of having a son who would be able to kill Droṇācārya. Droṇācārya knew this perfectly well, and yet, as a liberal *brāhmaṇa*, he did not hesitate to impart all his military secrets when the son of Drupada, Dhṛṣṭadyumna, was entrusted to him for military education. Now, on the Battlefield of Kurukṣetra, Dhṛṣṭadyumna took the side of the Pāṇḍavas, and it was he who arranged their military phalanx, after having learned the art from Droṇācārya. Duryodhana pointed out this mistake of Droṇācārya's so that Droṇācārya might be alert in the fighting. By this he wanted to point out also that Droṇācārya should not be lenient in fighting with the Pāṇḍavas, who were also his affectionate students. Arjuna, especially, was his most affectionate and brilliant student. He also warned that leniency in the fight with the other party would create havoc for themselves.

4. Here, in this army of the Pāṇḍavas, there are many heroic bowmen equal in fighting to Bhīma and Arjuna; there are also great fighters like Yuyudhāna, Virāṭa and Drupada.

5. There are also great, heroic, powerful fighters like Dhṛṣṭaketu, Cekitāna, Kāśirāja, Purujit, Kuntibhoja and Śaibya.

6. There are very powerful charioteers like Yudhāmanyu, Uttamaujā, the sons of Subhadrā and Draupadī.

7. O best of *brāhmaṇas*, for your information, let me tell you about the captains who are especially qualified to lead my military force.

8. These are personalities like yourself, Bhīṣma, Karṇa, Kṛpa, Aśvatthāmā, Vikarṇa and the son of Somadatta, called Bhūriśravā, who are always victorious in battle.

9. There are many other heroes who are prepared to lay down their lives for my sake. All of them are well equipped with different kinds of weapons, and all are experienced in military science.

10. Our strength is immeasurable, and we are perfectly protected by grandfather Bhīṣma, whereas the strength of the Pāṇḍavas, carefully protected by Bhīma, is limited.

PURPORT

Herein an estimation of comparative strength is made by Duryodhana. He thinks that the strength of his armed forces is immeasurable, being specifically protected by the most experienced general, grandfather Bhīṣma. On the other hand, the forces of the Pāṇḍavas are limited, being protected by a less experienced general, Bhīma, who is like a fig in the presence of Bhīṣma. Duryodhana was always envious of Bhīma because he knew perfectly well that if he should die at all, he would only be killed by Bhīma. But at the same time he was confident of his victory on account of the presence of Bhīṣma, who was a far superior general. His conclusion that he would come out of the battle victorious was well ascertained.

11. Now all of you, standing at your respective strategic points in the phalanx of the army, must give full support to grandfather Bhīṣma.

12. Thereafter, the great valiant grandsire of the Kuru dynasty, the grandfather of the fighters, blew his conchshell very loudly, like the sound of a lion, giving Duryodhana joy.

13. After that, the conchshells, bugles, trumpets and horns all suddenly vibrated simultaneously and the sound was tumultuous.

14. On the other side, both Lord Kṛṣṇa and Arjuna, being situated on a chariot yoked with white horses, sounded their transcendental conchshells.

PURPORT

In contrast with the conchshell blown by Bhīṣmadeva, the conchshells in the hands of Kṛṣṇa and Arjuna are described as transcendental. The sounding of the transcendental conchshells indicated that there was no hope of victory on the other side, because Kṛṣṇa was with the Pāṇḍavas. *Jayas tu pāṇḍu-putrāṇāṁ yeṣāṁ pakṣe janārdanaḥ.* Victory is always with persons like the sons of Pāṇḍu because Lord Kṛṣṇa is associated with them. And whenever the Lord is present, the goddess of fortune is also there because the goddess of fortune never lives alone without her husband. Therefore, victory and fortune were awaiting Arjuna, as indicated by the transcendental sound produced by the conchshell of Viṣṇu, or Lord Kṛṣṇa. Besides that, the chariot on which both the friends were seated was donated by Agni (the fire-god) to Arjuna, and this indicated that that chariot was meant for conquering all sides, wherever it was drawn, over all the three worlds.

15. Thereafter, Lord Kṛṣṇa blew His conchshell, named Pāñcajanya, Arjuna blew his, the Devadatta, and Bhīma, the voracious eater and performer of herculean tasks, blew his terrific conchshell, named Pauṇḍra.

PURPORT

Hṛṣīkeśa is a name for Lord Kṛṣṇa because He is the owner of all senses. The living entities are part and parcel of Him, and therefore the senses of the living entities are also part and parcel of His senses. The impersonalists cannot account for the senses of the living entities, and therefore they are always anxious to describe all living entities as senseless, or impersonal. The Lord, situated in the hearts of all living entities, directs their senses. But He directs in terms of the surrender of the living entity, and in the case of a pure devotee, He directly controls the senses. Here on the Battlefield of Kurukṣetra, the Lord directly controls the transcendental senses of Arjuna, and thus His particular name in that connection. The Lord has different names in terms of His activities. For example, His name is Madhusūdana because He kills the demon named Madhu; His name is Govinda because He gives pleasure to the cows and to the senses; His name is Vāsudeva because He appeared as the son of Vasudeva; His name is Devakīnandana because He accepted Devakī as His mother; His name is Yaśodānandana because He awarded His childhood pastimes to Yasodā at Vṛndāvana; His name is Pārtha-sārathi because He worked as charioteer of His friend Arjuna. Similarly, His name is Hṛṣīkeśa because He gave direction to Arjuna on the Battlefield of Kurukṣetra.

Dhanañjaya is a name for Arjuna because he helped his elder brother in fetching wealth when it was required by the King to make expenditures for different sacrifices. Similarly, Bhīma is known as Vṛkodara because he could eat as voraciously as he could perform herculean tasks, such as killing the demon Hiḍimba. So, the particular types of conchshell blown by the different personalities on the side of the Pāṇḍavas, beginning from the Lord's, were all very encouraging to the fighting soldiers. On the other side there were no such credits, nor was there the presence of Lord Kṛṣṇa, the supreme director, nor that of the goddess of fortune. So they were predestined to lose the battle, and that was the message announced by the sounds of the conchshells.

16-18. Prince Yudhiṣṭhira, Kuntī's son, blew his conchshell, named Anantavijaya, and Nakula and Sahadeva blew theirs, named Sughoṣa and Maṇipuṣpaka. That great archer the King of Kāśī, the great fighter Śikhaṇḍī, Dhṛṣṭadyumna, Virāṭa and the unconquerable Sātyaki, Drupada, the sons of Draupadī, and the others, O King, such as the son of Subhadrā, greatly armed, all blew their respective conchshells.

19. The blowing of all these different conchshells became uproarious, and, vibrating both in the sky and on the earth, it shattered the hearts of the sons of Dhṛtarāṣṭra.

PURPORT

When Bhīṣma and the others on the side of Duryodhana blew their respective conchshells, there was no heartaching on the part of the Pāṇḍavas; such occurrences are not mentioned. But in this particular verse it is mentioned that the hearts of the sons of Dhṛtarāṣṭra were shattered by the sounds vibrated by the Pāṇḍava's party. This is due to the Pāṇḍavas and their confidence in Lord Kṛṣṇa. One who takes shelter of the Supreme Lord has nothing to fear, even in the midst of the greatest calamity.

20. O King, at that time Arjuna, the son of Pāṇḍu, who was seated in his chariot, his flag marked with Hanumān, was taking up his bow and was about to shoot his arrows, looking at the sons of Dhṛtarāṣṭra. O King, he then spoke to Hṛṣīkeśa [Lord Kṛṣṇa] these words.

PURPORT

The battle was just about to begin. It is understood from the above statements that the sons of Dhṛtarāṣṭra were more or less disheartened by the unexpected military force of the Pāṇḍavas, who were endowed with the direct instructions of Lord Kṛṣṇa on the battlefield. The emblem of Hanumān on Arjuna's banners, as mentioned here, is another sign of victory because Hanumān cooperated with Lord Rāma in the battle between Rāma and Rāvaṇa, and Lord Rāma emerged victorious. Now both Rāma and Hanumān were present on the chariot of Arjuna to help him. Lord Kṛṣṇa is Rāma Himself, and wherever there is Lord Rāma, His eternal servitor Hanumān and His eternal consort Sītā, the goddess of fortune, are also present. Therefore, Arjuna had no cause to fear any enemies whatever. And, above all, the Lord of the senses, Lord Kṛṣṇa, was personally present to give him direction. Thus all good counsel was available for Arjuna in the matter of executing the battle. In such auspicious conditions, arranged by the Lord for His eternal devotee, lay the signs of assured victory.

21-22. O infallible one, please place my chariot between the two armies so that I may see who is present here, who is desirous of fighting, and with whom I must fight in this great trial of arms.

PURPORT

Although Lord Kṛṣṇa is the Supreme Personality of Godhead, out of His causeless mercy He was engaged in the service of His friend. He never fails in His affection for His devotees, and thus He is addressed herein as infallible. As charioteer, He had to carry out the orders of Arjuna. Since He did not hesitate to do so, He is addressed as infallible. Although He had accepted the position of a charioteer to His devotee, there was no chance of His supreme position's being challenged. In all circumstances, He is the Supreme Personality of Godhead, Hṛṣīkeśa, the Lord of the total senses. The relationship between the Lord and His servitor is very sweet and transcendental. The servitor is always ready to render a service to the Lord, and, similarly, the Lord is always seeking an opportunity to render some service to the devotee. He takes greater pleasure in His pure devotee's assuming the advantageous position of ordering Him than He does in being the giver of orders. Since He is the master, everyone is under His orders, and no one is above Him to order Him. But when he finds that a pure devotee is ordering Him, He obtains transcendental pleasure.

As a pure devotee of the Lord, Arjuna had no desire to fight with his cousin-brothers, but he was forced to come onto the battlefield by the obstinacy of Duryodhana, who was never agreeable to any terms of peaceful negotiation. Therefore, he was very anxious to see who the leading persons present on the battlefield were. Although there was no question of a peacemaking endeavor, he wanted to see them again and to see how much they were bent upon demanding an unwanted war.

23. Let me see those who have come here to fight, wishing to please the evil-minded son of Dhṛtarāṣṭra.

24. Sañjaya said, O descendant of Bharata, being thus addressed by Arjuna, Lord Kṛṣṇa drew the fine chariot up in the midst of the armies of both parties.

25. In the presence of Bhīṣma, Droṇa and all other chieftains of the world, Hṛṣīkeśa, the Lord, said, Just behold, O Pārtha, all the Kurus that are assembled here.

PURPORT

As the Supersoul of all living entities, Lord Kṛṣṇa could understand what was going on in the mind of Arjuna. The use of the word Hṛṣīkeśa in this connection indicates that He knew everything. And the word Pārtha, or the son of Pṛthā, is also similarly significant. As a friend He wanted to inform Arjuna that because Arjuna was the son of Pṛthā, the sister of His own father, Vasudeva, He had agreed to be charioteer to Arjuna. Now what did Arjuna mean by beholding the Kurus? Did he want to stop there and not fight? Kṛṣṇa never expected such things from the son of His aunt Pṛthā. The mind of Arjuna was thus predicated by the Lord in friendly joking.

26-28. There Arjuna could see, within the midst of both parties, fathers and grandfathers, brothers, sons, grandsons, friends, and also fathers-in-law and well-wishers—all present there. The son of Kuntī, Arjuna, after seeing all different grades of friends and relatives, became overwhelmed by compassion and spoke thus: My dear Kṛṣṇa, seeing my friends and relatives present before me with such a fighting spirit, I feel the limbs of my body quivering and my mouth drying up.

PURPORT

Any man who has genuine devotion to the Lord has all the good qualities found in godly persons or in the demigods, whereas the nondevotee, however advanced he may be in material qualifications through education and culture, will lack in godly qualities. As such, Arjuna, just after seeing his kinsmen, friends and relatives on the battlefield, was at once overwhelmed by compassion for those who had so decided to fight among themselves. So far as his soldiers were concerned, he was sympathetic from the beginning, but he felt compassion even for the soldiers of the opposite party, foreseeing their imminent death. Thus the limbs of his body began to quiver, and his mouth became dry. He was more or less astonished to see their fighting spirit. Practically the whole community, all in blood relationship with Arjuna, came there to fight against him. This was too much for a devotee like Arjuna. Although it is not mentioned here, still one can easily imagine that not only were Arjuna's bodily limbs quivering and his mouth drying up, but he was also crying out of compassion. Such symptoms in Arjuna were due not to weakness but to his softheartedness, a characteristic of a pure devotee of the Lord. It is said therefore: "One who has unflinching devotion for the Personality of Godhead has all the good qualities of the demigods. But one who is not a devotee of the Lord has only material qualifications, which are of little value. This is because he is hovering on the mental plane and is certain to be attracted by the glaring material energy."

29. My whole body is trembling, and my hairs are standing on end. My bow Gāṇḍīva is slipping from my hand, and my skin is burning.

30. I am now unable to stand here any longer. I am forgetting myself, and my mind is reeling. I foresee only evil, O killer of the Keśī demon.

PURPORT

Due to his impatience, Arjuna was unable to stay on the battlefield, and he was forgetting himself on account of the weakness of his mind. Excessive attachment for material things puts a man in such a bewildering condition of existence. Such fearfulness and loss of mental equilibrium take place in persons who are too much affected by material conditions. Arjuna envisioned only unhappiness in the battlefield—he was not going to be happy even by gaining victory over the foe. When a man sees only the frustration of his expectations, he thinks, "Why am I here?" Everyone is interested in himself and his own welfare. No one is interested in the Supreme Self, Kṛṣṇa. Arjuna is supposed to show disregard for self-interest by the will of the Lord. Real self-interest is Viṣṇu, or Kṛṣṇa. The conditioned soul forgets this and therefore suffers the symptoms of bodily degradations. Arjuna thought that his victory in the battle would only be a cause of lamentation for him.

31. I do not see how any good can come from killing my own kinsmen in this battle. Nor can I, my dear Kṛṣṇa, desire any consequent victory, kingdom or happiness.

PURPORT

Without knowing one's self-interest is Viṣṇu, conditioned souls are attracted by bodily relationships, hoping to be happy in such situations. By such a blind conception of life one forgets the causes of material happiness also. Arjuna appears to have even forgotten the moral codes for a warrior. It is said that two kinds of men—namely, the *kṣatriya* who dies directly in front of the battlefield and the person in the renounced order of life, absolutely devoted to spiritual culture—are eligible to enter into the sun-globe, which is so powerful and dazzling. Arjuna is reluctant even to kill his enemies, let alone his relatives. He thought that by killing his kinsmen there would be no happiness in his life, and therefore he was not willing to fight, just as a person who does not feel any hunger is not inclined to cook. He has now decided to go into the forest and live a secluded life in frustration. As a *kṣatriya,* he required a kingdom for his subsistence because warriors cannot engage themselves in any other occupation. But Arjuna had no kingdom. His sole opportunity for gaining one lay in fighting with his cousin-brothers and reclaiming the kingdom he originally inherited from his father, which he does not want to do. Therefore he considers himself fit for going to the forest and living a secluded life of frustration.

32-35. O Govinda, of what avail to us are kingdoms, happiness or even life itself when all those for whom we may desire them are now arrayed in this battlefield? O Madhusūdana, when teachers, fathers, sons, grandfathers, maternal uncles, fathers-in-law, grandsons, brothers-in-law and all relatives are ready to give up their lives and properties and are standing before me, then why should I wish to kill them, though I may survive? O maintainer of all living entities, I am not prepared to fight with them even in exchange for all the three worlds, let alone this earth.

PURPORT

Arjuna has addressed Lord Kṛṣṇa as Govinda because Kṛṣṇa is the object of all pleasures for the cows and for the senses. By using this significant word, Arjuna intends Kṛṣṇa to understand what will satisfy his senses. Actually, Govinda is not meant for satisfying our senses; but if we try to satisfy the senses of Govinda, then automatically our senses are satisfied. Materially everyone wants to satisfy his senses, and he wants God to be the order supplier for such satisfaction. The Lord can satisfy the senses of the living entities as much as they deserve, but not to the extent that one may covet. But when one takes the opposite way—when one tries to satisfy the senses of Govinda without desiring to satisfy one's own—then by the grace of Govinda all desires of the living entity are satisfied. Arjuna's deep affection for community and family members is exhibited herewith, partly due to his natural compassion for them. He is not, therefore, prepared to fight with them. Everyone wants to show his opulence to friends and relatives, but Arjuna fears that all his relatives and friends will be killed in the battlefield and that he will be unable to share his opulence after victory. This is a typical calculation of material life. The transcendental life, however, is apart from such calculations. Since a devotee wants to satisfy the desires of the Lord, he can, Lord willing, accept all kinds of opulence for the service of the Lord; and if the Lord is not willing, he should not accept a farthing. Arjuna did not want to kill his relatives, and if there were any need for killing them he desired that Kṛṣṇa kill them personally. At this point he did not know that Kṛṣṇa had already killed them before their coming onto the battlefield and that Arjuna was only to become an instrument for Kṛṣṇa. This fact is disclosed in the subsequent chapters of *Bhagavad-gītā.* As a natural devotee of the Lord, Arjuna did not want to retaliate against his miscreant cousins and brothers, but it was the Lord's plan that they all be killed. The devotee of the Lord does not retaliate against the wrongdoer, but the Lord does not tolerate any mischief done to the devotee by the miscreants. The Lord can excuse a person on His own account, but He excuses no one who has done harm to His devotees. Therefore the Lord was determined to kill the miscreants, although Arjuna wanted to excuse them.

36. Sin will overcome us by slaying such aggressors. Therefore it is not proper for us to kill the sons of Dhṛtarāṣṭra and his friends. What should

we gain, O Kṛṣṇa, O husband of the goddess of fortune? And how could we be happy by killing our own kinsmen?

PURPORT

According to Vedic injunctions there are six kinds of aggressors: (1) the poison giver, (2) the one who sets fire to the house, (3) one who attacks with deadly weapons, (4) one who plunders riches, (5) one who occupies another's land, and (6) one who kidnaps the wife. Such aggressors are at once to be killed, and no sin is incurred by killing such aggressors. The killing of aggressors is quite befitting any ordinary man; but Arjuna was not an ordinary person. He was saintly by character, and therefore he wanted to deal with them accordingly. Saintliness is not, however, for a *kṣatriya.* A responsible man involved in the administration of a state should not be cowardly. Of course, he is required to be saintly in his behavior. For example, Lord Rāma was so saintly that people were anxious to live in His kingdom (Rāma-rājya); yet Lord Rāma never showed any example of cowardliness. Rāvaṇa was an aggressor against Rāma, having kidnapped Lord Rāma's wife, Sītā, and Lord Rāma gave him sufficiently stern lessons, unparalleled in the history of the world. In Arjuna's case, however, one should consider the special type of aggressors—namely, his own grandfather, own teacher, friends, sons, grandsons, etc. Because of them, Arjuna thought that he should not take the severe steps necessary against ordinary aggressors. Besides that, saintly persons are advised to forgive. Such injunctions for saintly persons are more important than any political emergency. Arjuna considered that rather than kill his own kinsmen for political reasons, it would be better to forgive them on grounds of religion and saintly behavior. He did not, therefore, consider such killing business profitable simply for the matter of temporary bodily happiness. After all, kingdoms and the pleasures derived therefrom are not permanent, so why should he risk his life and eternal salvation by killing his own kinsmen? Arjuna's addressing of Kṛṣṇa as Mādhava, or the husband of the goddess of fortune, is also significant in this connection. He wanted to point out to Kṛṣṇa that, as husband of the goddess of fortune, He should not induce Arjuna to take up a matter which would ultimately bring about misfortune. Kṛṣṇa, however, never brings misfortune to anyone, much less to His devotees.

37-38. O Janārdana, although these men, overtaken by greed, see no fault in killing a family or fighting with friends, why should we, with knowledge of the sin, engage in these acts?

39. By the destruction of a dynasty, the eternal family tradition is vanquished, and thus the rest of the family becomes involved in irreligion.

PURPORT

In the system of the *varṇāśrama*, there are many principles and religious traditions to help the members of the family grow properly in spiritual values. The elder members are responsible for such purifying processes in the family, beginning from birth to death. But on the death of elderly members, such family traditions of purification might stop, and the remaining minor family members would develop irreligious habits, thereby losing their chance for spiritual salvation. Therefore, for no purpose should the elder members of the family be slain.

40. When irreligion is prominent in the family, O Kṛṣṇa, the ladies of the family become corrupt, and from the degradation of womanhood, O descendant of Vṛṣṇi, comes unwanted progeny.

PURPORT

Good population in human society is the basic principle for peace, prosperity and spiritual progress in life. The Vedic religion's principles were so designed that good population might prevail in society for the all-around spiritual progress of state and community. Such population in society depends on the chastity and faithfulness of its womanhood. As children are very prone to being misled, women are also very prone to degradation. Therefore, both children and women require protection by the elder members of the family. By being engaged in various religious practices, women will not be misled into adultery. According to the sage Cāṇakya Paṇḍita, women are generally not very intelligent and therefore not trustworthy. So the different family traditions of religious activities should always engage them, and thus their chastity and devotion will give birth to a good population, eligible for participating in the *varṇāśrama* system. On the failure of such *varṇāśrama-dharma*, naturally the women become free to act and free to mix with men, and thus adultery is indulged in at the risk of unwanted population.

41. When there is an increase of unwanted population, a hellish situation is created both for the family and for those who destroy the family tradition. In such corrupt families, there is no offering of oblations of food and water to the ancestors.

PURPORT

According to the rules and regulations of fruitive activities, there is the need for offering periodical food and water to the forefathers of the family. The offering is done by worship of Viṣṇu because eating the remnants of food offered to Viṣṇu can deliver one from all kinds of sinful actions. The forefathers may be suffering from various types of sinful reactions, and sometimes some of them cannot even acquire a gross material body, and are forced to remain in subtle bodies, as ghosts. Thus when remnants of *prasāda* food are offered to the forefathers by descendants, the forefathers are released from ghostly or other kinds of miserable life. Such help rendered to forefathers is a family tradition, and those who are not in devotional life are required to perform such rituals. One who is engaged in the devotional life is not required to perform such actions. Simply by performing devotional service, one can deliver hundreds and thousands of forefathers from all kinds of miserable life. It is stated in *Śrīmad-Bhāgavatam:* "Anyone who has taken shelter of the lotus feet of Mukunda, the giver of liberation, giving up all obligations, and has taken to the path in all seriousness, owes neither duties nor obligations to the demigods, sages, general living entities, family members, humankind or forefathers." Such obligations are automatically fulfilled by performance of devotional service to the Supreme Personality of Godhead.

42. By the evil deeds of the destroyers of family tradition, all kinds of community projects and family welfare activities are devastated.

PURPORT

The four orders of human society, combined with family welfare activities as they are set forth by the institution of the *sanātana-dharma*, or *varṇāśrama-dharma*, are designed to enable the human being to attain his ultimate salvation. Therefore, the breaking of the *sanātana-dharma* tradition by irresponsible leaders of society brings about chaos in that society, and consequently people forget the aim of life—Viṣṇu,

God. Such leaders are called blind, and persons who follow such leaders are sure to be brought into chaos.

43. O Kṛṣṇa, maintainer of the people, I have heard by disciplic succession that those who destroy family traditions dwell always in hell.

44. Alas, how strange it is that we are preparing ourselves to commit great sinful acts, driven by the desire to enjoy royal happiness.

45. I would consider it better for the sons of Dhṛtarāṣṭra to kill me unarmed and unresisting, rather than fight with them.

PURPORT

It is the custom, according to *kṣatriya* fighting principles, that an unarmed and unwilling foe should not be attacked. Arjuna, however, decided that in such an enigmatic position he would not fight even if attacked by the enemy. He did not care how much the other party was bent upon fighting. All these symptoms are due to softheartedness resulting from his being a great devotee of the Lord.

46. Sañjaya said: Arjuna, having thus spoken, cast aside his bow and arrows and sat down on the chariot, his mind overwhelmed with grief.

PURPORT

While observing the situation of his enemy, Arjuna stood up on the chariot, but he was by now so afflicted with lamentation that he sat down again, setting aside his bow and arrows. Such a kind and softhearted person, in the devotional service of the Lord, is fit for receiving self-knowledge.

Thus end the Bhaktivedanta purports to the First Chapter of the *Śrīmad Bhagavad-gītā* in the matter of Observing the Armies on the Battlefield of Kurukṣetra.

CHAPTER TWO

Contents of the Gītā Summarized

1. Sañjaya said: Seeing Arjuna full of compassion and very sorrowful, his eyes brimming with tears, Madhusūdana, Kṛṣṇa, spoke the following words.

2. The Supreme Personality of Godhead said: My dear Arjuna, how have these impurities come upon you? They are not at all befitting a man who knows the progressive values of life. They lead not to higher planets but to infamy.

PURPORT

The Sanskrit word *bhagavān* is explained by the great authority Parāśara Muni, the father of Vyāsadeva. The Supreme Personality who possesses all riches, entire strength, entire fame, entire beauty, entire knowledge and entire renunciation is called Bhagavān. There are many persons who are very rich, very powerful, very beautiful, very famous, very learned and very much detached, but no one can claim that he is possessor of all these opulences entirely. Such a claim is applicable to Kṛṣṇa only, and as such He is the Supreme Personality of Godhead. No living entity, including Brahmā, Lord Śiva, or even Nārāyaṇa, can possess opulences as fully as Kṛṣṇa. By analytical study of such possessions, it is concluded in the

Brahma-saṁhitā by Lord Brahmā himself that Lord Kṛṣṇa is the Supreme Personality of Godhead. No one is equal to or above Him. He is the primeval Lord, or Bhagavān, known as Govinda, and He is the supreme cause of all causes. It is stated as follows: "There are many personalities possessing the qualities of Bhagavān, but Kṛṣṇa is supreme because none can excel Him. He is the Supreme Person, and His body is eternal, full of knowledge and bliss. He is the primeval Lord Govinda and the cause of all causes."

In the *Bhāgavatam* also there is a list of many incarnations of the Supreme Personality of Godhead, but Kṛṣṇa is described therein as the original personality from whom many, many incarnations and Personalities of Godhead expand. It is stated in this way: "All the lists of the incarnations of Godhead submitted herewith are either plenary expansions or parts of the plenary expansions of the Supreme Personality of Godhead, but Kṛṣṇa is the Supreme Personality of Godhead Himself."

Therefore, Kṛṣṇa is the original Supreme Personality of Godhead, the Absolute Truth, the source of both Supersoul and the impersonal Brahman.

In the presence of the Supreme Person, Arjuna's lamentation for his kinsmen is certainly unbecoming, and therefore Kṛṣṇa expressed His surprise with the word *kutaḥ,* "wherefrom." Such unmanly sentiments were never expected from a person belonging to the civilized class of men known as Āryans. The word *āryan* is applicable to persons who know the value of life and have a civilization based on spiritual realization. Persons who are led by the material conception of life do not know that the aim of life is realization of the Absolute Truth, Viṣṇu, or Bhagavān. Such persons are captivated by the external features of the material world, and therefore they do not know what liberation is. Persons who have no knowledge of liberation from material bondage are called non-Āryans. Arjuna was trying to deviate from his prescribed duties, declining to fight, although he was a *kṣatriya,* or warrior. This act of cowardice is described as befitting the non-Āryans. Such deviation from duty does not help one in the progress of spiritual life, nor does it even give one the opportunity to become famous in this world. Lord Kṛṣṇa did not approve of the so-called compassion of Arjuna for his kinsmen.

3. O son of Pṛthā, do not yield to this degrading impotence. It does not become you. Give up such petty weakness of heart and arise, O chastiser of the enemy!

4. Arjuna said: O killer of Madhu [Kṛṣṇa], how can I counterattack with arrows in battle personalities like Bhīṣma and Droṇa, who are worthy of my worship?

5. It is better to live in this world by begging than to live at the cost of the lives of great souls who are my teachers. Even though they are avaricious, they are nonetheless superiors. If they are killed, our spoils will be tainted with blood.

6. Nor do we know which is better—conquering them or being conquered by them. The sons of Dhṛtarāṣṭra, whom if we killed we should not care to live, are now standing before us on this battlefield.

PURPORT

Arjuna became perplexed in this connection, not knowing whether he should execute the fighting with the risk of committing unnecessary violence, although it is the duty of the *kṣatriyas*, or whether he should not and prefer instead to live by begging. If he did not conquer the enemy, begging would be the only means left for his living. There was no certainty of victory because either side might emerge victorious. Even if there were victory awaiting them because their cause was justified, still, if the sons of Dhṛtarāṣṭra should die in battle, it would be very difficult to live in their absence. Under the circumstances, that would be another kind of defeat. All these considerations by Arjuna definitely prove that he was not only a great devotee of the Lord, but was also highly enlightened and had complete control over his mind and senses. His desire to live by begging, although he was born in the royal household, is another sign of detachment. He was fully in the quality of forbearance, as all these qualities, combined with his faith in the words of instruction of Śrī Kṛṣṇa (his spiritual master), give evidence. It is concluded that Arjuna was quite fit for liberation. Unless the senses are controlled, there is no chance of elevation to the platform of knowledge, and without knowledge and devotion there is no chance of liberation. Arjuna was competent in all these attributes, over and above his enormous attributes in his material relationships.

7. Now I am confused about duty and have lost all composure because of weakness. In this condition I am asking You to tell me clearly what is best for me. Now I am Your disciple, and a soul surrendered unto You. Please instruct me.

PURPORT

By nature's own way the complete system of material activities is a source of perplexity for everyone. In every step there is perplexity, and it behooves one therefore to approach the bona fide spiritual master who can give one the proper guidance for executing the purpose of life. All Vedic literatures advise us to approach a bona fide spiritual master to get free from the perplexities of life, which happen without our desire. They appear like a forest fire, which takes place without being set by anyone. Similarly, the world situation is such that perplexities of life automatically appear, without our wanting such confusion. Nobody wants fire, and yet it takes place, and we are perplexed. The Vedic wisdom therefore advises that in order to solve the perplexities of life and to understand the science of the solution, one must approach a spiritual master, who is in the disciplic succession. A person with a bona fide spiritual master is supposed to know everything. One should not therefore remain in material perplexities, but should approach such a teacher. This is the purport of this verse.

Who is the man in material perplexities? It is he who does not understand the problems of life. In the *Garga Upaniṣad* this is described as follows: "He is a miserly man who does not solve the problems of life as a human and who thus quits this world like the cats and dogs, without understanding the science of self-realization. He is called a miserly man." This human form of life is a most valuable asset for the living entity who can utilize it to solve the problems of life. Therefore, one who does not utilize this opportunity is a miser. On the other hand, there is the *brāhmaṇa*, or he who is intelligent enough to utilize this body for solving all the problems of life.

The *kṛpaṇas*, or miserly persons, waste their time in being overly affectionate for family, society, country, etc., in the material conception of life. One is often attached to family life, to wife, children, and other members, on the basis of "skin disease." The *kṛpaṇas* think that they are able to protect their family members from death; or the *kṛpaṇa* thinks that his family or society can save him from death. Such family attachment can be found even in the lower animals, who also take care of children. Being intelligent, Arjuna could understand that his affection for family members and his wish to protect them from death were the causes of his perplexities. Although he could understand that his duty to fight was awaiting him, still, on account of miserly weakness, he could not discharge the duty. He is therefore asking Lord Kṛṣṇa, the supreme spiritual master, to make a definite solution. He offers himself to Kṛṣṇa as a disciple; he wants to stop friendly talks. Talks between the master and disciple are serious, and now Arjuna wants to talk very seriously before the recognized spiritual master. Kṛṣṇa is therefore the original spiritual master in the science of *Bhagavad-gītā*, and Arjuna is the original disciple in understanding the *Gītā*. How Arjuna understands *Bhagavad-gītā* is stated in the *Gītā* itself. And yet foolish mundane scholars explain that one need not submit to Kṛṣṇa as a person, but to the unborn within Kṛṣṇa. There is no difference between Kṛṣṇa's within and without, and one who has no sense of this understanding is the greatest fool, the greatest pretender.

8. I can find no means to drive away this grief which is drying up my senses. I will not be able to destroy it even if I win an unrivaled kingdom on the earth with sovereignty like the demigods in heaven.

9. Sañjaya said: Having spoken thus, Arjuna, chastiser of enemies, told Kṛṣṇa, "Govinda, I shall not fight," and fell silent.

10. O descendant of Bharata, at that time Kṛṣṇa, smiling, in the midst of both the armies, spoke the following words to the grief-stricken Arjuna.

11. The Blessed Lord said: While speaking learned words you are mourning for what is not worthy of grief. Those who are wise lament neither for the living nor the dead.

PURPORT

The Lord at once took the position of the teacher and chastised the student, calling him, indirectly, a fool. The Lord said, you are talking like a learned man, but you do not know that one who is learned—one who knows what is body and what is soul—does not lament for any stage of the body, neither in the living nor in the dead condition. As explained in later chapters, it will be clear that knowledge means to know matter and spirit and the controller of both. Arjuna argued that religious principles should be given more importance than politics or sociology, but he did not know that knowledge of matter, soul and the Supreme is more important than religious formularies. And because he was lacking in that knowledge, he should not have posed himself as a very learned man. As he did not happen to be a very learned man, he was consequently lamenting for something unworthy of lamentation. The body is born and is destined to be vanquished today or tomorrow. Therefore, the body is not as important as the soul. One who knows this is actually learned, and for him there is no cause for lamentation in any stage of the material body.

12. Never was there a time when I did not exist, nor you, nor all these kings; nor in the future shall any of us cease to be.

PURPORT

In the *Vedas*, in the *Kaṭha Upaniṣad* as well as in the *Śvetāśvatara Upaniṣad*, it is said that the Supreme Personality of Godhead is the maintainer of innumerable living entities, in terms of their different situations, according to individual work and the reaction to work. That Supreme Personality of Godhead is also, by His plenary portions, alive in the heart of every living entity. Only saintly persons who can see, within and without, the same Supreme Personality of Godhead can actually attain to perfect peace eternal. The same Vedic truth is given here to Arjuna—and, in that connection, to all persons in the world who pose themselves as very learned but factually have but a poor fund of knowledge. The Lord says clearly that He Himself, Arjuna, and all the kings who are assembled on the battlefield are eternally individual beings, and that the Lord is eternally the maintainer of the individual living entities, both in their conditioned and in their liberated situation. The Supreme

Personality of Godhead is the supreme individual person, and Arjuna, the Lord's eternal associate, and all the kings assembled there are individual, eternal persons. It is not that they did not exist as individuals in the past, and it is not that they will not remain as eternal persons. Their individuality existed in the past, and their individuality will continue in the future without interruption. Therefore, there is no cause for lamentation for any one of the individual living entities.

The Māyāvāda, or impersonal, theory that after liberation the individual soul, separated by the covering of *māyā*, or illusion, will merge into the impersonal Brahman without individual existence is not supported herein by Lord Kṛṣṇa, the supreme authority. Nor is the theory that we only think of individuality in the conditioned state supported herein. Kṛṣṇa clearly says that in the future also the individuality of the Lord and others, as is confirmed in the *Upaniṣads*, will continue eternally. This statement of Kṛṣṇa is authoritative because Kṛṣṇa cannot be subject to illusion. If individuality is not a fact, then Kṛṣṇa would not have stressed it so much—even for the future. The Māyāvādī may argue that the individuality spoken of by Kṛṣṇa is not spiritual, but material. Even accepting the argument that the individuality is material, then how can one distinguish Kṛṣṇa's individuality? Kṛṣṇa affirms His individuality in the past and confirms His individuality in the future also. He has confirmed His individuality in many ways, and impersonal Brahman has been declared subordinate to Him. Kṛṣṇa has maintained spiritual individuality all along, and if He is accepted as an ordinary conditioned soul in individual consciousness, then His *Bhagavad-gītā* has no value as an authoritative scripture. A common man with all the defects of human frailty is unable to teach that which is worth hearing. *Bhagavad-gītā* is above such literature. No mundane book compares with *Bhagavad-gītā*. When one accepts Kṛṣṇa as an ordinary man, *Bhagavad-gītā* loses all importance. The Māyāvādī argues that the plurality mentioned in this verse is conventional and that the plurality refers to the body. But previous to this verse such a bodily conception has already been condemned. After condemning the bodily conception of the living entities, how was it possible for Kṛṣṇa to place a conventional proposition on the body again? Therefore, the plurality is on spiritual grounds, as is confirmed by great teachers like Śrī Rāmānuja. It is clearly mentioned in many places in *Bhagavad-gītā* that this spiritual plurality is understood by those who are devotees of the Lord. Those who are envious of Kṛṣṇa as the Supreme Personality of Godhead have no bona fide access to this great literature. The nondevotee's approach to the teachings of *Bhagavad-gītā* is something like that of a bee licking on a bottle of honey. One cannot have a taste of honey unless one can taste within the bottle. Similarly, the mysticism of *Bhagavad-gītā* can be understood only by devotees, and no one else can taste it, as is stated in the Fourth Chapter of the book. Nor can the *Gītā* be touched by persons who envy the very existence of the Lord. Therefore, the Māyāvāda explanation of the *Gītā* is a most misleading presentation of the whole truth. Lord Caitanya has forbidden us to read commentaries made by the Māyāvādīs and warns that one who takes to an understanding of the Māyāvāda philosophy loses all power to understand the real mystery of the *Gītā*. If individuality refers to the empirical universe, then there is no need for teaching by the Lord. The plurality of the individual souls and of the Lord is an eternal fact, and it is confirmed by the *Vedas* as above mentioned.

13. As the embodied soul continually passes, in this body, from boyhood to youth, and then to old age, the soul similarly passes into another body at death. The self-realized soul is not bewildered by such a change.

PURPORT

Since every living entity is an individual soul, each is changing his body at every moment, manifesting sometimes as a child, sometimes as a youth, and sometimes as an old man—although the same spirit soul is there and does not undergo any change. This individual soul finally changes the body itself, in transmigrating from one to another, and since it is sure to have another body in the next birth—either material or spiritual—there was no cause for lamentation by Arjuna on account of death, either over Bhīṣma or over Droṇa, for whom he was so concerned. Rather, he should rejoice at their changing bodies from old to new ones, thereby rejuvenating their energy. Such changes of body are meant for varieties of enjoyment or suffering by the living entity, according to one's own work in this life. So Bhīṣma and Droṇa, being noble souls, were surely going to have either spiritual bodies in the next life, or at least life in godly bodies for superior enjoyment of material existence. In either case, there was no cause for lamentation.

Any man who has perfect knowledge of the constitution of the individual soul, the Supersoul, and nature—both material and spiritual—is called a *dhīra*, or a most sober man. Such a man is never deluded by the change of bodies by the living entities.

14. O son of Kuntī, the nonpermanent appearance of heat and cold, happiness and distress, and their disappearance in due course, are like the appearance and disappearance of winter and summer seasons. They arise from sense perception, O scion of Bharata, and one must learn to tolerate them without being disturbed.

15. O best among men [Arjuna], the person who is not disturbed by happiness and distress and is steady in both is certainly eligible for liberation.

16. Those who are seers of the truth have concluded that, of the nonexistent there is no endurance, and of the eternal there is no cessation. Seers have concluded this by studying the nature of both.

PURPORT

There is no endurance of the changing body. As admitted by modern science, the body is changing every moment by the actions and reactions of different cells, and thus growth and old age are taking place. But the spiritual soul exists permanently, remaining the same in all the changing circumstances of the body and the mind. That is the difference between matter and spirit. By nature the body is ever changing, and the soul is eternal. This conclusion is established by all classes of seers of the truth, impersonalist and personalist. In the *Viṣṇu Purāṇa* also this truth has been established. It is stated there that Viṣṇu and His abodes all have self-illuminated spiritual existence. The words existent and nonexistent refer only to spirit and matter. That is the version of all seers of truth.

This is the beginning of the instruction by the Lord to the living entities who are bewildered by the influence of ignorance. Removal of this ignorance means reestablishment of the eternal relationship between the worshiper and the worshipable, and the consequent understanding of the difference between part and parcel living entities and the Supreme Personality of Godhead. One can understand the nature of the Supreme by thorough study of oneself, the difference between oneself and the Supreme Being understood as the relationship between the part and the whole. In the *Vedānta-sūtra,* as well as in *Śrīmad-Bhāgavatam,* the Supreme has been accepted as the origin of all emanations. Such emanations are experienced by superior and inferior natural sequences. The living entities belong to the superior nature, as will be revealed in the Seventh Chapter. Although there is no difference between the energy and the energetic, the energetic is accepted as the Supreme, and energy or nature is accepted as the subordinate. The relationship of the living entities, therefore, is to be always subordinate to the Supreme Lord, as in the case of the master and the servant, or the teacher and the taught. Such clear knowledge is impossible to grasp under the spell of ignorance, and to drive away such ignorance the Lord teaches *Bhagavad-gītā* for the enlightenment of all beings for all time.

17. That which pervades the entire body is indestructible. No one is able to destroy the imperishable soul.

PURPORT

This verse more clearly explains the real nature of the soul, which is spread all over the body. Anyone can understand what is spread all over the body: it is consciousness. Everyone is conscious about the pains and pleasures of the body in part or as a whole. This spreading of consciousness is limited within one's own body. The pains and pleasures of one body are unknown to another. Therefore, each and every body contains an individual soul, and the symptom of the soul's presence is perceived as individual consciousness.

18. Only the material body of the indestructible, immeasurable and eternal living entity is subject to destruction; therefore, fight, O descendant of Bharata.

19. He who thinks that the living entity is the slayer, or that the entity is slain, does not understand. One who is in knowledge knows that the self slays not nor is slain.

PURPORT

When an embodied being is hurt by fatal weapons, it is to be known that the living entity within the body is not killed. The spirit soul is so small that it is impossible to kill him by any material weapon. Nor is the living entity killable in any case because of his spiritual constitution. What is killed or is supposed to be killed is the body only. This, however, does not at all encourage killing of the body. The Vedic injunction is *Mā hiṁsyāt sarva-bhūtāni*, never commit violence to anyone. The understanding that a living entity is not killed does not encourage animal slaughter. Killing the body of anyone without authority is abominable and is punishable by the law of the state as well as by the law of the Lord. Arjuna, however, is being engaged in killing for the principle of religion, and not whimsically.

20. For the soul there is never birth nor death. Nor, having once been, does he ever cease to be. He is unborn, eternal, ever-existing, undying and primeval. He is not slain when the body is slain.

21. O Pārtha, how can a person who knows that the soul is indestructible, unborn, eternal and immutable kill anyone or cause anyone to kill?

PURPORT

Everything has its utility, and a man who is situated in complete knowledge knows how and where to apply a thing for its proper utility. Similarly, violence also has its use, and how to apply violence rests with the person in knowledge. Although the justice of the peace awards capital punishment to a person condemned for murder, the justice of the peace cannot be blamed because he orders violence to another according to the codes of justice. In the *Manu-saṁhitā*, the lawbook for mankind, it is supported that a murderer should be condemned to death so that in his next life he will not have to suffer for the great sin he has committed.

Therefore, the king's punishment of hanging a murderer is actually beneficial. Similarly, when Kṛṣṇa orders fighting, it must be concluded that violence is for supreme justice, and, as such, Arjuna should follow the instruction, knowing well that such violence, committed in the act of fighting for justice, is not at all violence because, at any rate, the man, or rather the soul, cannot be killed. For the administration of justice, so-called violence is permitted. A surgical operation is not meant to kill the patient, but is for his cure. Therefore, the fighting to be executed by Arjuna, under the instruction of Kṛṣṇa, is with full knowledge, and so there is no possibility of sinful reaction.

22. As a person puts on new garments, giving up old ones, similarly, the soul accepts new material bodies, giving up the old and useless ones.

PURPORT

Change of body by the atomic individual soul is an accepted fact. Even some of the modern scientists who do not believe in the existence of the soul, but at the same time cannot explain the source of energy from the heart, have to accept continuous changes of body which appear from childhood to boyhood, and from boyhood to youth, and again from youth to old age. From old age, the change is transferred to another body. This has already been explained in the previous verse.

Transference of the atomic individual soul to another body is also made possible by the grace of the Supersoul. The Supersoul fulfills the desire of the soul as one friend fulfills the desire of another. The *Vedas,* such as the *Muṇḍaka Upaniṣad,* as well as the *Śvetāśvatara Upaniṣad,* confirm this concept of two kinds of souls by comparing them to two friendly birds sitting on the same tree. One of the birds (the individual atomic soul) is eating the fruit of the tree, and the other bird is simply watching his friend. Of these two birds, although they are the same in quality, one is captivated by the fruits of the material tree, while the other is simply witnessing his activities. Kṛṣṇa is the witnessing bird, and Arjuna is the eating bird. Although they are friends, one is still the master, and the other is the servant. Forgetfulness of this relationship by the atomic soul is the cause of one's changing his position from one tree to another, or from one body to another. The *jīva* soul is struggling very hard on the tree of the material body, but as soon as he agrees to accept the other bird as the supreme spiritual master, as Arjuna has agreed to do by voluntary surrender unto Kṛṣṇa for instruction, the subordinate bird immediately becomes free from all lamentations. Both the *Kaṭha Upaniṣad* and the *Śvetāśvatara Upaniṣad* confirm this statement.

23. The soul can never be cut into pieces by any weapon, nor can he be burned by fire, nor moistened by water, nor withered by the wind.

24. This individual soul is unbreakable and insoluble, and can be neither burned nor dried. He is everlasting, all-pervading, unchangeable, immovable and eternally the same.

25. It is said that the soul is invisible, inconceivable, immutable and unchangeable. Knowing this, you should not grieve for the body.

PURPORT

As described above, the magnitude of the soul is such that, for our material calculation, he cannot be detected even by the most powerful microscope; therefore, he is invisible. As far as his existence is concerned, no one can establish his experimental stability beyond the proof of *śruti*, or Vedic wisdom. We have to accept this truth because there is no other source for understanding the existence of the soul, although it is a fact by perception. There are many things we have to accept solely on grounds of superior authority. No one can deny the existence of his father, based upon the authority of his mother; there is no other source of understanding the identity of the father except on the authority of the mother. Similarly, there is no other source of understanding the soul except by studying the *Vedas*. In other words, the soul is inconceivable to human experimental knowledge. The soul is consciousness and conscious—that also is the statement of the *Vedas*, and we have to accept that. Unlike the bodily changes, there is no change for the soul. As eternally unchangeable, he always remains atomic in comparison to the infinite Supreme Soul. The Supreme Soul is infinite, and the atomic soul is infinitesimal. Therefore, the infinitesimal soul, being unchangeable, can never become equal to the infinite soul, or the Supreme Personality of

Godhead. This concept is repeated in the *Vedas* in different ways, just to confirm the stability of the conception of the soul. Repetition of something is necessary in order that we understand the matter thoroughly, without error.

26. If, however, you think the soul is perpetually born and always dies, still you have no reason to lament, O mighty-armed.

PURPORT

There is always a class of philosophers, akin to the Buddhists, who do not believe in the existence of the soul beyond the body. When Lord Kṛṣṇa spoke *Bhagavad-gītā*, it appears that such philosophers existed and were known as the *lokayatikas* and *vaibhāṣikas*. These philosophers maintained that life symptoms take place at a certain mature condition of the material combination. The modern material scientist and materialistic philosophers think similarly. According to them, the body is a combination of physical elements, and at a certain stage the life symptoms develop by interaction of these elements. The science of anthropology is largely based on this philosophy. Currently, many pseudo-religions now becoming fashionable in America are also adhering to this concept, as well as to the nihilistic, nondevotional Buddhist sects.

Even if Arjuna did not believe in the existence of the soul—as in the Vaibhāṣika philosophy—there would still have been no cause for lamentation. No one would lament the loss of a certain bulk of chemicals and stop discharging his prescribed duties. On the other hand, in modern science and scientific warfare, so many tons of chemicals are wasted in achieving victory over the enemy. According to the Vaibhāṣika philosophy, the so-called soul or *ātmā* vanishes along with the deterioration of the body. So, in any case, whether Arjuna accepted the Vedic conclusion that there is an atomic soul, or whether he did not believe in the existence of the soul, he had no reason for lamenting. According to this theory, since there are so many entities generating out of matter every moment, and so many of them are being vanquished at every moment, there is no need to grieve for such an incidence. However, since he was not risking rebirth of the soul, Arjuna had no reason to be afraid of being affected with sinful activities due to killing his grandfather and teacher. But at the same time, Kṛṣṇa sarcastically addressed Arjuna as Mahābāho, mighty-armed, because He, at least, did not accept the theory of the Vaibhāṣikas, which leaves aside the Vedic wisdom. As a *kṣatriya,* Arjuna belonged to the Vedic culture, and it behooved him to continue to follow its principles.

27. For one who has taken his birth, death is certain; and for one who is dead, birth is certain. Therefore, in the unavoidable discharge of your duty, you should not lament.

PURPORT

According to logicians, one has to take birth according to one's activities of life. And after finishing one term of activities, one has to die to take birth for the next. In this way the cycle of birth and death is revolving, one after the other, without liberation. This cycle of birth and death does not, however, support unnecessary murder, slaughter and war. But at the same time, violence and war are inevitable factors in human society for keeping law and order. The Battle of Kurukṣetra, being the will of the Supreme, was an inevitable event, and to fight for the right cause is the duty of a *kṣatriya.* Why should he be afraid of, or aggrieved at, the death of his relatives, since he was discharging his proper duty? He did not deserve to break the law, thereby becoming subjected to the reactions of sinful acts, of which he was so afraid. By ceasing from the discharge of his proper duty, he would not be able to stop the death of his relatives, and he would be degraded on account of his selection of the wrong path of action.

28. All created beings are unmanifest in their beginnings, manifest in their interim state, and unmanifest again when they are annihilated. So what need is there for lamentation?

29. Some look on the soul as amazing, some describe him as amazing, and some hear of him as amazing, while others, even after hearing about him, cannot understand him at all.

30. O descendant of Bharata, he who dwells in the body is eternal and can never be slain. Therefore you need not grieve for any creature.

31. Considering your specific duty as a *kṣatriya,* you should know that there is no better engagement for you than fighting on religious principles; and so there is no need for hesitation.

32. O Pārtha, happy are the *kṣatriyas* to whom such fighting opportunities come unsought, opening for them the doors of the heavenly planets.

33. If, however, you do not fight this religious war, then you will certainly incur sin for neglecting your duties and thus lose your reputation as a fighter.

34. People will always speak of your infamy, and for one who has been honored, dishonor is worse than death.

35. The great generals who have highly esteemed your name and fame will think that you have left the battlefield out of fear only, and thus they will consider you a coward.

36. Your enemies will describe you in many unkind words and scorn your ability. What could be more painful for you?

37. O son of Kuntī, either you will be killed on the battlefield and attain the heavenly planets, or you will conquer and enjoy the earthly kingdom. Therefore, get up and fight with determination.

38. Do thou fight for the sake of fighting, without considering happiness or distress, loss or gain, victory or defeat—and, by so doing, you shall never incur sin.

PURPORT

Lord Kṛṣṇa now directly says that Arjuna should fight for the sake of fighting because Kṛṣṇa desires the battle. There is no consideration of happiness or distress, profit or gain, victory or defeat in the activities of Kṛṣṇa consciousness. That everything should be performed for the sake of Kṛṣṇa is transcendental consciousness; so there is no reaction from material activities. Anyone who acts for his sense gratification, either in goodness or in passion, is liable to the reaction, good or bad. Anyone who has completely surrendered himself in the activities of Kṛṣṇa consciousness is no longer obliged to anyone, nor is he a debtor to anyone, as we are in the ordinary course of activities. It is said: "Anyone who has completely surrendered unto Kṛṣṇa, Mukunda, giving up all other duties, is no longer a debtor, nor is he obliged to anyone—not the demigods, nor the sages, nor the people in general, nor kinsmen, nor humanity, nor forefathers." That is the indirect hint given by Kṛṣṇa to Arjuna in this verse, and the matter will be more clearly explained in the following verses.

39. Thus far I have declared to you the analytical knowledge of Sāṅkhya philosophy. Now listen to the knowledge of *yoga*, whereby one works without fruitive result. O son of Pṛthā, when you act by such intelligence, you can free yourself from the bondage of works.

40. In this endeavor there is no loss or diminution, and a little advancement on this path can protect one from the most dangerous type of fear.

PURPORT

Activity in Kṛṣṇa consciousness, or acting for the benefit of Kṛṣṇa without expectation of sense gratification, is the highest transcendental quality of work. Even a small beginning of such activity finds no impediment, nor can that small beginning be lost at any stage. Any work begun on the material plane has to be done nicely till the end, otherwise the whole attempt becomes a failure. But any work begun in Kṛṣṇa consciousness has a permanent effect, even though not finished. The performer of such work is therefore not at a loss even if his work in Kṛṣṇa consciousness is incomplete. One percent done in Kṛṣṇa consciousness bears permanent results,so that the next beginning is from the point of two percent, whereas in material activity without one hundred percent success there is no profit. There is a nice verse in this connection in

Śrīmad-Bhāgavatam. It says: "If someone gives up his occupational duties and works in Kṛṣṇa consciousness and then again falls down on account of not being complete in such activities, still what loss is there on his part? And what can one gain if one performs his material activities very perfectly?" Or, as the Christians say: "What profiteth a man if he gain the whole world yet suffers the loss of his eternal soul?"

Material activities, and the results of such actions, will end with the body. But work in Kṛṣṇa consciousness will carry the person again to Kṛṣṇa consciousness, even after the loss of this body. At least one is sure to have a chance in the next life of being born into human society, either in the family of a great cultured *brāhmaṇa* or else in a rich aristocratic family that will give one a further chance for elevation. That is the unique quality of work done in Kṛṣṇa consciousness.

41. Those who are on this path are resolute in purpose, and their aim is one. O beloved child of the Kurus, the intelligence of those who are irresolute is many-branched.

42-43. Men of small knowledge are very much attached to the flowery words of the *Vedas*, which recommend various fruitive activities for elevation to heavenly planets, resultant good birth, power, and so forth. Being desirous of sense gratification and opulent life, they say that there is nothing more than this.

44. In the minds of those who are too attached to sense enjoyment and material opulence, and who are bewildered by such things, the resolute determination for devotional service to the Lord does not take place.

PURPORT

Samādhi means "fixed mind." The Vedic dictionary, the *Nirukti*, says, "When the mind is fixed for understanding the self, this is called *samādhi.*" *Samādhi* is never possible for persons interested in material sense enjoyment, nor for those who are bewildered by such temporary things. They are more or less condemned by the process of material energy.

45. The *Vedas* mainly deal with the subject of the three modes of material nature. Rise above these modes, O Arjuna. Be transcendental to all of them. Be free from all dualities and from all anxieties for gain and safety, and be established in the self.

46. All purposes that are served by the small pond can at once be served by the great reservoirs of water. Similarly, all the purposes of the *Vedas* can be served to one who knows the purpose behind them.

47. You have a right to perform your prescribed duty, but you are not entitled to the fruits of action. Never consider yourself the cause of action, and never be attached to inaction.

PURPORT

There are three considerations here: prescribed duties, capricious work and inaction. Prescribed duties mean activities in terms of one's position in the modes of material nature. Capricious work means actions without the sanction of authority, and inaction means not performing one's prescribed duties. The Lord advised that Arjuna not be inactive, but that he be active in his duty without being attached to the result. One who is attached to the result of his work is also the cause of the action. Thus he is the enjoyer or sufferer of the result of such actions.

As far as prescribed duties are concerned, they can be fitted into three subdivisions: routine work, emergency work and desired activities. Routine work, in terms of the scriptural injunctions, is done without desire for results. As one has to do it, obligatory work is action in the mode of goodness. Work with results becomes the cause of bondage, and so such work is not auspicious. Everyone has his proprietary right in regard to his duties, but should act without attachment to the result; thus such disinterested obligatory duties doubtlessly lead one to the path of liberation.

Arjuna was advised by the Lord to fight as a matter of duty, without attachment to the result. His nonparticipation in the battle is another side of attachment. Such attachment never leads one to the path of salvation. Any attachment, positive or negative, is cause for bondage. Inaction is sinful. Therefore, fighting as a matter of duty was the only auspicious path to salvation for Arjuna.

48. Be steadfast in your duty, O Arjuna, and abandon all attachment to success or failure. Such evenness of mind is called *yoga.*

49. O Dhanañjaya, rid yourself of all fruitive activities by devotional service, and surrender fully to that consciousness. Those who want to enjoy the fruits of their work are misers.

50. A man engaged in devotional service rids himself of both good and bad actions even in this life. Therefore strive for this *yoga,* O Arjuna, which is the art of all work.

51. The wise, engaged in devotional service, take refuge in the Lord and free themselves from the cycle of birth and death by renouncing the fruits of action in the material world. In this way they can attain that state beyond all miseries.

52. When your intelligence has passed out of the dense forest of delusion, you will become indifferent to all that has been heard and all that is to be heard.

PURPORT

There are many good examples in the lives of the great devotees of the Lord of those who became indifferent to the rituals of the *Vedas* simply by devotional service to the Lord. When a person factually understands Kṛṣṇa and one's relationship with Kṛṣṇa, one naturally becomes completely indifferent to the rituals of fruitive activities, even though he may be an experienced *brāhmaṇa.* Śrī Mādhavendra Purī, a great devotee and *ācārya* in the line of devotees, says: "O Lord, in my prayers three times a day, all glory to You. Bathing, I offer my obeisances unto You. O demigods! O forefathers! Please excuse me for my inability to offer you my respects. Now wherever I sit I am able to remember the great descendant of the Yadu dynasty [Kṛṣṇa], the enemy of Kaṁsa, and thereby I can free myself from all sinful bondage. I think this is sufficient for me."

The Vedic rites and rituals, comprehending all kinds of prayer three times a day, taking a bath early in the morning, offering respects to the forefathers, and so on, are imperative for the beginning of human life.

But when one is fully in Kṛṣṇa consciousness and is engaged in His transcendental loving service, one becomes indifferent to all these regulative principles because he has already attained perfection. If one can reach the platform of understanding by service to the Supreme Lord Kṛṣṇa, he no longer has the duty to execute the different types of penances and sacrifices recommended in revealed scriptures. And similarly, if one has not understood that the purpose of the *Vedas* is to reach Kṛṣṇa and simply engages in the rituals, then he is uselessly wasting time in such engagements. Persons in Kṛṣṇa consciousness transcend the limit of *śabda-brahma*, or the range of the *Vedas* and *Upaniṣads.*

53. When your mind is no longer disturbed by the flowery language of the *Vedas* and when it remains fixed in the trance of self-realization, then you will have attained the divine consciousness.

54. Arjuna said: What are the symptoms of one whose consciousness is thus merged in Transcendence? How does he speak, and what is his language? How does he sit, and how does he walk?

55. The Supreme Personality of Godhead said: O Pārtha, when a man gives up all varieties of sense desire which arise of invention, and when his mind finds satisfaction in the self alone, then he is said to be in pure transcendental consciousness.

56. One who is not disturbed in spite of the threefold miseries, who is not elated when there is happiness, and who is free from attachment, fear and anger, is called a sage of steady mind.

PURPORT

The word *muni* means one who can agitate his mind in various ways for mental speculation, without coming to a factual conclusion. It is said that every *muni* has a different angle of vision, and unless one *muni* is different in view from another, he cannot be called a *muni* in the strict sense of the term. But a *sthita-dhī-muni,* the kind mentioned herein by the Lord, is different from an ordinary *muni.* The *sthita-dhī-muni* is always in Kṛṣṇa consciousness, for he has finished all his business with creative speculation. He is called *praśānta-nihśeṣa-manorathāntaram,* or one who has surpassed the stage of mental speculations and has come to the conclusion that Lord Śrī Kṛṣṇa, Vāsudeva, is everything. He is called the *muni* fixed in mind. Such a fully Kṛṣṇa conscious person is not at all disturbed by the onslaughts of the threefold miseries: those due to nature, to other beings, and to the frailties of one's own body. Such a *muni* accepts all miseries as the mercy of the Lord, thinking himself only worthy of more trouble due to his past misdeeds, and sees that his miseries, by the grace of the Lord, are minimized to the lowest. Similarly, when he is happy he gives credit to the Lord, thinking himself unworthy of that happiness. He realizes that it is due only to the Lord's grace that he is in such a comfortable condition and thus able to render better service to the Lord. And for the service of the Lord, he is always daring and active and is not influenced by attachment or detachment. Attachment means accepting things for one's own sense gratification, and detachment is the absence of such sensual attachment. But one fixed in Kṛṣṇa consciousness has neither attachment nor detachment because his life is dedicated in the service of the Lord. Consequently, he is not at all angry even when his attempts are unsuccessful. A Kṛṣṇa conscious person is always steady in his determination.

57. He who is without affection either for good or evil is firmly fixed in perfect knowledge.

PURPORT

There is always some upheaval in the material world which may be good or evil. One who is not agitated by such material upheavals, who is without affection for good or evil, is to be understood as fixed in Kṛṣṇa consciousness. As long as one is in the material world, there is always the possibility of good and evil because this world is full of duality. But one who is fixed in Kṛṣṇa consciousness is not affected by good and evil because he is simply concerned with Kṛṣṇa, who is all good absolute. Such consciousness in Kṛṣṇa situates one in a perfect transcendental position called, technically, *samādhi.*

58. One who is able to withdraw his senses from sense objects, as the tortoise draws his limbs within the shell, is to be understood as truly situated in knowledge.

59. The embodied soul may be restricted from sense enjoyment, though the taste for sense objects remains. But, ceasing such engagements by experiencing a higher taste, he is fixed in consciousness.

60. The senses are so strong and impetuous, O Arjuna, that they forcibly carry away the mind even of a man of discrimination who is endeavoring to control them.

61. One who restrains his senses and fixes his consciousness upon Me is known as a man of steady intelligence.

62. While contemplating the objects of the senses, a person develops attachment for them, and from such attachment lust develops, and from lust anger arises.

PURPORT

One who is not Kṛṣṇa conscious is subjected to material desires while contemplating the objects of senses. The senses require real engagements, and if they are not engaged in the transcendental loving service of the Lord, they will certainly seek engagement in the service of materialism. In the material world everyone, including Lord Śiva and Lord Brahmā, to say nothing of other demigods in the heavenly planets, is subjected to the influence of sense objects, and the only method to get out of this puzzle of material existence is to become Kṛṣṇa conscious. Lord Śiva once was deep in meditation, but when the beautiful maiden Pārvatī agitated him for sense pleasure, he agreed to the proposal, and as a result Kārttikeya was born. When Haridāsa Ṭhākura was a young devotee of the Lord, he was similarly allured by the incarnation of Māyādevī, but Haridāsa easily passed the test because of his unalloyed devotion to Lord Kṛṣṇa. A sincere devotee of the Lord learns to hate all material sense enjoyment due to his higher taste for spiritual enjoyment in the association of the Lord. That is the secret of success. One who is not, therefore, in Kṛṣṇa consciousness, however powerful he may be in controlling the senses by artificial repression, is sure ultimately to fall, for the slightest thought of sense pleasure will drive him to gratify his desires.

63. From anger, delusion arises, and from delusion bewilderment of memory. When memory is bewildered, intelligence is lost, and when intelligence is lost, one falls down again into the material pool.

64. One who can control his senses by regulated principles, and who is free from attachment and aversion, can obtain the mercy of God.

PURPORT

It is already explained that one may externally control the senses by some artificial process, but unless the senses are engaged in the transcendental service of the Lord, there is every chance of a fall. Although the person in full Kṛṣṇa consciousness may apparently be on the sensual plane, actually, because of his being Kṛṣṇa conscious, he has no attachment to, or detachment from, such sensual activities. The Kṛṣṇa conscious person is concerned only with the satisfaction of Kṛṣṇa, and nothing else. Therefore he is transcendental to all attachment or detachment. If Kṛṣṇa wants, the devotee can do anything which is ordinarily undesirable; and if Kṛṣṇa does not want, he will not do anything he would have ordinarily done for his own satisfaction. Therefore, to act or not to act is within his control because he acts only under the dictation of Kṛṣṇa. This consciousness is the causeless mercy of the Lord, which the devotee can achieve in spite of his being attached to the sensual platform.

65. For one who is so situated, the threefold miseries of material life exist no longer; in such a happy state, one's intelligence is steady.

66. One who is not in transcendental consciousness can have neither a controlled mind nor steady intelligence, without which there is no possibility of peace. And how can there be any happiness without peace?

67. As a boat on the water is swept away by a strong wind, even so one of the senses in which the mind becomes fixed can carry away a man's intelligence.

68. Therefore, O mighty-armed, one whose senses are restrained from their objects is certainly of steady intelligence.

69. What is night for all beings is the time of awakening for the self-controlled; and the time of awakening for all beings is night for the introspective sage.

PURPORT

There are two classes of intelligent men. The one is intelligent in material activities for sense gratification, and the other is introspective and awake to the cultivation of self-realization. Activities of the introspective sage, or thoughtful man, are night for persons materially absorbed. Materialistic persons remain asleep during such a night due to their ignorance of self-realization. The introspective sage, however, remains alert in that night of the materialistic men. Such sages feel transcendental pleasure in the gradual advancement of spiritual culture, whereas the man in materialistic activities, being asleep to self-realization, dreams of varieties of sense pleasure, feeling sometimes happy and sometimes distressed in his sleeping condition. The introspective man is always indifferent to materialistic happiness and distress. He goes on with his self-realization activities undisturbed by material reactions.

70. A person who is not disturbed by the incessant flow of desires—that enter like rivers into the ocean which is ever being filled but is always still—can alone achieve peace, and not the man who strives to satisfy such desires.

71. A person who has given up all desires for sense gratification, who lives free from desires, who has given up all sense of proprietorship, and is devoid of false ego—he alone can attain real peace.

72. That is the way of the spiritual and godly life, after attaining which a man is not bewildered. Being so situated, even at the hour of death, one can enter into the kingdom of God.

PURPORT

One can attain Kṛṣṇa consciousness or divine life at once, within a second—or one may not attain such a state of life even after millions of births. It is only a matter of understanding and accepting the fact.

Khaṭvāṅga Mahārāja attained this state of life just a few minutes before his death, by surrendering unto Kṛṣṇa. *Nirvāṇa* means ending the process of materialistic life. According to Buddhist philosophy, there is only void after this material life, but *Bhagavad-gītā* teaches differently. Actual life begins after the completion of this material life. For the gross materialist it is sufficient to know that one has to end this materialistic way of life, but for persons who are spiritually advanced, there is another life after this materialistic one. Therefore, before ending this life, if one fortunately becomes Kṛṣṇa conscious, certainly he at once attains the stage of *brahma-nirvāṇa.* There is no difference between the kingdom of God and the devotional service of the Lord. Since both of them are on the absolute plane, to be engaged in the transcendental loving service to the Lord is to have attained the spiritual kingdom. In the material world there are activities of sense gratification, whereas in the spiritual world there are activities of Kṛṣṇa consciousness. Therefore, attainment of Kṛṣṇa consciousness even during this life is immediate attainment of Brahman, and one who is situated in Kṛṣṇa consciousness has certainly already entered into the kingdom of God.

Śrīla Bhaktivinoda Ṭhākura has summarized this Second Chapter of the *Bhagavad-gītā* as being the contents for the whole text. In *Bhagavad-gītā* the subject matters are *karma-yoga, jñāna-yoga* and *bhakti-yoga.* In the Second Chapter, *karma-yoga* and *jñāna-yoga* have been clearly discussed, and a glimpse of *bhakti-yoga* has also been given.

Thus end the Bhaktivedanta purports to the Second Chapter of the *Śrīmad Bhagavad-gītā* in the matter of its Contents.

CHAPTER THREE

Karma-yoga

1. Arjuna said: O Janārdana, O Keśava, why do You urge me to engage in this ghastly warfare, if You think that intelligence is better than fruitive work?

PURPORT

The Supreme Personality of Godhead, Śrī Kṛṣṇa, has very elaborately described the constitution of the soul in the previous chapter, with a view to delivering His intimate friend Arjuna from the ocean of material grief. And the path of realization has been recommended: *buddhi-yoga*, or Kṛṣṇa consciousness. Sometimes this Kṛṣṇa consciousness is misunderstood to be inertia, and one with such a misunderstanding often withdraws to a secluded place to become fully Kṛṣṇa conscious by chanting the holy name of Lord Kṛṣṇa. But without being trained in the philosophy of Kṛṣṇa consciousness, it is not advisable to chant the holy name of the Lord in a secluded place, where one may acquire only cheap adoration from the innocent public. Arjuna thought of Kṛṣṇa consciousness or *buddhi-yoga*, intelligence in spiritual advancement of knowledge, as something like retirement from active life and the practice of penance and austerity at a secluded place. In other words, he wanted to skillfully avoid the fighting by using Kṛṣṇa consciousness as an excuse. But as a sincere student, he placed the matter before his master and questioned Kṛṣṇa as to his best course of action. In answer, Lord Kṛṣṇa elaborately explained *karma-yoga*, or work in Kṛṣṇa consciousness, in this Third Chapter.

2. My intelligence is bewildered by Your equivocal instructions. Therefore, please tell me decisively what is most beneficial for me.

PURPORT

In the previous chapter, as a prelude to *Bhagavad-gītā*, many different paths were explained, such as *sāṅkhya-yoga, buddhi-yoga*, controlling the senses by intelligence, work without fruitive desire, and the position of the neophyte. This was all presented unsystematically. A more organized outline of the path would be necessary for action and understanding. Arjuna, therefore, wanted to clear up these apparently confusing matters so that any common man could accept them without misinterpretation. Although Kṛṣṇa had no intention of confusing Arjuna by any jugglery of words, Arjuna could not follow the process of Kṛṣṇa consciousness, either by inertia or active service. In other words, by his questions he is clearing the path of Kṛṣṇa consciousness for all students who are serious about understanding the mystery of *Bhagavad-gītā*.

3. The Supreme Personality of Godhead said: O sinless Arjuna, I have already explained that there are two classes of men who realize the Self. Some are inclined to understand Him by empirical philosophical speculation, and others are inclined to know Him by devotional service.

PURPORT

In the Second Chapter, verse 39, the Lord has explained two kinds of procedure—namely *sāṅkhya-yoga* and *karma-yoga*, or *buddhi-yoga*. In this verse, the Lord explains the same more clearly. *Sāṅkhya-yoga*, or the analytical study of the nature of spirit and matter, is the subject for persons who are inclined to speculate and understand things by experimental knowledge and philosophy. The other class of men work in Kṛṣṇa consciousness, as is explained in verse 61 of the same Second Chapter. The Lord has explained, also in verse 39, that by working under the principles of *buddhi-yoga*, or Kṛṣṇa consciousness, one can be relieved from the bonds of action, and furthermore there is no flaw in the process. The same principle is more clearly explained in verse 61—to perform *buddhi-yoga* is to depend entirely on the Supreme (or, more specifically, on Kṛṣṇa), and in this way all the senses can be brought under control very easily. Therefore, both the *yogas* are interdependent, as religion and philosophy. Religion without philosophy is sentiment, or sometimes fanaticism, while philosophy without religion is mental speculation. The ultimate goal is Kṛṣṇa because the philosophers who are also sincerely searching after the Absolute Truth come in the end to Kṛṣṇa consciousness. This is also stated in *Bhagavad-gītā.* The whole process is to understand the real position of the self in relation to the Superself. The indirect process is philosophical speculation, by which, gradually, one may come to the point of Kṛṣṇa consciousness; and the other process is by directly connecting with everything in Kṛṣṇa consciousness. Out of these two, the path of Kṛṣṇa consciousness is better because the philosophical process does not purify the senses. Kṛṣṇa consciousness is itself the purifying process, and by the direct method of devotional service it is simultaneously easy and sublime.

4. Not by merely abstaining from work can one achieve freedom from reaction, nor by renunciation alone can one attain perfection.

PURPORT

The renounced order of life can be adopted upon being purified by the discharge of the prescribed form of duties. The prescribed form of duties is laid down just to purify the heart of materialistic men. Without the purifying process, one cannot attain success by abruptly adopting the fourth order of life (*sannyāsa*). According to the empirical philosophers, simply by adopting *sannyāsa,* or retiring from fruitive activities, one at once becomes as good as Nārāyaṇa, God; but Lord Kṛṣṇa does not approve this principle. Without purification of heart, *sannyāsa* is simply a disturbance to the social order. On the other hand, if someone takes to the transcendental service of the Lord, even without discharging his prescribed duties, whatever he may be able to advance in the cause is accepted by the Lord. *Svalpam apy asya dharmasya trāyate mahato bhayāt.* Even the slight performance of such a principle enables one to overcome great difficulties.

5. All men are forced to act helplessly, according to the impulses born of the modes of material nature; therefore no one can refrain from doing something, not even for a moment.

PURPORT

This is not a question of embodied life; it is the nature of the soul itself to be always active. The proof is that without the presence of the spirit soul there is no movement of the material body. The body is only a dead vehicle to be worked by the spirit soul, and therefore it is to be understood that the soul is always active and cannot stop even for a moment. As such, the spirit soul has to be engaged in the good work of Kṛṣṇa consciousness; otherwise it will be engaged in occupations dictated by the illusory energy. In contact with material energy, the spirit soul acquires material modes, and to purify the soul from such affinities it is necessary to engage it in the prescribed duties enjoined in the *śāstras*, or scriptures. But if the soul is engaged in his natural function of Kṛṣṇa consciousness, whatever he is able to do is good for him. *Śrīmad-Bhāgavatam* affirms this: "If someone takes to Kṛṣṇa consciousness, even though he may not follow the prescribed duties in the *śāstras* or execute the devotional service properly, or even if he falls down from the standard, there is no loss or evil for him. And even though he carries out all the injunctions for purification in the *śāstras*, what does it avail him if he is not Kṛṣṇa conscious?" So the purifying process is necessary for reaching this point. *Sannyāsa*, or any purifying process, is meant for helping one to reach the ultimate goal of becoming Kṛṣṇa conscious, without which everything is considered a failure.

6. One who restrains the senses and organs of action, but whose mind dwells on sense objects, certainly deludes himself and is called a pretender.

7. On the other hand, he who controls the senses by the mind and engages his active organs in works of devotion, without attachment, is by far superior.

PURPORT

Instead of becoming a pseudo-transcendentalist for the sake of wanton living and sense enjoyment, it is far better to remain in one's own business and execute the purpose of life, which is to get free from material bondage and enter into the kingdom of God. The *svārtha-gati,* or goal of self-interest, is to reach Viṣṇu. The whole *varṇa* and *āśrama* system is designed to help us reach this goal of life. A householder can also reach this destination by regulated service in Kṛṣṇa consciousness. For self-realization, one can live a controlled life, as prescribed in the *śāstras,* and continue carrying out his business without attachment, and that will lead him gradually to the progressive path. Such a sincere person who follows this method is far better situated than the false pretender who adopts show-bottle spiritualism to cheat the innocent public. A sincere sweeper in the street is far better than the charlatan meditator who meditates only for the sake of making a living.

8. Perform your prescribed duty, which is better than not working. A man cannot even maintain his physical body without work.

9. Work done as a sacrifice for Viṣṇu has to be performed, otherwise work binds one to this material world. Therefore, O son of Kuntī, perform prescribed duties for His satisfaction, and in that way you will always remain unattached and free from bondage.

PURPORT

Since one has to work even for the simple maintenance of the body, the prescribed duties for a particular social position and quality are so made that that purpose can be fulfilled. *Yajña* means Lord Viṣṇu, or sacrificial performances. All sacrificial performances are meant for the satisfaction of Lord Viṣṇu. The *Vedas* enjoin, *yajña vai viṣṇu.* In other words, the same purpose is served whether one performs prescribed *yajñas* or directly serves Lord Viṣṇu. Kṛṣṇa consciousness is therefore the performance of *yajña* as prescribed here in this verse. The *varṇāśrama* institution also aims at satisfying Lord Viṣṇu. *Varṇāśramācaravatā puruṣeṇa paraḥ pumān/ viṣṇur ārādhyate panthā nānyat tat-toṣa-kāraṇam.*

Therefore, one has to work for the satisfaction of Viṣṇu. Any other work done in this material world will be a cause of bondage, for both good and evil work have their reactions, and any reaction binds the performer. One has only to work in Kṛṣṇa consciousness, to satisfy Kṛṣṇa or Viṣṇu, and while performing such activities one is in a liberated stage. This is the great art of doing work, and in the beginning this process requires very good and expert guidance. One should therefore act very diligently, under the expert guidance of a devotee of Lord Kṛṣṇa, or under the direct instruction of Kṛṣṇa (under whom Arjuna had the opportunity to work). Nothing should be performed for sense gratification, but everything should be done for the satisfaction of Kṛṣṇa. This practice will not only save one from the reactions of work, but will also gradually raise one to the platform of the transcendental loving service of the Lord, which alone can uplift one to the kingdom of God.

10. In the beginning of creation, the Lord of all creatures sent forth generations of men and demigods, along with sacrifices for Viṣṇu, and blessed them by saying, "Be thou happy by this *yajña* [sacrifice] because its performance will bestow upon you all desirable things."

PURPORT

The material creation by the Lord of creatures (Viṣṇu) is a chance offered to the conditioned souls to come back home, back to Godhead. All living entities within the material creation are conditioned by material nature because of their forgetfulness of their relationship to Viṣṇu, or Kṛṣṇa, the Supreme Personality of Godhead. The Vedic principles are to help us understand this eternal relationship. The Lord says that the purpose of the *Vedas* is to understand Him. In the Vedic hymns it is said, *patiṁ viśvasya ātmā īśvaram:* the Lord of the living entities is the Supreme Personality of Godhead, Viṣṇu.

Viṣṇu is the Lord of all living creatures, all worlds, and all beauties, and the protector of everyone. The Lord created this material world for the conditioned souls to learn how to perform *yajñas* for the satisfaction of Viṣṇu, so that while in the material world they can live very comfortably without anxiety in life. Then, after finishing the present material body, they can enter into the kingdom of God. That is the whole program for the conditioned souls. By performance of *yajña*, the conditioned souls gradually become Kṛṣṇa conscious and become godly in all respects. In this Age of Kali, the *saṅkīrtana-yajña*, the chanting of the holy names of God, is recommended by the Vedic scriptures, and this transcendental system was introduced by Lord Caitanya Mahāprabhu for the deliverance of all men. *Saṅkīrtana-yajña* and Kṛṣṇa consciousness go well together. Lord Kṛṣṇa in His devotional form (as Lord Caitanya) is worshiped in *Śrīmad-Bhāgavatam* as follows, with special reference to the *saṅkīrtana-yajña:* "In this Age of Kali, people who are endowed with sufficient brain substance will worship the Lord, who is accompanied by His associates, by performance of *saṅkīrtana-yajña.*" Although other *yajñas* prescribed in the Vedic literature are not easy to perform in this Age of Kali, the *saṅkīrtana-yajña* is the easiest and is sublime for all purposes, as recommended in *Bhagavad-gītā.*

11. The demigods, being pleased by sacrifices, will also please you; thus nourishing one another, there will reign general prosperity for all.

PURPORT

The demigods are empowered administrators of material affairs. The supply of air, light, water and all other benedictions for maintenance of the body and soul of every living entity is entrusted to the demigods, who are innumerable assistants in different parts of the body of the Supreme Personality of Godhead. Their pleasures and displeasures are dependent on the performance of *yajñas* by human beings. Some of the *yajñas* are meant for satisfying the particular demigods, but even in so doing, Lord Viṣṇu is worshiped in all *yajñas* as the chief beneficiary. It is stated also in *Bhagavad-gītā* that Kṛṣṇa Himself is the beneficiary of all kinds of *yajñas. Bhoktāraṁ yajña-tapasām.* Therefore, ultimate satisfaction of the Lord is the chief purpose of all *yajñas.* When these sacrifices are perfectly performed, naturally the demigods in charge of the different departments of supply are pleased, and there is no scarcity in the flow of natural products.

Performance of *yajñas* has many side benefits, ultimately leading to liberation from material bondage. By performance of sacrifice, all activities become purified, as stated in the *Vedas.* As will be explained in the following verse, by performance of *yajñas,* one's eatables become sanctified, and by eating sanctified food, one's very existence becomes purified; by the purification of existence, finer tissues in the memory become sanctified, and when memory is sanctified, one can think of the path of liberation, and all these combined together lead to Kṛṣṇa consciousness, the great necessity of present-day society.

12. In charge of the various necessities of life, the demigods, being satisfied by the performance of *yajña,* supply all needs to man. But he who enjoys these gifts, without offering them to the demigods in return, is certainly a thief.

13. The devotees of the Lord are released from all sins because they eat food which is offered first for sacrifice. Others, who prepare food for personal sense enjoyment, verily eat only sin.

14. All living bodies subsist on food grains, food grains are produced from rains, rains come from performance of sacrifice, and sacrifice is born of prescribed duties.

15. Regulated activities arise from the *Vedas,* and the *Vedas* spring from the Supreme Godhead. Therefore, the all-pervading Transcendence is eternally situated in acts of sacrifice.

PURPORT

Yajñārtha-karma, or the necessity of work for the satisfaction of Viṣṇu only, is more expressly stated in this verse. If we have to work for the satisfaction of the *yajña-puruṣa,* Viṣṇu, then we must find the direction of work in Brahman, or the transcendental *Vedas.* The *Vedas* are therefore codes of working direction. Anything performed without the direction of the *Vedas* is called *vikarma,* or unauthorized sinful work. Therefore, one should always take direction from the *Vedas* to be saved from the reaction of work. As one has to work in ordinary life by the direction of the state, similarly one has to work under the direction of the supreme state of the Lord. Such instructions in the *Vedas* are directly manifested from the breathing of the Supreme Personality of Godhead. It is said: "All the four *Vedas*—namely the *Ṛg Veda, Yajur Veda, Sāma Veda* and *Atharva Veda*—are emanations from the breathing of the great Personality of Godhead." The Lord, being potent, can speak by breathing air, as is confirmed in the *Brahma-saṁhitā,* for the Lord has the omnipotence to perform through each of His senses the actions of all other senses. In other words, the Lord can speak through His breathing, and He can impregnate by His eyes. It is said that He glanced over the material nature and thus fathered all the living entities. So after impregnating the conditioned soul into the womb of material nature, He gave His direction in the Vedic wisdom as to how such conditioned souls can return home, back to Godhead. We should always remember that the conditioned souls in material nature are all eager for material enjoyment. And the Vedic directions are so made that one can satisfy one's perverted desires and then return to Godhead, having finished this so-called enjoyment. It is a chance for the conditioned souls to attain liberation; therefore the conditioned souls must try to follow the process of *yajña* by becoming Kṛṣṇa conscious. Those who have not followed the Vedic injunctions may adopt the principles of Kṛṣṇa consciousness, and that will take the place of performance of Vedic *yajñas*, or *karma.*

16. My dear Arjuna, a man who does not follow this prescribed Vedic system of sacrifice certainly leads a life of sin, for a person delighting only in the senses lives in vain.

PURPORT

The mammonist philosophy of work very hard and enjoy sense gratification is condemned herewith by the Lord. For those who want to enjoy this material world, the above-mentioned cycle of sacrifices is absolutely necessary. One who does not follow such regulations is living a very risky life, being condemned more and more. By nature's law, this human form of life is specifically meant for self-realization, in either of the three ways—namely *karma-yoga, jñāna-yoga* or *bhakti-yoga.* There is no necessity of rigidly following the performances of the prescribed *yajñas.* Such transcendentalists are above vice and virtue. But those who are engaged in sense gratification require purification by the above-mentioned cycle of *yajña* performances. There are different kinds of activities. Those who are not Kṛṣṇa conscious are certainly engaged in sensory consciousness, and therefore they need to execute pious work. The *yajña* system is planned in such a way that sensory conscious persons may satisfy their desires without becoming entangled in the reactions to such sense gratifying work. The prosperity of the world depends not on our own efforts, but on the background arrangement of the Supreme Lord, directly carried out by the demigods. Therefore, these sacrifices are directly aimed at the particular demigod mentioned in the *Vedas.* Indirectly, it is the practice of Kṛṣṇa consciousness because when one masters the performances of *yajñas*, one is sure to become Kṛṣṇa conscious. If, having performed *yajñas*, one does not become Kṛṣṇa conscious, such principles are counted as only moral codes. One should not, of course, limit his progress to the point of moral codes, but should transcend them, to attain Kṛṣṇa consciousness.

17. One who is, however, taking pleasure in the self, who is illumined in the self, who rejoices in and is satisfied with the self only, fully satiated—for him there is no duty.

PURPORT

A person who is *fully* Kṛṣṇa conscious, and by his acts in Kṛṣṇa consciousness is fully satisfied, no longer has anything to perform as his duty. Due to his becoming Kṛṣṇa conscious, all the dirty things within are instantly cleansed, ordinarily an effect of many, many thousands of *yajña* performances. By such clearing of consciousness one becomes fully confident of his eternal position in relationship with the Supreme. His duty thus becomes self-illuminated by the grace of the Lord, and therefore he no longer has anything to do in terms of the Vedic injunctions. Such a Kṛṣṇa conscious person is no longer interested in material activities and no longer takes pleasure in material arrangements like wine, women and similar infatuations.

18. A self-realized man has no purpose to fulfill in the discharge of his prescribed duties, nor has he any reason not to perform such work. Nor has he any need to depend on any other living being.

19. Therefore, without being attached to the fruits of activities, one should act as a matter of duty, for by working without attachment one attains the Supreme.

PURPORT

The Supreme is the Personality of Godhead for the devotees, and liberation for the impersonalists. A person acting for Kṛṣṇa, or in Kṛṣṇa consciousness, under proper guidance and without attachment to the result of the work, is certainly making progress toward the supreme goal of life. Indirectly, Arjuna is told that he should fight the Battle of Kurukṣetra without attachment, in the interest of Kṛṣṇa, because Kṛṣṇa wanted him to fight. To be a good man or a nonviolent man is also a personal attachment, but to act on behalf of the Supreme's desire is to act without attachment for the result. That is the perfect action of the highest degree, recommended by the Supreme Personality of Godhead, Śrī Kṛṣṇa.

Vedic rituals, like prescribed sacrifices, are performed by persons for purification of impious activities that were performed in the field of sense gratification. But a person who is acting in Kṛṣṇa consciousness is transcendental to the actions and reactions of good or evil work. A Kṛṣṇa conscious person has no attachment for the result, but acts on behalf of Kṛṣṇa alone. He engages in all kinds of activities, but is completely nonattached.

20. Even kings like Janaka attained the perfectional stage by performance of prescribed duties. Therefore, just for the sake of educating the people in general, you should perform your work.

PURPORT

Kings like Janaka and others were all self-realized souls; consequently they had no obligation to perform the prescribed duties in the *Vedas.* Nonetheless, they performed all prescribed activities just to set examples for the people in general. Janaka was the father of Sītā and father-in-law of Lord Śrī Rāma. As a great devotee of the Lord, King Janaka was transcendentally situated, but because he was the King of Mithilā (a subdivision of Behar province in India) he had to teach his subjects how to act. In the Battle of Kurukṣetra, the Lord wanted to teach people in general that violence is also necessary in a situation where good arguments fail. Before the Battle of Kurukṣetra there was every effort to avoid the war, even by the Supreme Personality of Godhead, but the other party was determined to fight. So for such a right cause, there is a necessity for fighting. Therefore, although one who is situated in Kṛṣṇa consciousness may not have any interest in the world, he still works to teach the public how to live and how to act. Experienced persons in Kṛṣṇa consciousness can act in such a way that others will follow, and this is explained in the following verse.

21. Whatever action a great man performs, common men follow. And whatever standards he sets by exemplary acts, all the world pursues.

22. O son of Pṛthā, no work is prescribed for Me within all the three planetary systems. Nor am I in want of anything, nor have I the need to obtain anything—and yet I am engaged in work.

PURPORT

Since everything is in full opulence in the Personality of Godhead and is naturally existing in full truth, there is no duty for the Supreme Personality of Godhead to perform. One who must receive the results of work has some designated duty, but one who has nothing to achieve within the three planetary systems certainly has no duty. And yet Lord Kṛṣṇa is engaged on the Battlefield of Kurukṣetra as the leader of the *kṣatriyas* because the *kṣatriyas* are duty-bound to give protection to the distressed. Although He is above all the regulations of revealed scriptures, He does not do anything that violates the revealed scriptures.

23. For if I did not engage in work, O Pārtha, certainly all men would follow My path.

24. If I should cease to work, then all these worlds would be put to ruination, and I would be the cause of creating unwanted population, and I would thereby destroy the peace of all sentient beings.

PURPORT

Varṇa-saṅkara is unwanted population which disturbs the peace of the general society. In order to check this social disturbance, there are prescribed rules and regulations by which the population can automatically become peaceful and organized for spiritual progress in life. When Lord Kṛṣṇa descends, naturally He deals with such rules and regulations in order to maintain the prestige and necessity of such important performances. The Lord is said to be the father of all living entities, and if the living entities are misguided, indirectly the responsibility goes to the Lord. Therefore, whenever there is a general disregard of such regulative principles, the Lord Himself descends and corrects the society. We should, however, note carefully that although we have to follow in the footsteps of the Lord, we still have to remember that we cannot imitate Him. Following and imitating are not on the same level. We cannot imitate the Lord by lifting Govardhana Hill as the Lord did in His childhood. It is impossible for any human being. We have to follow His instructions, but we may not imitate Him at any time. *Śrīmad-Bhāgavatam* affirms this as follows: "One should simply follow the instructions of the controllers and should not imitate them in their activities. Their instructions are all good for us, and any intelligent person must perform them as instructed. However, one should guard against trying to imitate their actions. One should not try to drink the ocean of poison, imitating Lord Śiva."

We should always remember the position of the *īśvaras*, those who can actually control the movements of the sun and moon. Without such power, one cannot imitate the *īśvaras*, or the superpowerful. The example set herein is very appropriate. Lord Śiva drank poison to the extent of swallowing an ocean, but if any common man tries to drink even a fragment of such poison, he will be killed. There are many pseudo-devotees of Lord Śiva who want to indulge in smoking *gañja* (marijuana) and similar intoxicating drugs, forgetting that by so imitating the acts of Lord Śiva they are calling death very near. Similarly, there are some pseudo-devotees of Lord Kṛṣṇa who prefer to imitate the Lord in His *rāsa-līlā*, or dance of love, forgetting their inability to lift the Govardhana Hill. It is best, therefore, that one not try to imitate the powerful, but simply endeavor to follow their instructions; nor should one try to occupy the post of the powerful without qualification. There are so many "incarnations" of God without the powers of the Supreme Godhead.

25. As the ignorant perform their duties with attachment to results, so the learned may also act, but without attachment, for the sake of leading people on the right path.

26. Let not the wise disrupt the minds of the ignorant who are attached to fruitive action. They should be encouraged not to refrain from work, but to engage in work in the spirit of devotion.

27. The bewildered spirit soul, under the influence of the three modes of material nature, thinks himself to be the doer of activities that are in actuality carried out by nature.

PURPORT

Two persons, one in Kṛṣṇa consciousness and the other in material consciousness, working on the same level, may appear to be working on the same platform, but there is a wide gulf of difference in their respective positions. The person in material consciousness is convinced by false ego that he is the doer of everything. With him there is no consideration that the mechanism of the body is produced by material nature, or that material nature is under the supervision of the Supreme Personality of Godhead. The materialistic person has no knowledge that ultimately he is under the control of Kṛṣṇa. The person in false ego takes all credit for doing everything independently, and that is the symptom of his nescience. He does not know that his gross and subtle body is the creation of material nature, under the order of the Supreme Personality of Godhead, and that as such his bodily and mental activities should be engaged in the service of Kṛṇṣa in Kṛṣṇa consciousness. He does not know that the Supreme Personality of Godhead is known as Hṛṣīkeśa, or the master of all senses. But due to his long misuse of the senses, he is factually bewildered by the false ego, and that is the cause of his forgetfulness of his eternal relationship with Kṛṣṇa.

28. One who is in knowledge of the Absolute Truth, O mighty-armed, does not engage himself in the senses and sense gratification, knowing well the difference between work in devotion and work for fruitive results.

PURPORT

The knower of the Absolute Truth is convinced of his awkward position in material association. He knows that he is part and parcel of the Supreme Personality of Godhead, Kṛṣṇa, and that his position should not be in the material creation. He knows his real identity as part and parcel of the Supreme, who is eternal bliss and knowledge, and he realizes that somehow or other he is now entrapped in the material conception of life.

In his pure state of existence he is meant to dovetail his activities in devotional service to the Supreme Personality of Godhead, Kṛṣṇa. He therefore engages himself in the activities of Kṛṣṇa consciousness and becomes naturally unattached to the activities of the material senses, which are all circumstantial and temporary. He knows that his material condition of life is under the supreme control of the Lord; consequently he is not disturbed by any kind of material reaction, which he considers to be the mercy of the Lord. According to *Śrīmad-Bhāgavatam,* one who knows the Absolute Truth in three different features—namely Brahman, Paramātmā and the Supreme Personality of Godhead—is called *tattvavit,* for he knows also his own factual position in relationship with the Supreme.

29. Bewildered by the modes of material nature, the ignorant fully engage themselves in material activities and become attached, but the wise should not unsettle them, although these duties are inferior due to the performers' lack of knowledge.

PURPORT

Men who are ignorant cannot appreciate activities in Kṛṣṇa consciousness, and therefore Lord Kṛṣṇa advises us not to disturb them and simply waste valuable time. But the devotees of the Lord are more kind than the Lord because they understand the purpose of the Lord. Consequently they undertake all kinds of risks, even to the point of approaching ignorant men to try to engage them in the acts of Kṛṣṇa consciousness, which are absolutely necessary for the human being.

30. Therefore, O Arjuna, surrendering all your works unto Me, with mind intent on Me, and without desire for gain and free from egoism and lethargy—fight.

PURPORT

This verse clearly indicates the whole purpose of *Bhagavad-gītā.* The Lord instructs that one has to become fully Kṛṣṇa conscious to discharge duties, as if in military discipline. Such an injunction may make things a little difficult, but that is the constitutional position of the living entity.

The living entity cannot be happy independent of the cooperation of the Supreme Lord because the eternal constitutional position of the living entity is to become subordinate to the desires of the Lord. Arjuna was therefore ordered by Śrī Kṛṣṇa to fight as if the Lord were his military commander. One has to sacrifice everything for the good will of the Supreme Lord, and at the same time discharge his prescribed duties without claims of proprietorship. Arjuna did not have to consider the order of the Lord; he had only to execute His order. The Supreme Lord is the Soul of all souls, therefore one who depends solely and wholly on the Supreme Soul without personal consideration, or in other words one who is fully Kṛṣṇa conscious, is called *adhyātma-cetas,* full of self-knowledge. One has to act on the order of the master. One should not expect any fruitive result. The cashier may count millions of dollars for his employer, but he does not claim a cent out of the great amount of money. Similarly, one has to take it for granted that nothing in the world belongs to any individual person, but everything belongs to the Supreme Personality of Godhead. That is the real purport of Kṛṣṇa's saying "unto Me." And when one acts in such Kṛṣṇa consciousness, certainly he does not claim proprietorship over anything; so this consciousness is called *nirmama,* or "nothing is mine." And if there is any reluctance to execute such a stern order, which is without consideration of so-called kinsmen in the bodily relationship, that reluctance should be thrown off; in this way one may become without feverish mentality or lethargy. Everyone, according to his quality and position, has a particular type of work to discharge, and all such duties may be discharged in Kṛṣṇa consciousness, as described above. That will lead one to the path of liberation.

31. One who executes his duties according to My injunctions and who follows this teaching faithfully becomes free from the bondage of fruitive actions.

PURPORT

This injunction of the Supreme Personality of Godhead, Kṛṣṇa, is the essence of all Vedic wisdom, and therefore is eternally true without exception. As the *Vedas* are eternal, so this truth of Kṛṣṇa consciousness is also eternal. One should have firm faith in this injunction, without envying the Lord. There are many so-called philosophers who write comments on the *Bhagavad-gītā* but have no faith in Kṛṣṇa. They will never be liberated from the bondage of fruitive action. But an ordinary man with firm faith in the eternal injunctions of the Lord, even though unable to execute such orders, becomes liberated from the bondage of the law of *karma*. In the beginning of Kṛṣṇa consciousness, one may not fully discharge the injunctions of the Lord, but because one is not resentful of this principle and works sincerely without consideration of defeat and hopelessness, he will surely be promoted to the stage of pure Kṛṣṇa consciousness.

32. But those who, out of envy, disregard these teachings and do not practice them regularly, are to be considered bereft of all knowledge, befooled, and doomed to ignorance and bondage.

33. Even a man of knowledge acts according to his own nature, for everyone follows his nature. What can repression accomplish?

34. Attraction and repulsion for sense objects are felt by embodied beings, but one should not fall under the control of senses and sense objects because they are stumbling blocks on the path of self-realization.

35. It is far better to discharge one's prescribed duties, even though they may be faulty, than another's duties. Destruction in the course of performing one's own duty is better than engaging in another's duties, for to follow another's path is dangerous.

36. Arjuna said: O descendant of Vṛṣṇi, by what is one impelled to sinful acts, even unwillingly, as if engaged by force?

PURPORT

A living entity, as part and parcel of the Supreme Personality, is originally spiritual and pure as well as free from all contaminations of matter. Therefore, by nature the living entity is not subjected to the sins of the material world. But factually, when the living entity is in contact with the material nature, he acts in many sinful ways without hesitation. As such, Arjuna's question to Kṛṣṇa is very sanguine, as to the perverted nature of the living entities. Although the living entity sometimes does not want to act in sin, he is still forced to act. This force is not, however, impelled by the Supersoul living with the living entity, but must be due to other causes. And that is explained in the next verse by the Lord.

37. The Supreme Personality of Godhead said: It is lust only, Arjuna, which is born of contact with the material modes of passion and later transformed into wrath, and which is the all-devouring, sinful enemy of this world.

38. As fire is covered by smoke, as a mirror is covered by dust, or as the embryo is covered by the womb, similarly, the living entity is covered by different degrees of this lust.

PURPORT

There are three degrees of covering of the pure living entity, and thereby the pure consciousness of the living entity, or Kṛṣṇa consciousness, is embarrassed by nonmanifestation. This covering is but lust, under different manifestations like smoke in fire, dust on a mirror, and the womb about the embryo. When lust is compared to smoke it is understood that the fire of the living spark can be a little perceived. In other words, when the living entity exhibits his Kṛṣṇa consciousness slightly, he may be likened to the fire covered by smoke. Although fire is necessary where there is smoke, there is no overt manifestation of fire in the early stage. This stage can be compared to the beginning of Kṛṣṇa consciousness. The comparison of the dust of the mirror refers to the cleansing process of the mirror of the mind by so many spiritual methods. The best process is to chant the holy names of the Lord. The comparison of the embryo covered by the womb is an analogy illustrating the most awkward position, for the child in the womb is so helpless that it cannot even move. This stage of living condition can be compared also to that of the trees. The trees are living entities, but they have been put into that condition of life by such a great exhibition of lust that they are almost void of all consciousness. The covered mirror is compared to the birds and beasts, and smoke-covered fire is compared to the human being. In the form of a human being, the living entity can perceive a little Kṛṣṇa consciousness, and if he makes further development, the fire of spiritual life can be kindled in the human form. By careful handling of the smoke in the fire, the fire can be made to blaze, and therefore the human form of life is a chance for the living entity to escape the entanglement of material existence. In the human form of life, one can conquer the enemy, lust, by culture of Kṛṣṇa consciousness under able guidance.

39. Thus, a man's pure consciousness is covered by his eternal enemy in the form of lust, which is never satisfied and which burns like fire.

40. The senses, the mind and the intelligence are the sitting places of this lust, which veils the real knowledge of the living entity and bewilders him.

41. Therefore, O Arjuna, best of the Bharatas, in the very beginning curb the great symbol of sin [lust] by regulating the senses, and slay this destroyer of knowledge and self-realization.

42. The working senses are superior to dull matter; mind is higher than the senses; intelligence is still higher than the mind; and he [the soul] is even higher than the intelligence.

43. Thus knowing oneself to be transcendental to material senses, mind and intelligence, one should control the lower self by the higher self and thus—by spiritual strength—conquer this insatiable enemy known as lust.

PURPORT

This Third Chapter of *Bhagavad-gītā* is conclusively directive to Kṛṣṇa consciousness, through knowing oneself as the eternal servitor of the Supreme Personality of Godhead, without considering impersonal voidness as the ultimate end. In the material existence of life, one is certainly influenced by propensities of lust and desire for dominating the resources of material nature. Such desires for overlording and sense gratification are the greatest enemies of the conditioned soul; but by the strength of Kṛṣṇa consciousness, one can conquer the material senses and the mind, along with the intelligence. One may not give up work and prescribed duties all of a sudden, but by gradually developing one's Kṛṣṇa consciousness, one can be situated in a transcendental position without being influenced by the material senses and the mind—by steady intelligence directed toward one's pure identity. This is the sum total of this chapter. In the immature stage of material existence, philosophical speculations and artificial attempts to control the senses by the so-called practice of yogic postures can never help a man toward spiritual life. He must be trained in Kṛṣṇa consciousness by higher intelligence.

Thus end the Bhaktivedanta purports to the Third Chapter of the *Śrīmad Bhagavad-gītā* in the matter of *Karma-yoga,* or the discharge of one's prescribed duty in Kṛṣṇa consciousness.

CHAPTER FOUR

Transcendental Knowledge

1. The Supreme Personality of Godhead said: I instructed this imperishable science of yoga to the sun-god Vivasvān, and Vivasvān instructed it to Manu, the father of mankind, and Manu in turn instructed it to Ikṣvāku.

PURPORT

Herein we find the history of the *Bhagavad-gītā* traced from a remote time when it was delivered to the kings of all planets. The royal order is especially dedicated to the protection of the inhabitants, and as such its members should also understand the science of *Bhagavad-gītā* in order to rule the citizens and protect them from the onslaught of material bondage to lust. Human life is meant for cultivation of spiritual knowledge, in eternal relationship with the Supreme Personality of Godhead, and the executive heads of all states and all planets are obliged to impart this lesson to the citizens by education, culture and devotion. In other words, the executive heads of all states are intended to spread the science of Kṛṣṇa consciousness so that the people may take advantage of this great science and pursue a successful path, utilizing the opportunity of the human form of life.

2. This supreme science was thus received through the chain of disciplic succession, and the saintly kings understood it in that way. But in course of time the succession was broken, and therefore the science as it is appears to be lost.

3. That very ancient science of the relationship with the Supreme is today told by Me to you because you are My devotee as well as My friend; therefore, you can understand the transcendental mystery of this science.

PURPORT

There are two classes of men, namely the devotee and the demon. The Lord selected Arjuna as the recipient of this great science owing to his being the devotee of the Lord, but for the demon it is not possible to understand this great, mysterious science. There are a number of editions of this great book of knowledge, and some of them are commented upon by the devotees, and some of them are commented upon by the demons. Commentary by the devotees is real, whereas that of the demons is useless. Arjuna is recognized by the Lord as a devotee; therefore, one who follows the line of Arjuna in understanding the *Gītā* will derive benefit from it. Otherwise, one will simply waste his valuable time in reading commentaries. Arjuna accepts Śrī Kṛṣṇa as the Supreme Personality of Godhead, and any commentary on the *Gītā* following in the footsteps of Arjuna is real devotional service to the cause of this great science. But the demons do not accept Lord Kṛṣṇa as He is. The demons concoct something out of their imaginations about Kṛṣṇa's instructions. Here is a warning regarding such misleading paths. One should try to follow the disciplic succession from Arjuna, and thus be benefited by this great science of *Śrīmad Bhagavad-gītā.*

4. Arjuna said: The sun-god Vivasvān is senior by birth to You. How am I to understand that in the beginning You instructed this science to him?

5. The Supreme Personality of Godhead said: Many, many births both you and I have passed. I can remember all of them, but you cannot, O subduer of the enemy!

PURPORT

In the *Brahma-saṁhitā* we have information of many, many incarnations of the Lord. It is stated there: "I worship the Supreme Personality of Godhead, Govinda [Kṛṣṇa], who is the original person—absolute, infallible, without beginning, although expanded into unlimited forms, still the same original, the oldest, and the person always appearing as a fresh youth. Such eternal, blissful, all-knowing forms of the Lord are usually understood by the best Vedic scholars, but they are always manifest to pure, unalloyed devotees."

It is also stated in the same scripture: "I worship the Supreme Personality of Godhead, Govinda [Kṛṣṇa], who is always situated in various incarnations such as Rāma, Nṛsiṁha, and many subincarnations as well, but who is the original Personality of Godhead known as Kṛṣṇa, and who incarnates personally also."

In the *Vedas* also it is said that the Lord, although He is one without a second, nevertheless manifests Himself in innumerable forms. He is like the *vaidūrya* stone, which changes color variously yet still is one. All those multiforms are understood by the pure, unalloyed devotees, but not by a simple study of the *Vedas*. Devotees like Arjuna are constant companions of the Lord, and whenever the Lord incarnates, the associate devotees also incarnate in order to serve the Lord in different capacities. Arjuna is one of these devotees, and in this verse it is understood that when Lord Kṛṣṇa spoke *Bhagavad-gītā* to the sun-god Vivasvān, Arjuna in a different capacity was also present there—some millions of years before. But the difference between the Lord and Arjuna is that the Lord remembered the incident, whereas Arjuna could not remember. That is the difference between the part and parcel living entity and the Supreme Personality of Godhead. Arjuna is addressed herein as the mighty hero who could subdue the enemies. At the same time, he is unable to recall what had happened in his various past births. Therefore, a living entity, however great he may be in a material estimation, can never equal the Supreme Lord. Anyone who is a constant companion of the Lord is certainly a liberated person, but he cannot be equal to the Lord. The Lord is described above in the *Brahma-saṁhitā* as infallible (*acyuta*), which means He never forgets Himself, even though He is in material contact. So the Lord and the living entity can never be equal in all respects, even if the living entity is as liberated as Arjuna. Although Arjuna is a devotee of the Lord, he sometimes forgets the nature of the Lord, but by the divine grace a devotee can at once understand the infallible condition of the Lord, whereas a nondevotee or a demon cannot understand this transcendental nature. Consequently, these descriptions in *Bhagavad-gītā* cannot be understood by demoniac brains. Kṛṣṇa remembered acts which were performed by Him millions of years before, but Arjuna could not, despite the fact that both Kṛṣṇa and Arjuna are eternal in nature. We may also note herein that a living entity forgets everything due to his change of body, but the Lord remembers because He does not change His *sac-cid-ānanda* body. He is *advaita,* which means there is no distinction between His body and Himself. Everything in relation to Him is spirit—whereas the conditioned soul is different from his material body. And because the Lord is identical in His body and Self, His position is always different from the ordinary living entity, even when He descends to the material platform. The demons cannot adjust themselves to this transcendental nature of the Lord, as the Lord explains in the following verse.

6. Although I am unborn and My transcendental body never deteriorates, and although I am the Lord of all sentient beings, I still appear in every millennium in My original transcendental form.

PURPORT

The Lord has spoken about the peculiarity of His birth: although He may appear like an ordinary person, He remembers everything of His many, many past "births," whereas a common man cannot remember what he has done even a few hours before. If someone is asked what he did exactly at the same time one day earlier, it would be very difficult for him to answer immediately. He would have to dredge his memory to recall what he was doing. And yet men often dare to claim to be God, or Kṛṣṇa. One should not be misled by such meaningless claims. Then again, the Lord explains His *prakṛti,* or His form. *Prakṛti* means nature as well as *svarūpa,* or one's own form. The Lord says that He appears in His own body. He does not change His body, as the common living entity does from one to another. The conditioned soul may have one kind of body in the present birth, but he has a different one in the next birth. In the material world, the living entity transmigrates in this way. The Lord, however, does not do so. Whenever He appears, He does so in the same original body, by His internal potency. In other words, Kṛṣṇa appears in this material world in His original eternal form, with two hands and holding a flute. He appears exactly in His eternal body, uncontaminated by this material world. Although He appears in the same transcendental body, it still appears that He has taken His birth like an ordinary living entity, although in fact He is the Lord of the universe. Despite the fact that Lord Kṛṣṇa has grown up from childhood to boyhood and from boyhood to youth, astonishingly enough He never ages beyond youth. On the Battlefield of Kurukṣetra, when He was present, He had many grandchildren at home; or, in other words, He had sufficiently aged by material calculations. Still He looked like a young man twenty or twenty-five years old. We have never seen a picture of Kṛṣṇa in old age because He never grows old like us, although He is the oldest person in the whole creation—past, present and future. Neither His body nor His intelligence ever deteriorates or changes. Therefore, it is clear herein that in spite of His being in the material world, He is the same unborn, eternal form of bliss and knowledge, changeless in His transcendental body and intelligence. Factually, His appearance and disappearance are like the sun's rising, moving before us, and then disappearing from our eyesight. When the sun is out of sight we think that the sun is set, and when the sun is before our eyes we think that the sun is on the horizon. Actually, the sun is always there, but owing to our defective, insufficient eyesight, we must calculate the appearance and disappearance of the sun in the sky. And because His appearance and disappearance are completely different from that of any ordinary, common living entity, it is evident that He is eternal, blissful knowledge by His internal potency—and He is not contaminated by material nature. The *Vedas* confirm that the Supreme Personality of Godhead is unborn, yet He still appears to be taking His birth in multimanifestations. The Vedic supplementary literature also confirms that even though the Lord appears to be taking His birth, He is still without change of body. In the *Bhāgavatam*, He appears before His mother as Nārāyaṇa, with four hands and the decorations of the six kinds of full opulences. His appearance in His original eternal form is His causeless mercy, according to the *Viśvakośa* dictionary. The Lord is conscious of all of His previous appearances and disappearances, but a common living entity forgets everything about his past body as soon as he gets another. He shows that He is the Lord of all living entities by performing wonderful and superhuman activities while on this earth.

The Lord is always the same Absolute Truth and is without differentiation between His form and Self, or between His quality and body. A question may now be raised as to why the Lord appears and disappears in this world at all. This is explained in the next verse.

7. Whenever and wherever there is a decline in religious practice, O descendant of Bharata, and a predominant rise of irreligion—at that time I descend Myself.

PURPORT

The word *sṛjāmi,* "manifest," is significant herein. *Sṛjāmi* cannot be used in the sense of creation because, according to the previous verse, there is no creation of the Lord's form or body, since all of the forms are eternally existent. Therefore, *sṛjāmi* means that the Lord manifests Himself as He is. Although the Lord appears on schedule, namely at the end of Dvāpara-yuga of the twenty-eighth millennium of the eighth Manu in one day of Brahmā, still He has no obligation to adhere to such rules and regulations because He is completely free to act many ways at His will. He therefore appears by His own will whenever there is a predominance of irreligion and a disappearance of true religion. Principles of religion are laid down in the *Vedas,* and any discrepancy in the matter of properly executing the rules of the *Vedas* makes one irreligious. In the *Bhāgavatam,* we find that such principles of religion are the laws of the Lord. Only the Lord can manufacture a system of religion. The *Vedas* are also accepted as originally spoken by the Lord Himself to Brahmā, from within his heart. Therefore, the principles of religion are the direct orders of the Supreme Personality of Godhead. These principles are clearly indicated throughout *Bhagavad-gītā.* The purpose of the *Vedas* is to establish such principles under the order of the Supreme Lord, and the Lord directly orders, at the end of *Bhagavad-gītā,* that the highest principle of religion is to surrender unto Him only, and nothing more. The Vedic principles push one toward complete surrender unto Him. And whenever such principles are disturbed by the demons, the Lord appears.

From the *Bhāgavatam* we understand that Lord Buddha is the incarnation of Kṛṣṇa who appeared when materialism was rampant and materialists were using the pretext of the authority of the *Vedas*. Although there are certain restrictive rules and regulations regarding animal sacrifice for particular purposes in the *Vedas*, people of demoniac tendency still took to animal sacrifice without reference to the Vedic principles. Lord Buddha appeared to stop this nonsense and to establish the Vedic principle of nonviolence. Therefore, each and every *avatāra*, or incarnation of the Lord, has a particular mission, and they are all described in the revealed scriptures. No one can be accepted as an *avatāra* without reference to such scriptural indications. It is not a fact that the Lord appears only on Indian soil. He can advent Himself anywhere and everywhere, and whenever He desires to appear. In each and every incarnation, He speaks as much about religion as can be understood by the particular people under their particular circumstances. But the mission is the same—to lead people to God consciousness and obedience to the principles of religion. Sometimes He descends personally, and sometimes He sends His bona fide representative in the form of His son or servant, or Himself in some disguised form. The principles of *Bhagavad-gītā* were spoken to Arjuna, and, for that matter, to other highly elevated persons, because they were highly advanced compared to ordinary men in other parts of the world. Two plus two equals four is a mathematical principle, and it is true both in the infant's arithmetic class and in the master's degree class as well. Still, there are higher and lower mathematics. In all incarnations of the Lord, therefore, the same principles are taught, but they appear to be higher and lower under varied circumstances. The higher principles of religion begin with the acceptance of the four orders and the four ranks of social life, as will be explained later. The whole purpose of the mission of incarnations is to arouse Kṛṣṇa consciousness everywhere.

8. To deliver the pious and to annihilate the miscreants, as well as to reestablish the principles of religion, I advent Myself millennium after millennium.

9. One who knows the transcendental nature of My appearance and activities does not, upon leaving the body, take his birth again in this material world, but attains My eternal abode, O Arjuna.

PURPORT

The Lord's descent from His transcendental abode is already explained in the sixth verse. One who can understand the truth of the appearance of the Personality of Godhead is already liberated from material bondage, and therefore he returns to the kingdom of God immediately after quitting this present material body. Such liberation of the living entity from material bondage is not at all easy. The impersonalists and the *yogīs* attain liberation only after much trouble and many, many births. Even then, the liberation they achieve—merging into the impersonal *brahma-jyoti* effulgence of the Lord—is only partial, and there is the risk of returning again to this material world. But the devotee, simply by understanding the transcendental nature of the body and activities of the Lord, attains the abode of the Lord after ending this body and does not run the risk of returning again to this material world. In the *Brahma-saṁhitā* it is stated that the Lord has many, many forms and incarnations. *Advaitam acyutam anādim ananta-rūpam.* Although there are many transcendental forms of the Lord, they are still one and the same Supreme Personality of Godhead. One has to understand this fact with conviction, although it is incomprehensible to mundane scholars and empiric philosophers. As stated in the *Vedas, eko devo nitya-līlānurakto bhakta-vyāpī hṛdy antarātmā:* "The one Supreme Personality of Godhead is eternally engaged in many, many transcendental forms, in relationships with His unalloyed devotees." This Vedic version is confirmed in this verse of *Bhagavad-gītā* personally by the Lord. Anyone who accepts this truth on the strength of the authorities of the *Vedas* and of the Supreme Personality of Godhead, and who does not waste time in philosophical speculations, attains the highest perfectional stage of liberation. Simply by acceptance of this truth on faith, one can, without a doubt, attain liberation. The Vedic version *tat tvam asi* is actually applied in this case. Anyone who understands Lord Kṛṣṇa to be the Supreme, or who says unto the Lord, "You are the same Supreme Brahman, the Personality of Godhead," is certainly liberated instantly, and consequently his entrance into the transcendental association of the Lord is guaranteed. In other words, such a faithful devotee of the Lord attains perfection, and this is confirmed by the following Vedic assertion: *tam eva viditvātimṛtyum eti nānyaḥ panthā vidyate 'yanāya.* One can attain the perfect stage of liberation from birth and death simply by knowing the Lord, the

Supreme Personality of Godhead. There is no alternative means because anyone who does not understand Lord Kṛṣṇa as the Supreme Personality of Godhead is surely in the mode of ignorance. Consequently, he will not attain salvation, simply, so to speak, by licking the outer surface of the bottle of honey, or by interpreting the texts of *Bhagavad-gītā* according to his own mundane scholarship. Such empiric philosophers may assume very important roles in the material world, but they are not necessarily eligible for liberation. Such puffed-up mundane scholars have to wait for the causeless mercy of the devotee of the Lord. One should, therefore, accept the principle of Kṛṣṇa consciousness with faith and knowledge, and in this way one can attain the perfection of life.

10. Being freed from attachment, fear and anger, being fully absorbed in Me and taking refuge in Me, many, many persons in the past became purified, and thus they all attained transcendental love for Me.

PURPORT

As described above, it is very difficult for a person who is too materially affected to understand the personal nature of the Supreme Absolute Truth. Generally, people who are attached to the bodily concept of life are so absorbed in materialism that it is almost impossible for them to understand how the Supreme can be a person. Such materialists cannot even imagine that there is a transcendental body which is nonperishable, full of knowledge and eternally blissful. In the materialistic concept, the body is perishable, full of ignorance and completely miserable. Therefore, people in general keep this same bodily idea in mind when they are informed of the personal form of the Lord. For such materialistic men, the form of the gigantic material manifestation is supreme; therefore, they imagine that the Supreme is impersonal. And because they are too materially absorbed, the concept of retaining the personality after liberation from matter frightens them. When such materialistic men are informed that spiritual life is also individual and personal, they are afraid of becoming persons again, and so they naturally prefer a kind of merging into an impersonal void. Generally, they compare the living entities to the bubbles of the ocean, which merge into the ocean. That is the highest perfection of spiritual existence attainable without individual personality. This is a fearful stage of life, devoid of perfect knowledge of spiritual existence. Furthermore, there are many persons who cannot understand spiritual existence at all. Being embarrassed by so many theories and by contradictions of various types of philosophical speculation, they become disgusted or angry and foolishly conclude that there is no supreme cause and that everything is ultimately void. Such people are in diseased conditions of life. Some of them are too materially attached and therefore do not give attention to spiritual life, some of them want to merge into the supreme spiritual cause, and some of them disbelieve in everything, being angry at all sorts of spiritual speculation out of hopelessness. This last class of men take to the shelter of some kind of intoxication, and their affective hallucinations are sometimes accepted as spiritual visions. One has to get rid of all three stages of attachment to the material world: negligence of spiritual life, fear of a spiritual personal identity, and the concept of void that underlies the frustration of life. To get free of these three stages in the material concept of life, one has to take complete shelter of the Lord, guided by the bona fide spiritual master, and follow the penances of disciplinary and regulative principles of devotional life. The last stage of such devotional life is called *bhāva*, or transcendental love of Godhead.

According to *Bhakti-rasāmṛta-sindhu*, the science of devotional service, in the beginning one must have a preliminary desire for self-realization. This will bring one to the stage of trying to associate with persons who are spiritually elevated. The next stage is that one becomes initiated by an elevated spiritual master, and under the instruction of the spiritual master, the neophyte devotee begins the process of devotional service. By execution of devotional service under the guidance of the spiritual master, one becomes free from all material attachment, attains steadiness in self-realization, and acquires a taste for hearing about the absolute Personality of Godhead, Śrī Kṛṣṇa. This taste leads one further forward to the attachment for Kṛṣṇa consciousness, and this Kṛṣṇa consciousness is matured in *bhāva*, or the preliminary stage of transcendental love of Godhead. When the devotee reaches the stage of real love for Godhead it is called *prema*, the highest perfection of life. In the *prema* stage there is a constant engagement in the transcendental loving service of the Lord. So, by the slow process of devotional service, under the guidance of the bona fide spiritual master, one can attain the *bhāva* stage, being freed from all material attachment, from fear of one's individual spiritual personality, and from the frustration of voidness. And when one is actually free from such lower stages of life, one can attain to the abode of the Supreme Personality of Godhead.

11. All of them—as they surrender unto Me—I reward accordingly. Everyone follows My path in all respects, O son of Pṛthā.

PURPORT

Everyone is searching after Kṛṣṇa in the different aspects of His manifestations. Kṛṣṇa, the Supreme Personality of Godhead, is partially realized in His impersonal *brahmajyoti,* or shining effulgence. Kṛṣṇa is also partially realized as the all-pervading Supersoul dwelling within everything, even in the particles of atoms. But Kṛṣṇa is fully realized only by His pure devotees. Therefore, Kṛṣṇa is the object of everyone's realization, and, as such, anyone and everyone is satisfied according to one's desire to have Him. One devotee may want Kṛṣṇa as the supreme master, another as his personal friend, another as his son, and still another as his lover. Kṛṣṇa rewards equally all the devotees, in their different intensities of love for Him. In the material world, the same reciprocations of feelings are there, and they are equally exchanged by the Lord with the different types of worshipers. The pure devotees both here and in the transcendental abode associate with Him in person and are able to render personal service to the Lord and thus derive transcendental bliss in His loving service. As for those who are impersonalists and who want to commit spiritual suicide by annihilating the individual existence of the living entity, Kṛṣṇa helps them also, by absorbing them into His effulgence. Such impersonalists do not agree to accept the eternal, blissful Personality of Godhead, and consequently they cannot relish the bliss of transcendental personal service to the Lord, having extinguished their individuality. Some of them, who are not situated even in the impersonal existence, return to this material field to exhibit their dormant desires for activities. They are not admitted into the spiritual planets, but they are again given a chance to act on the material planets. For those who are fruitive workers, the Lord, as the *yajñeśvara,* awards the desired results of their prescribed duties, and those who are *yogīs* seeking mystic powers are awarded such powers. In other words, everyone is dependent for success upon His mercy alone, and all kinds of spiritual processes are but different degrees of success on the same path.

Unless, therefore, one comes to the highest perfection of Kṛṣṇa consciousness, all attempts remain imperfect, as stated in *Śrīmad-Bhāgavatam:* "Whether one is without desire [the condition of the devotees], or is desirous of all fruitive results, or is after liberation, one should with all efforts try to worship the Supreme Personality of Godhead for complete perfection, culminating in Kṛṣṇa consciousness."

12. Men in this world desire success in fruitive activities, and therefore they worship the demigods. Quickly, of course, men get results from fruitive work in this world.

13. According to the three modes of material nature and the work ascribed to them, the corresponding four divisions of human society were created by Me. And although I am the creator of this system, you should know that I am yet the nondoer, being unchangeable.

PURPORT

The Lord is the creator of everything. Everything is born of Him, everything is sustained by Him, and everything, after annihilation, rests in Him. He is therefore the creator of the four divisions of the social order, beginning with the intelligent class of men, technically called the *brāhmaṇas* due to their being situated in the mode of goodness. Next is the administrative class, technically called the *kṣatriyas* due to their being situated in the mode of passion. The mercantile men, called the *vaiśyas,* are situated in the mixed modes of passion and ignorance, and the *śūdras,* or the laborer class, are situated in the ignorant mode of material nature. In spite of His creating the four divisions of human society, Lord Kṛṣṇa does not belong to any of these divisions because He is not one of the conditioned souls, a section of whom form human society. Human society is the same as animal society, but to elevate men from the animal status, the above-mentioned divisions are created by the Lord for the systematic development of Kṛṣṇa consciousness. The tendency of a particular man toward work is determined by the modes of material nature he has acquired. Such symptoms of life, according to different modes of material nature, are described in the Eighteenth Chapter of this book. A person in Kṛṣṇa consciousness, however, is above even the *brāhmaṇas* because a *brāhmaṇa* by quality is supposed to know about

Brahman, the Supreme Absolute Truth. Most of them approach the impersonal Brahman manifestation of Lord Kṛṣṇa, but only a man who transcends the limited knowledge of a *brāhmaṇa* and reaches the knowledge of the Supreme Personality of Godhead, Lord Śrī Kṛṣṇa, becomes a person in Kṛṣṇa consciousness, or, in other words, a Vaiṣṇava. Kṛṣṇa consciousness includes knowledge of all different plenary expansions of Kṛṣṇa, such as Rāma, Nṛsiṁha and Varāha. As Kṛṣṇa is transcendental to this system of the four divisions of human society, a person in Kṛṣṇa consciousness is also transcendental to the mundane divisions of human society, whether we consider the divisions of community, nation or species.

14. There is no work that affects Me, nor do I aspire for the fruits of action. One who understands this truth about Me does not become entangled in the fruitive reactions of work.

15. All the liberated souls in ancient times acted with this understanding and so attained liberation. Therefore, as did the ancients, you should perform your duty in this divine consciousness.

PURPORT

There are two classes of men. Some of them are full of polluted material things within their hearts, and some of them are materially free. Kṛṣṇa consciousness is equally beneficial for both of these persons. Those who are full of dirty things can take to the line of Kṛṣṇa consciousness for a gradual cleansing process, following the regulative principles of devotional service. Those who are already cleansed of the impurities may continue to act in the same Kṛṣṇa consciousness so that others may follow their exemplary activities and thereby be benefited. Foolish persons or neophytes in Kṛṣṇa consciousness often want to retire from activities without having knowledge of Kṛṣṇa consciousness. Arjuna's desire to retire from activities on the battlefield was not approved by the Lord. One need only know how to act. To retire from activities and to sit aloof making a show of Kṛṣṇa consciousness is less important than actually engaging in the field of activities for the sake of Kṛṣṇa. Arjuna is here advised to act in Kṛṣṇa consciousness, following in the footsteps of the Lord's previous disciples, such as the sun-god Vivasvān, as mentioned hereinbefore. The Supreme Lord knows all His past activities, as well as those of persons who acted in Kṛṣṇa consciousness in the past. Therefore He recommends the acts of the sun-god, who learned this art from the Lord some millions of years before. All such students of Lord Kṛṣṇa are mentioned here as past liberated persons, engaged in the discharge of duties allotted by Kṛṣṇa.

16. Even the intelligent are bewildered in determining what is action and what is inaction. Now I shall explain to you what action is, knowing which you shall be liberated from all sins.

17. The intricacies of action are very hard to understand. Therefore, one should know properly what action is, what forbidden action is, and what inaction is.

PURPORT

If one is serious about liberation from material bondage, one has to understand the distinctions between action, inaction and unauthorized actions. One has to apply oneself to such an analysis of action, reaction and perverted actions because it is a very difficult subject matter. To understand Kṛṣṇa consciousness and action according to the modes, one has to learn one's relationship with the Supreme. One who has learned perfectly knows that every living entity is an eternal servitor of the Lord, and consequently he acts in Kṛṣṇa consciousness. The entire *Bhagavad-gīta* is directed toward this conclusion. Any other conclusions, against this consciousness and its attendant reactions, are *vikarmas*, or prohibitive actions. To understand all this one has to associate with authorities in Kṛṣṇa consciousness and learn the secret from them; this is as good as learning from the Lord directly. Otherwise, even the most intelligent person will be bewildered.

18. One who sees inaction in action, and action in inaction, is intelligent among men, and he is in the transcendental position, although engaged in all sorts of activities.

PURPORT

A person acting in Kṛṣṇa consciousness is naturally free from the resultant action of work. His activities are all performed for Kṛṣṇa, and therefore he does not enjoy or suffer any of the effects of work. Consequently, he is intelligent in human society, even though he is engaged in all sorts of activities for Kṛṣṇa. *Akarma* means without reaction to work. The impersonalist ceases fruitive activities out of fear, so that the resultant action may not be a stumbling block on the path of self-realization, whereas the personalist knows rightly his position as the eternal servitor of the Supreme Personality of Godhead. Therefore, he engages himself in the activities of Kṛṣṇa consciousness. Because everything is done for Kṛṣṇa, he enjoys only transcendental happiness in the discharge of this service. Those who are engaged in this process are without desire for personal sense gratification. The sense of eternal servitorship to Kṛṣṇa makes one immune to all the reactionary elements of work.

19. One is understood to be in full knowledge whose every act is devoid of desire for sense gratification. He is said by sages to be a worker whose fruitive action is burned up by the fire of perfect knowledge.

20. Abandoning all attachment to the results of his activities, ever satisfied and independent, he performs no fruitive action, although engaged in all kinds of undertakings.

21. Such a man of understanding acts with mind and intelligence perfectly controlled, gives up all sense of proprietorship over his possessions, and acts only for the bare necessities of life. Thus working, he is not affected by sinful reactions.

22. He who is satisfied with gain which comes of its own accord, who is free from duality and does not envy, who is steady both in success and failure, is never entangled, although performing actions.

PURPORT

A Kṛṣṇa conscious person does not make much endeavor even to maintain his body. He is satisfied with gains obtained of their own accord. He neither begs nor borrows, but he labors honestly as far as is in his power, and is satisfied with whatever is obtained by his own honest labor. A Kṛṣṇa conscious person is therefore independent in his livelihood. He does not allow anyone's service to hamper his own service to Kṛṣṇa.

However, for the service of the Lord he can participate in any kind of action without being disturbed by the duality of the material world. The duality of the material world is felt in terms of heat and cold, or misery and happiness. A Kṛṣṇa conscious person is above this duality because he does not hesitate to act in any way for the satisfaction of Kṛṣṇa. Therefore he is steady both in success and in failure. These signs are visible when one is full in transcendental knowledge.

23. The work of a man who is unattached to the modes of material nature and who is fully situated in transcendental knowledge merges entirely into transcendence.

24. A person who is fully absorbed in Kṛṣṇa consciousness is sure to attain the spiritual kingdom through his full contribution to spiritual activities, for the consummation is absolute and the things offered are also of the same spiritual nature.

PURPORT

How activities in Kṛṣṇa consciousness can lead one ultimately to the spiritual goal is described here. There are various activities in Kṛṣṇa consciousness, and all of them will be described in the following verses. But, for the present, just the principle of Kṛṣṇa consciousness is described. A conditioned soul, entangled in material contamination, is sure to act in the material atmosphere, and yet he has to get out of such an environment. The process by which the conditioned soul can get out of the material atmosphere is Kṛṣṇa consciousness. For example, a patient who is suffering from a disorder of the bowels due to overindulgence in milk products is cured by another milk product, curd. Similarly, the materially absorbed conditioned soul can be cured by Kṛṣṇa consciousness, as prescribed here in *Bhagavad-gītā.* This process is generally known as *yajña,* or activities simply meant for the satisfaction of Viṣṇu or Kṛṣṇa. Therefore, the more the activities of the material world are performed in Kṛṣṇa consciousness, or for Viṣṇu only, the more the atmosphere becomes spiritualized by complete absorption. Brahman means spiritual. The Lord is spiritual, and the rays of His transcendental body are called *brahmajyoti,* His spiritual effulgence. Everything that exists is situated in that *brahmajyoti,* and when the *jyoti* is covered by the illusion of *māyā,* or sense gratification, it is called material. This material feature can be removed at once by Kṛṣṇa consciousness, wherein the offering for the cause of Kṛṣṇa consciousness, the consuming agent of such an offering or contribution, the process of consumption, the contributor, and the result of such activities, are—all combined together—Brahman, or the Absolute Truth. The Absolute Truth covered by *māyā* is called matter. Matter dovetailed for the cause of the Absolute Truth regains its spiritual quality. Kṛṣṇa consciousness is the process of converting the illusory consciousness into Brahman, or the Supreme. When the mind is fully absorbed in such Kṛṣṇa consciousness, it is said to be in *samādhi*, or trance. Anything done in such transcendental consciousness is called *yajña*, or sacrifice for the Absolute. In that condition of spiritual consciousness, the contributor, the contribution, the consumption, the performer or leader of the performance, and the result or ultimate gain—everything—becomes one in the Absolute, the Supreme Brahman. That is the explanation of Kṛṣṇa consciousness.

25. Some *yogīs* perfectly worship the demigods by offering different sacrifices to them, and some of them offer sacrifices in the fire of the Supreme Brahman.

PURPORT

As described above, a person engaged in discharging duties in Kṛṣṇa consciousness is also called a perfect *yogī*, or a first-class mystic. But there are others also, who perform similar sacrifices in the worship of demigods, and still others who sacrifice to the Supreme Brahman, or the impersonal feature of the Supreme Lord. So there are different kinds of sacrifices in terms of different categories. Such different categories of sacrifice by different types of performers only superficially demark varieties of sacrifice. Factual sacrifice means to satisfy the Supreme Lord, Viṣṇu, and is also known as *yajña*. All the different varieties of sacrifice can be placed within two primary divisions—sacrifice of worldly possessions and sacrifice in pursuit of transcendental knowledge. Those who are in Kṛṣṇa consciousness sacrifice all material possessions for the satisfaction of the Supreme Lord, while others, who want some temporary material happiness, sacrifice their material possessions to satisfy demigods such as Indra and the sun. And others, who are impersonalists, sacrifice in the sense of merging into the existence of impersonal Brahman. The demigods are powerful living entities appointed by the

Supreme Lord for the maintenance and supervision of all material functions like the heating, watering and lighting of the universe. Those who are interested in such supplies of material benefits worship the demigods by various sacrifices according to the Vedic rituals. They are called *bahv-īśvara-vādī*, or believers in many gods. But others, who stick to the impersonal feature of the Absolute Truth and regard the forms of the demigods as temporary, sacrifice their individual selves in the supreme fire and thus end their individual existences by merging into the existence of the Supreme. Such impersonalists relinquish their time in philosophical speculation for understanding the transcendental nature of the Supreme. In other words, the fruitive workers sacrifice their material possessions for material enjoyment, whereas the impersonalist sacrifices his material designations with a view to merging into the existence of the Supreme. For the impersonalist, the fire altar of sacrifice is the Supreme Brahman, and the offering is the self being consumed by the fire of Brahman. The Kṛṣṇa conscious person, however, sacrifices everything for the satisfaction of Kṛṣṇa, and as such all his material possessions as well as his own self—everything—are sacrificed for Kṛṣṇa (as with Arjuna). Thus, he is the first-class *yogī*, but he does not lose his individual existence.

26. Some of them sacrifice the hearing process and the senses in the fire of the controlled mind, and others sacrifice the objects of the senses, such as sound, in the fire of sacrifice.

PURPORT

The four divisions of human life, namely *brahmacarya, gṛhastha, vānaprastha* and *sannyāsa,* are all meant to help men become perfect *yogīs* or transcendentalists. Since human life is not meant for our enjoying sense gratification like the animals, the four orders of human life are fixed so that one may become perfect in spiritual life. The *brahmacārīs,* or students under the care of a bona fide spiritual master, control the mind by abstaining from sense gratification. Furthermore, a *brahmacārī* hears only words concerning Kṛṣṇa consciousness. Hearing is the basic principle for understanding, and therefore the pure *brahmacārī* engages fully in chanting and hearing the glories of the Lord. He restricts himself from vibrations of material sound, and his hearing is engaged in the transcendental sound vibration Hare Kṛṣṇa, Hare Kṛṣṇa. Similarly, the householders, who have some license for sense gratification, perform such acts with great restraint. Sex life, intoxication and meat-eating are general tendencies of human society, but a regulated householder does not indulge in unrestricted sex life and other sense gratifications. Marriage on principles of religious life is therefore current in all civilized human society because that is the way for restricted sex life. This restricted, unattached sex life is also a kind of *yajña* because the restricted householder sacrifices his general tendency toward sense gratification for higher transcendental life.

27. And some offer the work of the senses and the work of the life-force, controlling them in *yoga*, to obtain knowledge of the self.

28. There are others who, enlightened by sacrificing their material possessions in severe austerities, take strict vows and practice the *yoga* of eightfold mysticism, and others study the *Vedas* for the advancement of transcendental knowledge.

29. And there are even others who are inclined to the process of breath restraint to remain in trance, and they practice stopping the movement of the outgoing breath into the incoming, and incoming breath into the outgoing, and thus at last remain in trance, stopping all breathing. Some of them, curtailing the eating process, offer the outgoing breath into itself, as a sacrifice.

30. All these performers who know the meaning of sacrifice become cleansed of sinful reactions, and, having tasted the nectar of the remnants of such sacrifices, they go to the supreme eternal atmosphere.

PURPORT

From the foregoing explanations of different types of sacrifice (namely sacrifice of one's possessions, study of the *Vedas* or philosophical doctrines, and performance of the *yoga* system), it is found that the common aim of all is to control the senses. Sense gratification is the root cause of material existence, and, therefore, unless and until one is situated on a platform apart from sense gratification, there is no chance of being elevated to the eternal platform of full knowledge, full bliss and full life.

This stage of life is called the eternal atmosphere, or Brahman atmosphere. All the above-mentioned sacrifices help one to become cleansed of the sinful reactions of material existence. By this advancement in life, not only does one become happy and opulent in this life, but also, at the end, he enters into the eternal kingdom of God, either merging into the impersonal Brahman or associating with the Supreme Personality of Godhead, Kṛṣṇa.

31. O best of the Kuru dynasty, without sacrifice one can never live happily on this planet or in this life: what then of the next?

PURPORT

Whatever form of material existence one is in, one is invariably ignorant of the real situation of his living condition. In other words, existence in the material world is due to the multiple reactions to our sinful lives. Ignorance is the cause of sinful life, and sinful life is the cause of one's dragging on in material existence. The human form of life is the only loophole by which one may get out of this entanglement. The *Vedas*, therefore, give us a chance for escape by pointing out the paths of religion, economic comfort, regulated sense gratification, and, at last, the means to get out of the miserable condition entirely. The path of religion, the different kinds of sacrifice recommended above, automatically solves our economic problems. By performance of *yajña* we can have enough food, enough milk, etc.—even if there is a so-called increase of population. When the body is fully supplied, naturally the next stage is to satisfy the senses. The *Vedas* prescribe, therefore, sacred marriage for regulated sense gratification. Thereby one is gradually elevated to the platform of release from material engagement. The ultimate goal of life is to get liberation from material bondage, and the highest perfection of liberated life is to associate with the Supreme Lord. All these different stages of perfection are achieved by performance of *yajña*, as described above. Now, if a person is not inclined to perform *yajña* in terms of the Vedic literature, how can he expect a happy life even in this body, and what to speak of another body on another planet? There are different grades of material comforts in different heavenly planets, and on all of them there is immense happiness for the persons engaged in different kinds of *yajña*. But the highest kind of happiness that a man can achieve is to be promoted to the spiritual planets by practice of Kṛṣṇa consciousness. A life of Kṛṣṇa consciousness is therefore the solution to all problems of material existence.

32. All these different types of sacrifice are approved by the *Vedas*, and all of them are born of different types of work. Knowing them as such, you will become liberated.

33. O chastiser of the enemy, the sacrifice of knowledge is greater than the sacrifice of material possessions. O son of Pṛthā, after all, the sacrifice of work culminates in transcendental knowledge.

PURPORT

The whole purpose of different types of sacrifice is to arrive gradually at the status of complete knowledge, then to gain release from material miseries, and, ultimately, to engage in loving transcendental service to the Supreme Personality of Godhead (Kṛṣṇa). Nonetheless, there is a mystery about all these different activities of sacrifice, and one should know this mystery. Sacrifices sometimes take different forms according to the particular faith of the performer. When his faith reaches the stage of the sacrifice of knowledge, the performer should be considered more advanced than those who simply sacrifice material possessions, for without attainment of knowledge, sacrifices remain on the material platform and bestow no spiritual benefit. Real knowledge is Kṛṣṇa consciousness, the highest stage of transcendental awareness. Without the elevation of knowledge, sacrifices are simply material activities. When, however, they are elevated to the level of transcendental knowledge, all such activities enter onto the spiritual platform. Depending on differences in consciousness, such activities are sometimes called *karma-kāṇḍa*, fruitive activities, and sometimes they are called *jñāna-kāṇḍa*, knowledge in the pursuit of truth. It is better when the end is knowledge.

34. Just try to learn the truth by approaching a spiritual master. Inquire from him submissively and render service unto him. The self-realized soul can impart knowledge unto you because he has seen the truth.

PURPORT

The path of spiritual realization is undoubtedly difficult. The Lord therefore advises us to approach a bona fide spiritual master in the line of disciplic succession from the Lord Himself. No one can be a bona fide spiritual master without following this principle of disciplic succession. The Lord is the original spiritual master, and a person in the disciplic succession can convey the message of the Lord as it is to his disciple. No one can be spiritually realized by manufacturing his own process, as is the fashion of foolish pretenders. The *Bhāgavatam* says, *dharmaṁ tu sākṣād bhagavat-praṇītam:* the path of religion is directly enunciated by the Lord. Therefore, mental speculation or dry arguments cannot help one progress in spiritual life. One has to approach a bona fide spiritual master to receive the knowledge. Such a teacher should be accepted in full surrender, and one should serve the spiritual master like a menial servant, without false prestige. Satisfaction of the self-realized spiritual master is the secret of advancement in spiritual life. Inquiries and submission constitute the proper combination for spiritual understanding. Unless there is submission and service, inquiries from the learned spiritual master will not be effective. One must be able to pass the test of the spiritual master, and when the spiritual master sees the genuine desire of the disciple he automatically blesses the disciple with genuine spiritual understanding. In this verse, both blind following and absurd inquiries are condemned. One should not only hear submissively from the spiritual master, but one must also get a clear understanding from him, in submission and service and inquiries. A bona fide spiritual master is by nature very kind toward the disciple, and, therefore, when the student is submissive and is always ready to render service, the reciprocation of knowledge and inquiries becomes perfect.

35. And when you have thus learned the truth, you will know that all living beings are but part of Me—and that they are in Me, and are Mine.

36. Even if you are considered to be the most sinful of all sinners, when you are situated in the boat of transcendental knowledge, you will be able to cross over the ocean of miseries.

37. As the blazing fire turns wood to ashes, O Arjuna, so does the fire of knowledge burn to ashes all reactions to material activities.

38. In this world, there is nothing so sublime and pure as transcendental knowledge. Such knowledge is the mature fruit of all mysticism. And one who has achieved this enjoys the self within himself in due course of time.

39. A faithful man who is absorbed in transcendental knowledge and who subdues his senses quickly attains the supreme spiritual peace.

PURPORT

Such knowledge in Kṛṣṇa consciousness can be achieved by a faithful person who believes firmly in Kṛṣṇa. One is called a faithful man who thinks that simply by acting in Kṛṣṇa consciousness one can attain the highest perfection. This faith is attained by the discharge of devotional service, and by chanting Hare Kṛṣṇa, Hare Kṛṣṇa, Kṛṣṇa Kṛṣṇa, Hare Hare/ Hare Rāma, Hare Rāma, Rāma Rāma, Hare Hare, which cleanses one's heart of all material dirt. Over and above this, one should control the senses. A person who is faithful and controls the senses can easily attain perfection in the knowledge of Kṛṣṇa consciousness without delay.

40. But ignorant and faithless persons who doubt the revealed scriptures do not attain God consciousness. For the doubting soul there is happiness neither in this world nor in the next.

41. Therefore, one who has renounced the fruits of his actions, whose doubts are destroyed by transcendental knowledge, and who is situated firmly in the self, is not bound by works, O conquerer of riches.

PURPORT

One who follows the instruction of *Bhagavad-gītā* as it is imparted by the Lord, the Personality of Godhead Himself, becomes free from all doubts by grace of transcendental knowledge. He, as a part and parcel of the Lord, in full Kṛṣṇa consciousness, is already fully conversant with self-knowledge. As such, he is undoubtedly above the reactions to whatever activities he may carry out.

42. Therefore, the doubts which have arisen in your heart out of ignorance should be slashed by the weapon of knowledge. Armed with *yoga*, O Bharata, stand and fight.

PURPORT

The *yoga* system instructed in this chapter is called *sanātana-yoga*, or eternal activities performed by the living entity. This *yoga* has two divisions of action, called sacrifices. The one is called sacrifice of one's material possessions, and the other is called knowledge of self, which is pure spiritual activity. If sacrifice of one's material possessions is not dovetailed for spiritual realization, then such sacrifice becomes material. But one who performs such sacrifices with a spiritual objective, or in devotional service, makes a perfect sacrifice. When we come to spiritual activities, we find that these are also divided into two: namely understanding of one's own self (or one's constitutional position), and the truth regarding the Supreme Personality of Godhead. One who follows the path of *Bhagavad-gītā* as it is can very easily understand these two important divisions of spiritual knowledge. For him there is no difficulty in obtaining perfect knowledge of the self as part and parcel of the Lord. And such understanding is beneficial for such a person who easily understands the transcendental activities of the Lord. In the beginning of this chapter, the transcendental activities of the Lord were discussed by the Supreme Lord Himself. One who does not understand the instructions of the *Gītā* is faithless and is considered to be misusing the fragmental independence awarded to him by the Lord. In spite of such instructions, one who does not understand the real nature of the Lord as the eternal, blissful, all-knowing Personality of Godhead is certainly fool number one. This ignorance of the so-called student of *Bhagavad-gītā* can be removed by gradual acceptance of the principles of Kṛṣṇa consciousness. Kṛṣṇa consciousness is awakened by different types of sacrifice to the demigods, sacrifice to Brahman, sacrifice in celibacy, sacrifice in household life, sacrifice in controlling the senses, sacrifice in practicing mystic *yoga*, sacrifice in penance, sacrifice of material possessions, sacrifice in studying the *Vedas*, and sacrifice in observing the scientific social institution called *varṇāśrama-dharma* (or the divisions of human society). All of these are known as sacrifice, but all of them are based on regulated action. And within all these activities, the important factor is self-realization. One who seeks *that* objective is the real student of *Bhagavad-gītā*, but one who doubts the authority of Kṛṣṇa falls back. One is therefore advised to study *Bhagavad-gītā* or any other scripture with a bona fide spiritual master, with service and surrender. A bona fide spiritual master is in the disciplic succession from time eternal, and there is not the slightest deviation from the instruction of the Personality of Godhead, as it was imparted millions of years ago to the sun-god, from whom the instruction of *Bhagavad-gītā* has come down to the earthly kingdom. One should, therefore, follow the path of *Bhagavad-gītā* as it is expressed in the *Gītā* itself and beware of self-interested people seeking personal aggrandizement who deviate others from the actual path. The Lord is definitely the Supreme Person, and His activities are transcendental. One who understands this is a liberated person from the very beginning of his study of the *Gītā.*

Thus end the Bhaktivedanta purports to the Fourth Chapter of the *Śrīmad Bhagavad-gītā* in the matter of Transcendental Knowledge.

CHAPTER FIVE

Karma-yoga— Action in Kṛṣṇa Consciousness

1. Arjuna said: O Kṛṣṇa, first of all You ask me to renounce work, and then again You recommend work with devotion. Now will You kindly tell me definitely which of the two is more beneficial?

2. The Blessed Lord said: The renunciation of work and work in devotion are both good for liberation. But of the two, work in devotional service is better than renunciation of works.

PURPORT

Fruitive activities (seeking sense gratification) are causes for material bondage. As long as one is engaged in activities aimed at improving the standard of bodily comfort, one is sure to transmigrate to different types of bodies, thereby continuing material bondage perpetually. *Śrīmad-Bhāgavatam* confirms this as follows: "People are mad after sense gratification, and they do not know that this present body, which is full of miseries, is a result of one's fruitive activities in the past. Although this body is temporary, it is always giving one trouble in many ways. Therefore, to act for sense gratification is not good. One is considered to be a failure in life as long as he makes no inquiry about the nature of work for fruitive results, for as long as one is engrossed in the consciousness of sense gratification, one has to transmigrate from one body to another. Although the mind may be engrossed in fruitive activities and influenced by ignorance, one must develop a love for devotional service to Vāsudeva. Only then can one have the opportunity to get out of the bondage of material existence."

Therefore, *jñāna* (knowledge that one is not this material body but spirit soul) is not sufficient for liberation. One has to act in the status of spirit soul, otherwise there is no escape from material bondage. Action in Kṛṣṇa consciousness is not, however, action on the fruitive platform. Activities performed in knowledge strengthen one's advancement in knowledge. Without Kṛṣṇa consciousness, mere renunciation of fruitive activities does not actually purify the heart of a conditioned soul. As long as the heart is not purified, one has to work on the fruitive platform. But action in Kṛṣṇa consciousness automatically helps one escape the result of fruitive action, so that one need not descend to the material platform. Therefore, action in Kṛṣṇa consciousness is always superior to renunciation, which entails a risk of falling. Renunciation without Kṛṣṇa consciousness is incomplete, as confirmed by Śrīla Rūpa Gosvāmī in his *Bhakti-rasāmṛta-sindhu:* "To achieve liberation, renunciation of things which are related to the Supreme Personality of Godhead, though they are material, is called incomplete renunciation." Renunciation is complete when it is in the knowledge that everything in existence belongs to the Lord and that no one should claim proprietorship over anything. One should understand that, factually, nothing belongs to anyone. Then where is the question of renunciation? One who knows that everything is Kṛṣṇa's property is always situated in renunciation. Since everything belongs to Kṛṣṇa, everything should be employed in the service of Kṛṣṇa. This perfect form of action in Kṛṣṇa consciousness is far better than any amount of artificial renunciation.

3. One who neither hates nor desires the fruits of activities is known to be always renounced. Such a person, liberated from all dualities, easily overcomes material bondage and is completely liberated, O mighty-armed Arjuna.

PURPORT

One who is fully in Kṛṣṇa consciousness is always a renouncer because he feels neither hatred nor desire for the results of his actions. Such a renouncer, dedicated to the transcendental loving service of the Lord, is fully qualified in knowledge because he knows his constitutional position in his relationship with Kṛṣṇa. He knows fully well that Kṛṣṇa is the whole and that he is part and parcel of Kṛṣṇa. Such knowledge is perfect because it is qualitatively and quantitatively correct. The concept of oneness with God is incorrect because the part cannot be equal to the whole. Knowledge that one is identical in quality yet different in quantity is correct transcendental knowledge leading one to become full in himself, having nothing to aspire to or lament over. There is no duality in his mind because whatever he does, he does for Kṛṣṇa. Being thus freed from the platform of dualities, he is liberated—even in this material world.

4. Only the ignorant speak of *karma-yoga* and devotional service as being different from the analytical study of the material world [*sāṅkhya*]. Those who are actually learned say that he who applies himself well to one of these paths achieves the results of both.

PURPORT

The aim of the analytical study of the material world is to find the soul of existence. The soul of the material world is Viṣṇu, or the Supersoul. Devotional service to the Lord in Kṛṣṇa consciousness involves engagement in the service of the soul of the material universe. One process is to find the root of the tree, and the other to water the root. The real student of *sāṅkhya* philosophy finds the root of the material world, Viṣṇu, and then, in perfect knowledge, engages himself in the service of the Lord. Therefore, in essence, there is no difference between the two because the aim of both is Viṣṇu. Those who do not know the ultimate end say that the purposes of *sāṅkhya* and *karma-yoga* are not the same, but one who is learned knows the unifying aim in these different processes.

5. One who knows that the position reached by means of renunciation can also be attained by devotional service, and who therefore sees that *sāṅkhya* and *yoga* are on the same level, sees things as they are.

PURPORT

The real purpose of philosophical research is to find the ultimate goal of life. Since the ultimate goal of life is self-realization, there is no difference between the conclusions reached by the two processes. By *sāṅkhya* philosophical research one comes to the conclusion that a living entity is not a part and parcel of the material world, but that he is part and parcel of the supreme spirit whole. Consequently, the spirit soul has nothing to do with the material world; his actions must be in some relationship with the Supreme. When he acts in Kṛṣṇa consciousness, he is actually in his constitutional position. In the first process of *sāṅkhya*, one has to become detached from matter, and in the devotional *yoga* process one has to attach himself to the work of Kṛṣṇa. Factually, both processes are the same, although superficially one process appears to be detachment and the other process appears to be attachment. Detachment from matter and attachment to Kṛṣṇa are one and the same. One who can see this sees things as they are.

6. Unless one is engaged in the devotional service of the Lord, mere renunciation of activities cannot make one happy. The sage, purified by works of devotion, achieves the Supreme without delay.

PURPORT

There are two classes of *sannyāsīs*, or persons in the renounced order of life. Māyāvādī *sannyāsīs* are engaged in the study of *sāṅkhya* philosophy, whereas Vaiṣṇava *sannyāsīs* are engaged in the study of *Bhāgavatam* philosophy, which affords the proper commentary on the *Vedānta-sūtras*. Māyāvādī *sannyāsīs* also study the *Vedānta-sūtras*, but use their own commentary, called the *Śārīraka-bhāṣya*, written by Śaṅkarācārya. The students of the *Bhāgavatam* school are engaged in devotional service of the Lord, according to *pañcarātrikī* regulations, and therefore Vaiṣṇava *sannyāsīs* have multiple engagements in the transcendental service of the Lord. Vaiṣṇava *sannyāsīs* have nothing to do with material activities, and yet they perform various activities in their devotional service to the Lord. But Māyāvādī *sannyāsīs*, engaged in the studies of *sāṅkhya* and Vedānta and speculation, cannot relish the transcendental service of the Lord. Because their studies become very tedious they sometimes grow tired of Brahman speculation, and thus they take shelter of the *Bhāgavatam* without proper understanding. Consequently, their study of *Śrīmad-Bhāgavatam* becomes troublesome. Dry speculations and impersonal interpretations by artificial means are all useless for the Māyāvādī *sannyāsīs*. Vaiṣṇava *sannyāsīs*, who are engaged in devotional service, are happy in the discharge of their transcendental duties, and they have the guarantee of ultimate entrance into the kingdom of God. Māyāvādī *sannyāsīs* sometimes fall down from the path of self-realization and again enter into material activities of a philanthropic and altruistic nature, which are nothing but material engagements. Therefore, the conclusion is that those who are engaged in Kṛṣṇa consciousness are better situated than the *sannyāsīs* engaged in simple Brahman speculation, although they too come to Kṛṣṇa consciousness, after many births.

7. One who works in devotion, who is a pure soul, and who controls his mind and senses, is dear to everyone, and everyone is dear to him. Though always working, such a man is never entangled.

PURPORT

One who is on the path of liberation by Kṛṣṇa consciousness is very dear to every living being, and every living being is dear to him. This is due to his Kṛṣṇa consciousness. Such a person cannot think of any living being as separate from Kṛṣṇa, just as the leaves and branches of a tree are not separate from the tree. He knows very well that by pouring water on the root of the tree, the water will be distributed to all the leaves and branches, or by supplying food to the stomach, the energy is automatically distributed throughout the body. Because one who works in Kṛṣṇa consciousness is servant to all, he is very dear to everyone. And because everyone is satisfied by his work, he is pure in consciousness. Because he is pure in consciousness, his mind is completely controlled. And because his mind is controlled, his senses are also controlled. Because his mind is always fixed on Kṛṣṇa, there is no chance of his being deviated from Kṛṣṇa. Nor is there a chance that he will engage his senses in matters other than the service of the Lord. He does not like to hear anything except topics relating to Kṛṣṇa, he does not like to eat anything which is not offered to Kṛṣṇa, and he does not wish to go anywhere if Kṛṣṇa is not involved. Therefore, his senses are controlled. A man of controlled senses cannot be offensive to anyone. One may ask, "Why then was Arjuna offensive (in battle) to others? Wasn't he in Kṛṣṇa consciousness?" Arjuna was only superficially offensive because (as has already been explained in the Second Chapter) all the assembled persons on the battlefield would continue to live individually, as the soul cannot be slain. So, spiritually, no one was killed on the Battlefield of Kurukṣetra. Only their dresses were changed by the order of Kṛṣṇa, who was personally present. Therefore, Arjuna, while fighting on the Battlefield of Kurukṣetra, was not really fighting at all; he was simply carrying out the orders of Kṛṣṇa in full Kṛṣṇa consciousness. Such a person is never entangled in the reactions of work.

8-9. A person in the divine consciousness, although engaged in seeing, hearing, touching, smelling, eating, moving about, sleeping and breathing, always knows within himself that he actually does nothing at all. Because while evacuating, receiving, opening or closing his eyes, he always knows that only the material senses are engaged with their objects and that he is aloof from them.

10. One who performs his duty without attachment, surrendering the results unto the Supreme God, is not affected by sinful action, as the lotus leaf is untouched by water.

11. The *yogīs*, abandoning attachment, act with body, mind, intelligence, and even with the senses, only for the purpose of purification.

PURPORT

By acting in Kṛṣṇa consciousness for the satisfaction of the senses of Kṛṣṇa, any action, whether of the body, mind, intelligence, or even of the senses, is purified of material contamination. There are no material reactions resulting from the activities of a Kṛṣṇa conscious person. Therefore, purified activities, which are generally called *sadācara*, can be easily performed by acting in Kṛṣṇa consciousness. Śrī Rūpa Gosvāmī in his *Bhakti-rasāmṛta-sindhu* describes this as follows: A person acting in Kṛṣṇa consciousness (or, in other words, in the service of Kṛṣṇa) with his body, mind, intelligence and words, is a liberated person even within the material world, although he may be engaged in many so-called material activities. He has no false ego, nor does he believe that he is this material body, or that he possesses the body. He knows that he is not this body and that this body does not belong to him. He himself belongs to Kṛṣṇa, and the body too belongs to Kṛṣṇa. When he applies everything produced of the body, mind, intelligence, words, life, wealth, etc.—whatever he may have within his possession—to Kṛṣṇa's service, he at once becomes dovetailed with Kṛṣṇa. He is one with Kṛṣṇa and is devoid of the false ego that would lead him to believe that he is the body. This is the perfect stage of Kṛṣṇa consciousness.

12. The steadily devoted soul attains unadulterated peace because he offers the results of all activities to Me; whereas a person who is not in harmony with the Divine, who is greedy for the fruits of his labor, becomes entangled.

PURPORT

The difference between a person in Kṛṣṇa consciousness and a person in bodily consciousness is that the former is attached to Kṛṣṇa, whereas the latter is attached to the results of his activities. The person who is attached to Kṛṣṇa and works for Him only is certainly a liberated person, and such a person is not anxious for fruitive rewards. In the *Bhāgavatam*, anxiety over the result of an activity is explained as being due to one's functioning within the conception of duality, that is, without knowledge of the Absolute Truth. Kṛṣṇa is the Supreme Absolute Truth, the Personality of Godhead. In Kṛṣṇa consciousness, there is no duality. All that exists is a product of Kṛṣṇa's energy, and Kṛṣṇa is all good. Therefore, activities in Kṛṣṇa consciousness are on the absolute plane; they are transcendental and have no material effect. One is filled with peace in Kṛṣṇa consciousness. One who is, however, entangled in profit calculation for sense gratification cannot have that peace. This is the secret of Kṛṣṇa consciousness—realization that there is no other existence besides Kṛṣṇa is the platform of peace and fearlessness.

13. When the embodied living being neither does nor causes to be done, mentally renouncing all actions, he resides happily in the city of nine gates [the material body].

PURPORT

The embodied soul lives in the city of nine gates. The activities of the body, or the figurative city of body, are conducted automatically by the particular modes of nature. The soul, although subjecting himself to the conditions of the body, can be beyond those conditions, if he so desires. Owing only to forgetfulness of his superior nature, he identifies with the material body and therefore suffers. By Kṛṣṇa consciousness, he can revive his real position, and thus he can come out of his embodiment. Therefore, when one takes to Kṛṣṇa consciousness, one at once becomes completely aloof from bodily activities. In such a controlled life, in which his deliberations are changed, he lives happily within the city of nine gates. The nine gates are described as follows: "The Supreme Personality of Godhead, who is living within the body of a living entity, is the controller of all living entities all over the universe. The body consists of nine gates: two eyes, two nostrils, two ears, the mouth, the anus and the genitals. The living entity in his conditioned stage identifies himself with the body, but when he identifies himself with the Lord within himself, he becomes just as free as the Lord, even while in the body."

Therefore, a Kṛṣṇa conscious person is free from both the outer and inner activities of the material body.

14. The embodied spirit, master of the city of his body, does not create activities, nor does he induce people to act, nor does he create the fruits of action. All this is enacted by the modes of material nature.

15. Nor does the Supreme Spirit assume anyone's sinful or pious activities. Embodied beings, however, are bewildered because of the ignorance which covers their real knowledge.

PURPORT

The Sanskrit word *vibhu* means the Supreme Lord who is full of unlimited knowledge, riches, strength, fame, beauty and renunciation. He is always satisfied in Himself, undisturbed by sinful or pious activities. He does not create a particular situation for any living entity, but the living entity, bewildered by ignorance, desires to be put into certain conditions of life, and thereby his chain of action and reaction begins. A living entity is, by superior nature, full of knowledge. Nevertheless, he is prone to be influenced by ignorance due to his limited power. The Lord is omnipotent, but the living entity is not. The Lord is *vibhu*, or omniscient, but the living entity is *aṇu*, or atomic. Because he is a living soul, he has the capacity to desire by his free will. Such desire is fulfilled only by the omnipotent Lord. And so when the living entity is bewildered in his desires, the Lord allows him to fulfill those desires, but the Lord is never responsible for the actions and reactions of the particular situation which may be desired. Being in a bewildered condition, therefore, the embodied soul identifies himself with the circumstantial material body and becomes subjected to the temporary misery and happiness of life. The Lord is the constant companion of the living entity as Paramātmā, or the Supersoul, and therefore He can understand the desires of the individual soul, as one can smell the flavor of a flower by being near it. Desire is a subtle form of conditioning of the living entity. The Lord fulfills his desire as he deserves: Man proposes and God disposes. The individual is not, therefore, omnipotent in fulfilling his desires. The Lord, however, can fulfill all desires, and the Lord, being neutral to everyone, does not interfere with the desires of the minutely independent living entities. However, when one desires in terms of Kṛṣṇa consciousness, the Lord takes special care of him and encourages him to desire in a particular way by which one can gradually attain to Him and be eternally happy. The Vedic hymn therefore declares: "The Lord engages the living entity in pious activities so he may be elevated. The Lord engages him in impious activities so he may go to hell. The living entity is completely dependent in his distress and happiness. By the will of the Supreme he can go to heaven or hell, as a cloud is driven by the air."

Therefore, the embodied soul, by his immemorial desire to avoid Kṛṣṇa consciousness, causes his own bewilderment. Consequently, although he is constitutionally eternal, blissful and cognizant, due to the littleness of his existence he forgets his constitutional position of service to the Lord and is thus entrapped by nescience. And, under the spell of ignorance, the living entity claims that the Lord is responsible for his conditional existence. The *Vedānta-sūtras* confirm this: "The Lord neither hates nor likes anyone, though He appears to."

16. When, however, one is enlightened with the knowledge by which nescience is destroyed, then his knowledge reveals everything, as the sun lights up everything in the daytime.

PURPORT

Those who have forgotten Kṛṣṇa must certainly be bewildered, but those who are in Kṛṣṇa consciousness are not bewildered at all. Knowledge is always highly esteemed. And what is knowledge? Perfect knowledge is achieved when one surrenders unto Kṛṣṇa, as is said in the *Bhagavad-gītā. Bahūnāṁ janmanām ante jñānavān māṁ prapadyate:* after passing through many, many births, when one perfect in knowledge surrenders unto Kṛṣṇa, or when one attains Kṛṣṇa consciousness, then everything is revealed to him, as the sun reveals everything in the daytime. The living entity is bewildered in so many ways. For instance, when a living entity thinks himself God, unceremoniously, he actually falls into the last snare of nescience. If a living entity is God, then how can he become bewildered by nescience? Does God become bewildered by nescience? If so, then nescience, or Satan, is greater than God.

Real knowledge can be obtained from a person who is in perfect Kṛṣṇa consciousness. Therefore, one has to seek out a bona fide spiritual master and, under him, learn what Kṛṣṇa consciousness is. Kṛṣṇa consciousness will certainly drive away all nescience, as the sun drives away darkness. Even though a person may be in full knowledge that he is not this body but is transcendental to the body, he still may not be able to discriminate between the soul and the Supersoul. However, he can know everything well if he cares to take shelter of the perfect, bona fide Kṛṣṇa conscious spiritual master. One can know God and one's relationship with God only when one actually meets a representative of God. A representative of God never claims that he is God, although he is paid all the respect ordinarily paid to God because he has knowledge of God. One has to learn the distinction between God and the living entity. The Lord, Śrī Kṛṣṇa, therefore stated in the Second Chapter, verse 12, that every living being is individual and that the Lord also is individual. They were all individuals in the past, they are individuals at present, and they will continue to be individuals in the future, even after liberation. At night we see everything as one in the darkness, but in day when the sun is up, we see everything in its real identity. Identity with individuality in spiritual life is real knowledge.

17. When one's intelligence, mind, faith and refuge are all fixed in the Supreme, then one becomes fully cleansed of misgivings through complete knowledge and thus proceeds straight on the path of liberation.

18. The humble sage sees with equal vision a learned and gentle *brāhmaṇa*, a cow, an elephant, a dog and a dog-eater [outcaste].

19 Those whose minds are established in sameness and equanimity have already conquered the conditions of birth and death. They are flawless like Brahman, and as such they are already situated in Brahman.

20. A person who neither rejoices upon achieving something pleasant nor laments upon obtaining something unpleasant, who is self-intelligent, unbewildered, and who knows the science of God, is to be understood as already situated in transcendence.

PURPORT

The symptoms of the self-realized person are given herein. The first symptom is that he is not illusioned by the false identification of the body with his true self. He knows perfectly well that he is not this body, but is the fragmental portion of the Supreme Personality of Godhead. He is therefore not joyful in achieving something, nor does he lament in losing anything related to this body. This steadiness of mind is called *sthira-buddhi*, or self-intelligence. He is therefore never bewildered by mistaking the gross body for the soul, nor does he accept the body as permanent and disregard the existence of the soul. This knowledge elevates him to the station of knowing the complete science of the Absolute Truth, namely Brahman, Paramātmā and Bhagavān. He thus knows his constitutional position perfectly well, without falsely trying to become one with the Supreme in all respects. This is called Brahman realization, or self-realization. Such steady consciousness is called Kṛṣṇa consciousness.

21. Such a liberated person is not attracted to material sense pleasure, but is always in trance, enjoying the pleasure within. In this way, the self-realized person enjoys unlimited happiness, for he concentrates on the Supreme.

22. An intelligent person does not take part in the sources of misery, which are due to contact with the material senses. O son of Kuntī, such pleasures have a beginning and an end, and so the wise man does not delight in them.

23. Before giving up this present body, if one is able to tolerate the urges of the material senses and check the force of desire and anger, he is a *yogī* and is happy in this world.

24. One whose happiness is within, who is active within, who rejoices within and is illumined within, is actually the perfect mystic. He is liberated in the Supreme, and ultimately he attains the Supreme.

25. One who is beyond duality and doubt, whose mind is engaged within, who is always busy working for the welfare of all sentient beings, and who is free from all sins, achieves liberation in the Supreme.

PURPORT

Only a person who is fully in Kṛṣṇa consciousness can be said to be engaged in welfare work for all living entities. When a person is actually in knowledge that Kṛṣṇa is the fountainhead of everything, then when he acts in that spirit he acts for everyone. The sufferings of humanity are due to forgetfulness of Kṛṣṇa as the supreme enjoyer, the supreme proprietor and the supreme friend. Therefore, to act to revive this consciousness within the entire human society is the highest welfare work. One cannot be engaged in first-class welfare work without being liberated in the Supreme. A Kṛṣṇa conscious person has no doubt about the supremacy of Kṛṣṇa. He has no doubt because he is completely freed from all sins. This is the state of divine love.

A person engaged only in administering to the physical welfare of human society cannot factually help anyone. Temporary relief of the external body and the mind of the living entity is not satisfactory. The real cause of his difficulties in the hard struggle for life may be found in his forgetfulness of his relationship with the Supreme Lord. When a man is fully conscious of his relationship with Kṛṣṇa, he is actually a liberated soul, although he may be in the material tabernacle.

26. Those who are free from anger and all material desires, who are self-realized, self-disciplined, and constantly endeavoring for perfection, are assured of liberation in the Supreme in the very near future.

27-28. Shutting out all external sense objects, keeping the eyes and vision concentrated between the two eyebrows, suspending the inward and outward breaths within the nostrils and thus controlling the mind, senses and intelligence, the transcendentalist becomes free from desire, fear and anger. One who is always in this state is certainly liberated.

29. The sages, knowing Me as the ultimate purpose of all sacrifices and austerities, the Supreme Lord of all planets and demigods, and the benefactor and well-wisher of all living entities, attain peace from the pangs of material miseries.

PURPORT

The conditioned souls within the clutches of illusory energy are all anxious to attain peace in the material world. But they do not know the formula for peace, which is explained in this part of *Bhagavad-gītā*. The peace formula is this: Lord Kṛṣṇa is the beneficiary in all human activities. Man should offer everything to the transcendental service of the Lord because He is the proprietor of all planets and the demigods thereon. No one is greater than He. He is greater than the greatest of the demigods, Lord Śiva and Lord Brahmā. Under the spell of illusion, living entities are trying to be lords of all they survey, but actually they are dominated by the material energy of the Lord. The Lord is the master of material nature, and the conditioned souls are under the stringent rules of that nature. Unless one understands these bare facts, it is not possible to achieve peace in the world either individually or collectively. This is the sense of Kṛṣṇa consciousness: Lord Kṛṣṇa is the supreme predominator, and all living entities, including the great demigods, are His subordinates. One can attain perfect peace only in complete Kṛṣṇa consciousness.

This Fifth Chapter is a practical explanation of Kṛṣṇa consciousness, generally known as *karma-yoga*. The question of mental speculation as to how *karma-yoga* can give liberation is answered herewith. To work in Kṛṣṇa consciousness is to work with the complete knowledge of the Lord as the predominator. Such work is not different from transcendental knowledge. Direct Kṛṣṇa consciousness is *bhakti-yoga*, and *jñāna-yoga* is a path leading to *bhakti-yoga*. Kṛṣṇa consciousness means to work in full knowledge of one's relationship with the Supreme Absolute, and the perfection of this consciousness is full knowledge of Kṛṣṇa, or the Supreme Personality of Godhead. A pure soul is the eternal servant of God as His fragmental part and parcel. He comes into contact with *māyā* (illusion) due to the desire to lord it over *māyā*, and that is the cause of his many sufferings. As long as he is in contact with matter, he has to execute work in terms of material necessities. Kṛṣṇa consciousness, however, brings one into spiritual life even while one is within the jurisdiction of matter, for it is an arousing of spiritual existence by practice in the material world. The more one is advanced, the more he is freed from the clutches of matter. There is no partiality of the Lord toward anyone. Everything depends on one's own practical performance of duties in Kṛṣṇa consciousness in an effort to control the senses and conquer the influence of desire and anger. And, remaining in Kṛṣṇa consciousness by controlling the above-mentioned passions, one remains factually in the transcendental stage, or *brahma-nirvāṇa*. The eightfold *yoga* mysticism is automatically practiced in Kṛṣṇa consciousness because the ultimate purpose is served. There is a gradual elevation in the practice of *yama, niyama, āsana, pratyāhāra, dhyāna, dhāraṇā, prāṇāyāma* and *samādhi*. But these only preface perfection by devotional service, which alone can award peace to the human being. It is the highest goal of life.

Thus end the Bhaktivedanta purports to the Fifth Chapter of the *Śrīmad Bhagavad-gītā* in the matter of *Karma-yoga*, or acting in Kṛṣṇa consciousness.

CHAPTER SIX

Sāṅkhya-yoga

1. The Supreme Personality of Godhead said: One who is unattached to the fruits of his work and who works as he is obligated is in the renounced order of life, and he is the true mystic, not he who lights no fire and performs no work.

PURPORT

In this chapter the Lord explains that the process of the eightfold *yoga* system is a means to control the mind and the senses. However, this is very difficult for people in general to perform, especially in this Age of Kali. Although the eightfold *yoga* system is recommended in this chapter, the Lord emphasizes that the process of *karma-yoga*, or acting in Kṛṣṇa consciousness, is better. Everyone acts in this world to maintain his family and their paraphernalia, but no one is working without some self-interest, some personal gratification, be it concentrated or extended. The criterion of perfection is to act in Kṛṣṇa consciousness, and not with a view to enjoying the fruits of work. To act in Kṛṣṇa consciousness is the duty of every living entity because we are constitutionally parts and parcels of the Supreme. The parts of the body work for the satisfaction of the whole body. The limbs of the body do not act for self-satisfaction, but for the satisfaction of the complete whole. Similarly, the living entity, acting for the satisfaction of the supreme whole, not for personal satisfaction, is the perfect *sannyāsī*, the perfect *yogī.*

Sannyāsīs sometimes artificially think that they have become liberated from all material duties, and therefore they cease to perform *agnihotra-yajñas* (fire sacrifices), but actually they are self-interested because their goal is to become one with the impersonal Brahman. Such a desire is greater than any material desire, but it is not without self-interest. Similarly, the mystic *yogī* who practices the *yoga* system with half-open eyes, ceasing all material activities, desires some satisfaction for his personal self. But a person acting in Kṛṣṇa consciousness works for the satisfaction of the whole, without self-interest. A Kṛṣṇa conscious person has no desire for self-satisfaction. His criterion of success is the satisfaction of Kṛṣṇa and thus he is the perfect *sannyāsī*, or perfect *yogī.* Lord Caitanya, the highest perfectional symbol in Kṛṣṇa consciousness, prays in this way: "O almighty Lord, I have no desire to accumulate wealth, nor to enjoy beautiful women, nor do I want any number of followers. What I want only is the causeless mercy of Your devotional service in my life, birth after birth."

2. What is called renunciation is the same as *yoga*, or linking oneself with the Supreme, for no one can become a *yogī* unless he renounces the desire for sense gratification.

3. For one who is a neophyte in the eightfold *yoga* system, work is said to be the means; and for one who has already attained to *yoga*, cessation of all material activities is said to be the means.

4. A person is said to have attained to *yoga* when, having renounced all material desires, he neither acts for sense gratification nor engages in fruitive activities.

PURPORT

When a person is fully engaged in the transcendental loving service of the Lord, he is pleased in himself, and thus he is no longer engaged in sense gratification or in fruitive activities. Otherwise, one must be engaged in sense gratification, since one cannot live without engagement.

Without Kṛṣṇa consciousness, one must be always seeking self-centered or extended selfish activities. But a Kṛṣṇa conscious person can do everything for the satisfaction of Kṛṣṇa and thereby be perfectly detached from sense gratification. One who has no such realization must mechanically try to escape material desires before being elevated to the top rung of the *yoga* ladder.

5. A man must elevate himself by his own mind, not degrade himself. The mind is the friend of the conditioned soul, and his enemy as well.

PURPORT

The Sanskrit word *ātmā* (self) denotes body, mind and soul—depending upon different circumstances. In the *yoga* system, the mind of the conditioned soul is especially important. Since the mind is the central point of *yoga* practice, *ātmā* here refers to the mind. The purpose of the *yoga* system is to control the mind and to draw it away from attachment to sense objects. It is stressed herewith that the mind must be so trained that it can deliver the conditioned soul from the mire of nescience. In material existence one is subjected to the influence of the mind and the senses. In fact, the pure soul is entangled in the material world because of the mind's ego, which desires to lord it over material nature. Therefore, the mind should be trained so that it will not be attracted by the glitter of material nature, and in this way the conditioned soul may be saved. One should not degrade oneself by attraction to sense objects. The more one is attracted by sense objects, the more one becomes entangled in material existence. The best way to disentangle oneself is always to engage the mind in Kṛṣṇa's service.

The Sanskrit word *hi* in this verse is used to emphasize this point, i.e., that one must do this. It is also said: "For man, mind is the cause of bondage and mind is the cause of liberation. Mind absorbed in sense objects is the cause of bondage, and mind detached from the sense objects is the cause of liberation." Therefore, the mind which is always engaged in Kṛṣṇa consciousness is the cause of supreme liberation.

6. For he who has conquered his mind, it is the best of friends; but for one who has failed to do so, his very mind will be the greatest enemy.

7. For one who has conquered the mind, the Supersoul is already reached, for he has attained tranquility. To such a man happiness and distress, heat and cold, honor and dishonor are all the same.

8. A person is said to be established in self-realization and is called a *yogī* [or mystic] when he is fully satisfied by virtue of acquired knowledge and realization. Such a person is situated in transcendence and is self-controlled. He sees everything—whether it be pebbles, stones or gold—as the same.

PURPORT

Book knowledge without realization of the Supreme Truth is useless. This is said as follows in the *Padma Purāṇa:* "No one can understand the transcendental nature of the name, form, quality and pastimes of Śrī Kṛṣṇa through his materially contaminated senses. Only when one becomes spiritually saturated by transcendental service to the Lord are the transcendental name, form, quality and pastimes of the Lord revealed to him."

This *Bhagavad-gītā* is the science of Kṛṣṇa consciousness. No one can become Kṛṣṇa conscious simply by mundane scholarship. One must be fortunate enough to associate with a person who is in pure consciousness. A Kṛṣṇa conscious person has realized knowledge, by the grace of Kṛṣṇa, because he is satisfied with pure devotional service. By realized knowledge, one becomes perfect. By such perfect knowledge one can remain steady in his convictions, but by academic knowledge one is easily deluded and is confused by apparent contradictions. It is the realized soul who is actually self-controlled because he has nothing to do with mundane scholarship.

9. A person is said to be still further advanced when he regards all—the honest well-wisher, friends and enemies, the envious, the pious, the sinner and those who are indifferent and impartial—with an equal mind.

10. A transcendentalist should always try to concentrate his mind on the Supreme Self; he should live alone in a secluded place and should always carefully control his mind. He should be free from desires and possessiveness.

Plate 20 One who engages in devotional service to the Supreme Personality of Godhead achieves the same results as one who engages in the analytical study of the material world (*sāṅkhya*). *(pp.91–92)*

Plate 21 The humble sage sees with equal vision a learned and gentle *brāhmaṇa*, cow, an elephant, a dog, and a dog-eater (outcaste). *(p.99)*

Plate 22 The perfection of *yoga* is to meditate on the Supreme Personality of Godhead within one's heart and make Him the ultimate goal of life. (p.107)

Plate 23 Always expecting the mercy of the Lord, one should practice *yoga* with the same undeviating determination shown by the sparrow trying to retrieve her eggs from the ocean. *(pp.109–110)*

Plate 24 The individual self is the passenger in the chariot of the material body, and intelligence is the driver. Mind is the driving instrument, and the senses are the horses. The self is thus the enjoyer or sufferer in the association of the mind and senses. *(pp.113–114)*

Plate 25 Kṛṣṇa, who is called Śyāmasundara, is the beautiful color of a cloud. His lotuslike face as effulgent as the sun, His dress brilliant with jewels, and His body garlanded by flowers, He is the object of the ideal *yogī's* meditation. *(pp.117–119)*

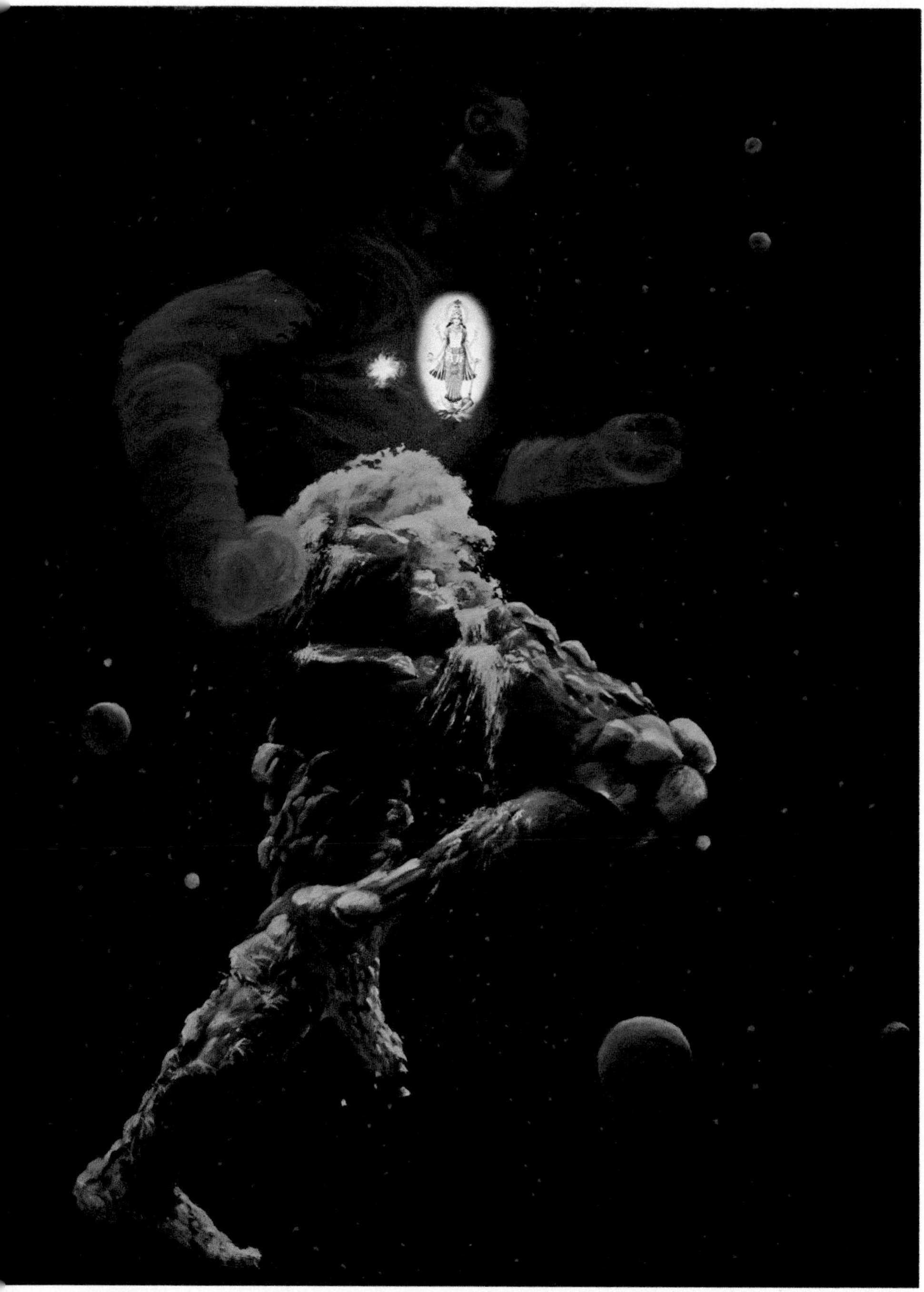

Plate 26 Kṛṣṇa's material and spiritual energies. *(pp.124–125)*

Plate 27 The process of creation, conducted by Lord Kṛṣṇa's Viṣṇu expansions
(p.124)

Plate 28 Four kinds of pious men surrender to Kṛṣṇa, and four kinds of impious men do not. *(pp.129–134)*

Plate 29 Men of small intelligence seek favors from the demigods and obtain thei desires, but in actuality these benefits are bestowed by the Supreme Lord alone
(pp.135–136)

'late 30 The abode of Lord Kṛṣṇa, known as Goloka Vṛndāvana, is full of palaces nade of touchstone. There the trees are called desire trees, the cows are called *surabhi*, ınd the Lord is served by hundreds and thousands of goddesses of fortune. *(p.148)*

Plate 31 The foolish mock at the Supreme Lord Śrī Kṛṣṇa when He descends like human being. They do not know His transcendental nature and His supreme dominio over all that be. (p.155)

Plate 32 If with love and devotion one offers the Supreme Lord Śrī Kṛṣṇa a leaf, a flower, fruit, or water, He will accept it. *(pp.157–159)*

Plate 33 Arjuna addressed Kṛṣṇa: "You are the Supreme Brahman, the ultimate, th supreme abode and purifier." *(pp.168–169)*

Plate 34 The opulence of the Absolute Lord, Śrī Kṛṣṇa. *(pp.169–176)*

Plate 35 The playmates of Kṛṣṇa are so immersed in pure love that they do not even realize that Kṛṣṇa is the Supreme Personality of Godhead. *(p.180)*

11-12. To practice *yoga*, one should go to a secluded place and should lay *kuśa* grass on the ground and then cover it with a deerskin and a soft cloth. The seat should neither be too high nor too low and should be situated in a sacred place. The *yogī* should then sit on it very firmly and should practice *yoga* by controlling the mind and the senses, purifying the heart and fixing the mind on one point.

PURPORT

"Sacred place" refers to places of pilgrimage. In India the *yogīs*, the transcendentalists or the devotees all leave home and reside in sacred places such as Prayāga, Mathurā, Vṛndāvana, Hṛṣīkeśa and Hardwar and practice *yoga* there. A sacred place is where the sacred rivers like the Yamunā and the Ganges flow. Any bank on the Ganges or Yamunā is naturally sacred. One should select a place which is secluded and undisturbed. The so-called *yoga* societies in big cities may be successful in earning material benefit, but they are not at all suitable for the actual practice of *yoga*. One who is not self-controlled and whose mind is not undisturbed cannot practice meditation. Therefore, in the *Bṛhannaradīya Purāṇa* it is said that in the Kali-yuga (the present *yuga*, or age), when people in general are short-living, slow in spiritual realization and always disturbed by various anxieties, the best means of spiritual realization is to chant the holy name of the Lord. "In this age of quarrel and hypocrisy the only means of deliverance is to chant the holy name of the Lord. There is no other way to success."

13-14. One should hold one's body, neck and head erect in a straight line and stare steadily at the tip of the nose. Thus with an unagitated, subdued mind, devoid of fear, completely free from sex life, one should meditate upon Me within the heart and make Me the ultimate goal of life.

15. By meditating in this manner, always controlling the body, mind and activities, the mystic transcendentalist attains to the kingdom of God through cessation of material existence.

PURPORT

The ultimate goal in practicing *yoga* is now clearly explained. *Yoga* practice is not meant for attaining any kind of material facility. One who seeks an improvement in health or aspires after material perfection is no *yogī*, according to *Bhagavad-gītā.* Cessation of material existence does not mean entering into an existence of void, which is only a myth. There is no void anywhere within the creation of the Lord. Rather, the cessation of material existence enables one to enter into the spiritual sky, the abode of the Lord. The abode of the Lord is also clearly described in *Bhagavad-gītā* as that place where there is no need of sun or moon, nor of electricity. All the planets in the spiritual kingdom are self-luminous like the sun in the material sky. The kingdom of God is everywhere, but the spiritual sky and the planets thereof are called *paraṁ dhāma*, or superior abodes.

A consummate *yogī*, who is perfect in understanding Lord Kṛṣṇa, as clearly stated herein by the Lord Himself, can attain real peace and can ultimately reach His supreme abode, Kṛṣṇaloka, known as Goloka Vṛndāvana. In the *Brahma-saṁhitā* it is clearly stated that the Lord, although He resides always in His abode called Goloka, is the all-pervading Brahman and the localized Paramātmā as well, through His superior spiritual energies. No one can reach the spiritual sky or enter into the eternal abode of the Lord without the proper understanding of Kṛṣṇa and His plenary expansion Viṣṇu. Therefore, a person working in Kṛṣṇa consciousness is the perfect *yogī* because his mind is always absorbed in Kṛṣṇa's activities. In the *Vedas* also we learn: "One can overcome the path of birth and death only by understanding the Supreme Personality of Godhead." In other words, perfection of the *yoga* system is the attainment of freedom from material existence, and not some magical jugglery or gymnastic feats to befool innocent people.

16. There is no possibility of one's becoming a *yogī*, O Arjuna, if one eats too much or eats too little, sleeps too much or does not sleep enough.

17. He who is regulated in his habits of eating, sleeping, working and recreation can mitigate all material pains by practicing the *yoga* system.

18. When the *yogī*, by practice of *yoga*, disciplines his mental activities and becomes situated in transcendence—devoid of all material desires—he is said to have attained *yoga*.

19. As a lamp in a windless place does not waver, so the transcendentalist, whose mind is controlled, remains always steady in his meditation on the transcendent self.

20-23. In the state of perfection called trance, or *samādhi*, one's mind is completely restrained from material mental activities by practice of *yoga*. This is characterized by one's ability to see the self by the pure mind and to relish and rejoice in the self. In that joyous state, one is situated in boundless transcendental happiness and enjoys himself through transcendental senses. Established thus, one never departs from the truth, and upon gaining this he thinks there is no greater gain. Being situated in such a position, one is never shaken, even in the midst of the greatest difficulty. This, indeed, is actual freedom from all miseries arising from material contact.

24. One should engage oneself in the practice of *yoga* with undeviating determination and faith. One should abandon, without exception, all material desires born of false ego and thus control all the senses on all sides by the mind.

PURPORT

The *yoga* practitioner should be determined and should patiently prosecute the practice without deviation. One should be sure of success at the end and pursue this course with great perseverence, not becoming discouraged if there is any delay in the attainment of success. Success is sure for the rigid practitioner. Regarding *bhakti-yoga*, Rūpa Gosvāmī says: "The process of *bhakti-yoga* can be executed successfully with full-hearted enthusiasm, perseverance and determination by following the prescribed duties in the association of devotees and by engaging completely in activities of goodness."

As for determination, one should follow the example of the sparrow who lost her eggs in the waves of the ocean. A sparrow laid her eggs on the shore of the ocean, but the big ocean carried them away on its waves. The sparrow became very upset and asked the ocean to return her eggs. The ocean did not even consider her appeal, and so she decided to dry up the ocean. She began to pick out the water in her small beak, and everyone laughed at her for her impossible determination. The news of her activity spread, and at last Garuḍa, the gigantic bird carrier of Lord Viṣṇu, heard it. He became compassionate toward his small sister bird, and so he came to see the small sparrow, and he promised his help. Thus Garuḍa at once asked the ocean to return her eggs, lest he himself take up the work of the sparrow. The ocean was frightened at this and returned the eggs. Thus the sparrow became happy by the grace of Garuḍa.

Similarly, the practice of *yoga*, especially *bhakti-yoga* in Kṛṣṇa consciousness, may appear to be a very difficult job. But if anyone follows the principles with great determination the Lord will surely help, for God helps those who help themselves.

25. Gradually, step by step, with full conviction, one should become situated in trance by means of intelligence, and thus the mind should be fixed on the self alone and should think of nothing else.

26. From whatever and wherever the mind wanders due to its flickering and unsteady nature, one must certainly withdraw it and bring it back under the control of the self.

PURPORT

The nature of the mind is flickering and unsteady. But a self-realized *yogī* has to control the mind; the mind should not control him. One who controls the mind (and therefore the senses as well) is called *gosvāmī*, or *svāmī*, and one who is controlled by the mind is called *godāsa*, or the servant of the senses. A *gosvāmī* knows the standard of sense happiness. In transcendental sense happiness, the senses are engaged in the service of Hṛṣīkeśa, the supreme owner of the senses, Kṛṣṇa. Serving Kṛṣṇa with purified senses is called Kṛṣṇa consciousness. That is the way of bringing the senses under full control. What is more, that is the highest perfection of *yoga* practice.

27. The *yogī* whose mind is fixed on Me verily attains the highest happiness. By virtue of his identity with Brahman, he is liberated; his mind is peaceful, his passions are quieted, and he is freed from sin.

28. Steady in the self, being freed from all material contamination, the *yogī* achieves the highest perfectional stage of happiness in touch with the Supreme Consciousness.

29. A true *yogī* observes Me in all beings, and also sees every being in Me. Indeed, the self-realized man sees Me everywhere.

30. For one who sees Me everywhere and sees everything in Me, I am never lost, nor is he ever lost to Me.

PURPORT

A person in Kṛṣṇa consciousness certainly sees Lord Kṛṣṇa everywhere, and he sees everything in Kṛṣṇa. Such a person may appear to see all separate manifestations of the material nature, but in each and every instance he is conscious of Kṛṣṇa, knowing that everything is a manifestation of Kṛṣṇa's energy. Nothing can exist without Kṛṣṇa, and Kṛṣṇa is the Lord of everything—this is the basic principle of Kṛṣṇa consciousness. Kṛṣṇa consciousness is the development of love of Kṛṣṇa—a position transcendental even to material liberation. It is the stage after self-realization, at which the devotee becomes one with Kṛṣṇa in the sense that Kṛṣṇa becomes everything for the devotee and the devotee becomes full in loving Kṛṣṇa. An intimate relationship between the Lord and the devotee then exists. In that stage, there is no chance that the living entity will be annihilated. Nor is the Personality of Godhead ever out of the sight of the devotee. To merge in Kṛṣṇa is spiritual annihilation. A devotee takes no such risk. It is stated in the *Brahma-saṁhitā:* "I worship the primeval Lord, Govinda, who is always seen by the devotee whose eyes are anointed with the pulp of love. He is seen in His eternal form of Śyāmasundara, situated within the heart of the devotee."

At this stage Lord Kṛṣṇa never disappears from the sight of the devotee, nor does the devotee ever lose sight of the Lord. In the case of a *yogī* who sees the Lord as Paramātmā within the heart, the same applies. Such a *yogī* turns into a pure devotee and cannot bear to live for a moment without seeing the Lord within himself.

31. The *yogī* who knows that I and the Supersoul within all creatures are one worships Me and remains always in Me in all circumstances.

PURPORT

A *yogī* who is practicing meditation on the Supersoul within himself sees the plenary portion of Kṛṣṇa as Viṣṇu—with four hands, holding conchshell, wheel, club and lotus flower. The *yogī* should know that Viṣṇu is not different from Kṛṣṇa. Kṛṣṇa in this form of Supersoul is situated in everyone's heart. Furthermore, there is no difference between the innumerable Supersouls present in the innumerable hearts of living entities. Nor is there a difference between a Kṛṣṇa conscious person always engaged in the transcendental loving service of Kṛṣṇa and a perfect *yogī* engaged in meditation on the Supersoul. The *yogī* in Kṛṣṇa consciousness, even though he may be engaged in various activities while in material existence, remains always situated in Kṛṣṇa. A devotee of the Lord, always acting in Kṛṣṇa consciousness, is automatically liberated. In the *Nārada-pañcarātra* this is confirmed in this way: "By concentrating one's attention on the transcendental form of Kṛṣṇa, who is all-pervading and beyond time and space, one becomes absorbed in thinking of Kṛṣṇa and then attains the happy state of transcendental association with Him."

Kṛṣṇa consciousness is the highest stage of trance in *yoga* practice. This very understanding that Kṛṣṇa is present as Paramātmā in everyone's heart makes the *yogī* faultless. The *Vedas* confirms this inconceivable potency of the Lord as follows: "Viṣṇu is one, and yet He is certainly all-pervading. By His inconceivable potency, in spite of His one form, He is present everywhere. Like the sun, He appears in many places at once."

32. He is a perfect *yogī* who, by comparison to his own self, sees the true equality of all living entities, both in their happiness and distress, O Arjuna!

33. Arjuna said: O Madhusūdana, the system of *yoga* which You have summarized appears impractical and unendurable to me, for the mind is restless and unsteady.

PURPORT

The system of mysticism described by Lord Kṛṣṇa to Arjuna is here being rejected by Arjuna out of a feeling of inability. It is not possible for an ordinary man to leave home and go to a secluded place in the mountains or jungles to practice *yoga* in this Age of Kali. The present age is characterized by a bitter struggle for a life of short duration. People are not serious about self-realization even by simple, practical means, and what to speak of this difficult *yoga* system, which regulates the mode of living, the manner of sitting, selection of place, and detachment of the mind from material engagements? As a practical man, Arjuna thought it was impossible to follow this system of *yoga*, even though he was favorably endowed in many ways. He belonged to the royal family and was highly elevated in terms of numerous qualities; he was a great warrior, he had great longevity, and, above all, he was the most intimate friend of Lord Kṛṣṇa, the Supreme Personality of Godhead. Five thousand years ago, Arjuna had much better facilities than we do, yet he rejected this system of *yoga*. In fact, we do not find any record in history of his practicing it at any time. Therefore this system must be considered impossible, especially in this Age of Kali. Of course, it may be possible for some very few, rare men, but for the people in general it is an impossible proposal. If this was so five thousand years ago, then what to speak of the present day? Those who are imitating this *yoga* system in different so-called schools and societies, although complacent, are certainly wasting their time. They are completely in ignorance of the desired goal.

34. For the mind is restless, turbulent, obstinate and very strong, O Kṛṣṇa, and to subdue it is, it seems to me, more difficult than controlling the wind.

PURPORT

The mind is so strong and obstinate that sometimes it overcomes the intelligence. For a man in the practical world who has to fight so many opposing elements, the mind is certainly very difficult to control. Artificially, one may establish a mental equilibrium toward both friend and enemy, but ultimately no worldly man can do so, for this is more difficult than controlling the raging wind. In the Vedic literatures it is said: "The individual is the passenger in the car of the material body, and intelligence is the driver. Mind is the driving instrument, and the senses are the horses. The self is thus the enjoyer or sufferer in the association of the mind and senses. So it is understood by great thinkers." Intelligence is supposed to direct the mind. But the mind is so strong and obstinate that it surpasses even one's own intelligence, as an acute infection may surpass the efficacy of medicine. Such a strong mind is supposed to be controlled by the practice of *yoga*. But such practice is never practical for a worldly person like Arjuna. And what can we say of modern man? The difficulty is neatly expressed. One cannot capture the blowing wind, and it is even more difficult to capture the agitating mind.

35. The Blessed Lord said: O mighty-armed son of Kuntī, it is undoubtedly very difficult to curb the restless mind, but it is possible by constant practice and by detachment.

36. For one whose mind is unbridled, self-realization is difficult work. But he whose mind is controlled and who strives by right means is assured of success. That is My judgment.

PURPORT

The Supreme Personality of Godhead declares that one who does not accept the proper treatment to detach the mind from material engagement can hardly achieve success in self-realization. Trying to practice *yoga* while engaging the mind in material enjoyment is like trying to ignite a fire while pouring water on it. Similarly, *yoga* practice without mental control is a waste of time. Such a show of *yoga* practice may be materially lucrative, but it is useless as far as spiritual realization is concerned. Therefore, the mind must be controlled by engaging it constantly in the transcendental loving service of the Lord. Unless one is engaged in Kṛṣṇa consciousness, he cannot steadily control the mind. A Kṛṣṇa conscious person easily achieves the result of *yoga* practice without separate endeavor, but a *yoga* practitioner cannot achieve perfect success without becoming Kṛṣṇa conscious.

37. Arjuna said: What is the destination of the man of faith who does not persevere, who in the beginning takes to the process of self-realization but who later desists due to worldly-mindedness and thus does not attain perfection in mysticism?

PURPORT

The path of self-realization or mysticism is described in *Bhagavad-gītā*. The basic principle of self-realization is knowledge that the living entity is not this material body, but that he is different from it and that his happiness is in eternal life, bliss and knowledge. These are transcendental, beyond both body and mind. Self-realization is sought by the path of knowledge, by the practice of the eightfold system, or by *bhakti-yoga.* In each of these processes one has to realize the constitutional position of the living entity, his relationship with God, and the activities whereby he can reestablish the lost link and achieve the highest perfectional stage of Kṛṣṇa consciousness. Following any of the above-mentioned three methods, one is sure to reach the supreme goal sooner or later. This was asserted by the Lord in the Second Chapter: even a little endeavor on the transcendental path of *bhakti-yoga* is especially suitable for this age because it is the most direct method of God realization. To be doubly assured, Arjuna is asking Lord Kṛṣṇa to confirm His former statement. One may sincerely accept the path of self-realization, but the process of cultivation of knowledge and the practice of the eightfold *yoga* system are generally very difficult for this age. Therefore, in spite of one's earnest endeavor, one may fail for many reasons. The primary reason is one's not being sufficiently serious about following the process. To pursue the transcendental path is more or less to declare war on illusory energy. Consequently, whenever a person tries to escape the clutches of the illusory energy, she tries to defeat the practitioner by various allurements. A conditioned soul is already allured by the modes of material energy, and there is every chance of being allured again while performing such transcendental practice. This is called *yogāc calita-mānasaḥ*, deviation from the transcendental path. Arjuna is inquisitive to know the results of deviation from the path of self-realization.

38. O mighty-armed Kṛṣṇa, does not such a man, being deviated from the path of Transcendence, perish like a riven cloud, with no position in any sphere?

39. This is my doubt, O Kṛṣṇa, and I ask You to dispel it completely. But for Yourself, no one is to be found who can destroy this doubt.

40. The Blessed Lord said: Son of Pṛthā, a transcendentalist engaged in auspicious activities does not meet with destruction, either in this world

or in the spiritual world; one who does good, My friend, is never overcome by evil.

41. The unsuccessful *yogī*, after many, many years of enjoyment on the planets of the pious living entities, is born into the family of righteous people, or into a family of rich aristocracy.

42. Or he takes his birth in a family of transcendentalists who are surely great in wisdom. Verily, such a birth is rare in this world.

43. On taking such a birth, he again revives the divine consciousness of his previous life, and he tries to make further progress in order to achieve complete success, O son of Kuru.

PURPORT

King Bharata, who took his third birth in the family of a good *brāhmaṇa*, is an example of good birth for the revival of previous consciousness in transcendental realization or *yoga* perfection. King Bharata was the emperor of the world, and since his time this planet has been known among the demigods as Bhārata-varṣa. Formerly it was known as Ilāvṛta-varṣa. The emperor, at an early age, retired for spiritual perfection but failed to achieve success. In his next life he took birth in the family of good *brāhmaṇa* and was known as Jaḍa Bharata because he always remained secluded and did not talk to anyone. And later on, he was discovered as the greatest transcendentalist by King Rahūgaṇa. From his life it is understood that transcendental endeavors, or the practice of *yoga*, never go in vain. By the grace of the Lord such a transcendentalist gets repeated opportunities for complete perfection in Kṛṣṇa consciousness.

44. By virtue of the divine consciousness of his previous life, he automatically becomes attracted to the yogic principles—even without seeking them. Such an inquisitive transcendentalist, striving for *yoga*, stands always above the ritualistic principles of the scriptures.

45. But when the *yogī* engages himself with sincere endeavor in making further progress, being washed of all contaminations, then

ultimately, after many, many births of practice, he attains the supreme goal.

PURPORT

A person born in a particularly righteous, aristocratic or sacred family becomes conscious of his favorable condition for executing *yoga* practice. With determination, therefore, he begins his unfinished task, and thus he completely cleanses himself of all material contaminations. When he is finally free from all contaminations, he attains the supreme perfection—Kṛṣṇa consciousness. Kṛṣṇa consciousness is the perfect stage, being freed of all contaminations. This is confirmed in *Bhagavad-gītā:* "After many, many births in execution of pious activities, when one is completely freed from all contaminations and from all illusory dualities, one then becomes engaged in the transcendental loving service of the Lord."

46. A *yogī* is greater than the ascetic, greater than the empiricist and greater than the fruitive worker. Therefore, O Arjuna, in all circumstances, be a *yogī.*

47. And of all *yogīs,* he who always abides in Me with great faith, worshiping Me in transcendental loving service, is most intimately united with Me in *yoga* and is the highest of all.

PURPORT

The Sanskrit word *bhajate* is significant here. *Bhajate* has its root in the verb *bhaj,* which is used when there is need of service. The English word "worship" cannot be used in the same sense as *bhaj.* Worship means to adore, or to show respect and honor to the worthy one. But service with love and faith is especially meant for the Supreme Personality of Godhead. One can avoid worshiping a respectable man or demigod and may be called discourteous, but one cannot avoid serving the Supreme Lord without being thoroughly condemned. Every living entity is part and parcel of the Supreme Personality of Godhead, and as such every living entity is intended to serve the Supreme Lord by his own constitution. Failing to do this, he falls down. The *Bhāgavatam* confirms this as follows: "Anyone who does not render service and who neglects his duty unto the primeval Lord, who is the source of all living entities, will certainly fall down from his constitutional position."

In this verse from *Śrīmad-Bhāgavatam* the word *bhajanti* is used also. *Bhajanti* is applicable to the Supreme Lord only, whereas the word "worship" can be applied to demigods or to any other common living entity. The word *avajānanti* used in this verse of *Śrīmad-Bhāgavatam* is also found in *Bhagavad-gītā. Avajānanti māṁ mūḍhāḥ:* "Only the fools and rascals deride the Supreme Personality of Godhead, Lord Kṛṣṇa." Such fools take it upon themselves to write commentaries on *Bhagavad-gītā* without an attitude of service to the Lord. Consequently they cannot properly distinguish between the word *bhajanti* and the word "worship."

The culmination of all kinds of *yoga* practice lies in *bhakti-yoga.* All other *yogas* are but means to come to the point of *bhakti-yoga. Yoga* actually means *bhakti-yoga;* all other *yogas* are progressions toward this destination. From the beginning of *karma-yoga* to the end of *bhakti-yoga* is a long way to self-realization. *Karma-yoga,* without fruitive results, is the beginning of this path. When *karma-yoga* increases in knowledge and renunciation, the stage is called *jñāna-yoga.* When *jñāna-yoga* increases in meditation on the Supersoul by different physical processes, and the mind is on Him, it is called *aṣṭāṅga-yoga.* And when one surpasses *aṣṭāṅga-yoga* and comes to the point of the Supreme Personality of Godhead, Kṛṣṇa, it is called *bhakti-yoga,* the culmination. Factually, *bhakti-yoga* is the ultimate goal, but to analyze *bhakti-yoga* minutely one has to understand these other minor *yogas.* The *yogī* who is progressive is therefore on the true path of eternal auspiciousness. One who sticks to a particular point and does not make further progress is called by that particular name: *karma-yogī, jñāna-yogī, dhyāna-yogī, rāja-yogī* or *haṭha-yogī.* But if one is fortunate enough to come to the point of *bhakti-yoga,* it is to be understood that he has surpassed all the different *yogas.* Therefore, to become Kṛṣṇa conscious is the highest stage of *yoga,* just as, when we speak of Himalayan, we refer to the world's highest mountains of which the highest peak, Mount Everest, is considered the culmination.

It is by great fortune that one comes to Kṛṣṇa consciousness on the path of *bhakti-yoga* and is well situated according to the Vedic direction. The ideal *yogī* concentrates his attention on Kṛṣṇa, who is called Śyāmasundara, who is as beautifully colored as a cloud, whose lotuslike face is as effulgent as the sun, whose dress is brilliant with jewels, and whose body is flower garlanded. Illuminating all sides is His gorgeous luster, which is called the *brahmajyoti.* He incarnates in different forms such as Rāma, Varāha, and Kṛṣṇa, the Supreme Personality of Godhead. He descends like a human being, as the son of mother Yaśodā, and He is known as Kṛṣṇa, Govinda and Vāsudeva. He is the perfect child, husband, friend and master, and He is full with all opulences and transcendental qualities. If one remains fully conscious of these features of the Lord, he is called the highest *yogī.* This stage of highest perfection in *yoga* can be attained only by *bhakti-yoga,* as confirmed in all Vedic literature.

Thus end the Bhaktivedanta purports to the Sixth Chapter of the *Śrīmad Bhagavad-gītā* in the matter of *Sāṅkhya-yoga Brahma-vidyā.*

CHAPTER SEVEN

Knowledge of the Absolute

1. The Supreme Personality of Godhead said: Now hear, O son of Pṛthā [Arjuna], how by practicing *yoga* in full consciousness of Me, with mind attached to Me, you can know Me in full, free from doubt.

PURPORT

In the first six chapters of *Bhagavad-gītā*, the living entity has been described as a nonmaterial spirit soul who is capable of elevating himself to self-realization by different types of *yogas*. At the end of the Sixth Chapter, it has been clearly stated that the steady concentration of the mind upon Kṛṣṇa, or in other words Kṛṣṇa consciousness, is the highest form of all *yoga*. By concentrating one's mind upon Kṛṣṇa one is able to know the Absolute completely, but not otherwise. Impersonal *brahmajyoti* or localized Paramātmā is not perfect knowledge of the Absolute Truth because it is partial. Full and scientific knowledge is Kṛṣṇa, and everything is revealed to the person in Kṛṣṇa consciousness. In complete Kṛṣṇa consciousness one knows that Kṛṣṇa is ultimate knowledge beyond any doubts. Different types of *yoga* are only stepping-stones on the path of Kṛṣṇa consciousness. One who takes directly to Kṛṣṇa consciousness knows automatically about *brahmajyoti* and Paramātmā in full. By practice of Kṛṣṇa consciousness *yoga*, one can know everything in full—namely the Absolute Truth, the living entities, the material nature and their manifestations with paraphernalia.

One should therefore begin *yoga* practice as directed in the last verse of the Sixth Chapter. Concentration of the mind upon Kṛṣṇa, the Supreme, is made possible by prescribed devotional service in nine different forms, of which *śravaṇa*, hearing, is the first and most important. The Lord therefore says to Arjuna, *tat śṛṇu*, or "Hear from Me." No one can be a greater authority than Kṛṣṇa, and therefore by hearing from Him one receives the greatest opportunity for progress in Kṛṣṇa consciousness. One therefore has to learn from Kṛṣṇa directly or from a pure devotee of Kṛṣṇa—and not from a nondevotee upstart, puffed up with academic education.

In *Śrīmad-Bhāgavatam* this process of understanding Kṛṣṇa, the Supreme Personality of Godhead, the Absolute Truth, is described in the Third Chapter of the First Canto as follows: "To hear about Kṛṣṇa from Vedic literature, or to hear from Him directly through *Bhagavad-gītā*, is itself righteous activity. And for one who hears about Kṛṣṇa, Lord Kṛṣṇa, who is dwelling in everyone's heart, acts as a well-wishing friend and purifies the devotee. In this way, a devotee naturally develops his dormant transcendental knowledge. As he hears more about Kṛṣṇa from the *Bhāgavatam* and from the devotees, he becomes fixed in the devotional service of the Lord. By development of devotional service one becomes freed from the modes of ignorance and passion, and thus material lusts and avarice are diminished. When these impurities are wiped away, the candidate remains steady in his position of pure goodness, becomes enlivened by devotional service, and understands the science of God perfectly. Thus *bhakti-yoga* severs the hard knot of material affection, and one comes at once to the stage of *asaṁśayaṁ samagram*, understanding of the Supreme Absolute Personality of Godhead."

Therefore, only by hearing from Kṛṣṇa or from His devotee in Kṛṣṇa consciousness can one understand the science of Kṛṣṇa.

2. I shall now declare unto you in full this knowledge both phenomenal and noumenal, by knowing which there shall remain nothing further to be known.

3. Out of many thousands among men, one may endeavor for perfection, and of those who have achieved perfection, hardly one knows Me in truth.

PURPORT

There are various grades of men, and out of many thousands, one may be sufficiently interested in transcendental realization to try to know what is the self, what is the body, and what is the Absolute Truth. Generally, mankind is simply engaged in animal propensities—eating, sleeping, defending and mating—and hardly anyone is interested in transcendental knowledge. The first six chapters of the *Gītā* are meant for those who are interested in transcendental knowledge, in understanding the self, the Superself, and the process of realization by *jñāna-yoga*, *dhyāna-yoga* and discrimination of the self from matter.

However, Kṛṣṇa Himself can be known only by persons who are in Kṛṣṇa consciousness. Other transcendentalists may achieve impersonal Brahman realization, for this is easier than understanding Kṛṣṇa. Kṛṣṇa is the Supreme Person, but at the same time He is beyond the knowledge of Brahman and Paramātmā. *Yogīs* and *jñānīs* are confused in their attempts to understand Kṛṣṇa. Although the greatest of the impersonalists, Śrīpāda Śaṅkarācārya, has admitted in his *Gītā* commentary that Kṛṣṇa is the Supreme Personality of Godhead, his followers do not accept Kṛṣṇa as such, for it is very difficult to know Kṛṣṇa even though one has transcendental realization of impersonal Brahman.

Kṛṣṇa is the Supreme Personality of Godhead, the cause of all causes, the primeval Lord Govinda. He is very difficult for the nondevotees to know. Although nondevotees declare that the path of *bhakti*, or devotional service, is very easy, they cannot practice it. If the path of *bhakti* is so easy, as the nondevotee class of men proclaim, then why do they take up the difficult path? Actually, the path of *bhakti* is not easy. The so-called path of *bhakti* practiced by unauthorized persons without knowledge of *bhakti* may be easy, but when it is practiced factually, according to the rules and regulations, the speculative scholars and philosophers fall away from the path. Śrīla Rūpa Gosvāmī writes in his *Bhakti-rasāmṛta-sindhu:* "Devotional service to the Lord that ignores the authorized Vedic literatures like the *Upaniṣads*, *Purāṇas* and *Nārada-pañcarātra* is simply an unnecessary disturbance in society."

It is not possible for the Brahman-realized impersonalist or the Paramātmā-realized *yogī* to understand Kṛṣṇa, the Supreme Personality of Godhead, as the son of mother Yaśodā or the charioteer of Arjuna. Even the great demigods are sometimes confused about Kṛṣṇa. "No one knows Me as I am," the Lord says. And if anyone knows Him, then: "Such a great soul is very rare." Therefore, unless one practices devotional service to the Lord, he cannot know Kṛṣṇa as He is, even though he may be a great scholar or philosopher. Only the pure devotees can know something of the inconceivable transcendental qualities in Kṛṣṇa, in the cause of all causes, in His omnipotence and opulence, and in His wealth, fame, strength, beauty, knowledge and renunciation, because Kṛṣṇa is benevolently inclined to His devotees. He is the last word in Brahman realization, and the devotees alone can realize Him as He is. Therefore, it is said: "No one can understand Kṛṣṇa as He is by the blunt material senses. But He reveals Himself to the devotees, being pleased with them for their transcendental loving service unto Him."

4. Earth, water, fire, air, ether, mind, intelligence and false ego—all together these eight comprise My separated material energies.

PURPORT

The science of God analyzes the constitutional position of the Lord and His diverse energies. Material nature is called *prakṛti,* or the energy of the Lord in His different incarnations (expansions) as described in the *Sātvata-tantra:* "For material creation, Lord Kṛṣṇa's plenary expansion assumes three Viṣṇus. The first one, Mahā-Viṣṇu, creates the total material energy, known as the *mahat-tattva.* The second, Garbhodakaśāyī Viṣṇu, enters into all the universes to create diversities in each of them. The third, Kṣīrodakaśāyī Viṣṇu, is diffused as the all-pervading Supersoul in all the universes and is known as Paramātmā, who is present even within the atoms. Anyone who knows these three Viṣṇus can be liberated from material entanglements."

This material world is a temporary manifestation of one of the energies of the Lord. All the activities of the material world are directed by the above-mentioned three Viṣṇu expansions of Lord Kṛṣṇa. These are called incarnations.

5. Besides this inferior nature, O mighty Arjuna, there is a superior energy of Mine, which consists of all living entities who are struggling with material nature and who are sustaining the universe.

PURPORT

Here it is clearly mentioned that living entities belong to the superior nature (or energy) of the Supreme Lord. The inferior energy is matter manifested in different elements, namely earth, water, fire, air, sky, mind, intelligence and false ego. Both forms of material nature, namely gross (earth, etc.) and subtle (mind, etc.), are products of the inferior energy. The living entities, who are exploiting these inferior energies for different purposes, are the superior energy of the Supreme Lord. Energies are always controlled by the energetic, and therefore living entities are always controlled by the Lord—they have no independent existence. They are never equally powerful, as men with a poor fund of knowledge think. The distinction between the living entities and the Lord is described in the *Śrīmad-Bhāgavatam* as follows: "O supreme eternal! If the embodied living entities were eternal and all-pervading like You, then they would not be under Your supreme control. But if the living entities are accepted as minute energies of Your Lordship, then they are at once subjected to Your supreme control. Therefore, real liberation entails surrender by the living entities to Your control, and that surrender will make them happy. Only in that constitutional position can they be controllers. Therefore, men with limited knowledge who advocate the monistic theory that God and the living entities are equal in all respects are actually misleading themselves and others."

The Supreme Lord Kṛṣṇa is the only controller, and all living entities are controlled by Him. These living entities are His superior energy because the quality of their existence is one and the same with the Supreme, but they are never equal with the Lord in quantity of power. While exploiting the gross and subtle inferior energy (matter), the superior energy (the living entity) forgets his real spiritual mind and intelligence. This forgetfulness is due to the influence of matter upon the living entity. But when the living entity becomes free from the influence of the illusory material energy, he attains the stage called *mukti*, or liberation. The false ego, under the influence of material illusion, thinks,

"I am matter, and material acquisitions are mine." His actual position is realized when he is liberated from all material ideas, including the conception of his becoming one in all respects with God. Therefore one may conclude that the *Gītā* confirms the living entity to be only one of the multi-energies of Kṛṣṇa; and when this energy is freed from material contamination, it becomes fully Kṛṣṇa conscious, or liberated.

6. Of all that is material and all that is spiritual in this world, know for certain that I am both the origin and dissolution.

7. O conqueror of wealth [Arjuna], there is no truth superior to Me. Everything rests upon Me, as pearls are strung on a thread.

8. O son of Kuntī [Arjuna], I am the taste of water, the light of the sun and the moon, the syllable *om* in Vedic *mantras;* I am the sound in ether and ability in man.

PURPORT

The taste of water is the active principle of water. No one likes to drink seawater because the pure taste of water is mixed with salt. Attraction for water depends on the purity of the taste, and this pure taste is one of the energies of the Lord. The impersonalist perceives the presence of the Lord in water by its taste, and the personalist also glorifies the Lord for His kindly supplying water to quench man's thirst. That is the way of perceiving the Supreme. Practically speaking, there is no controversy between personalism and impersonalism. One who knows God knows that the impersonal conception and personal conception are simultaneously present in everything and that there is no contradiction. Therefore, Lord Caitanya established His sublime doctrine: simultaneously one and different. The light of the sun and moon are also originally emanating from the *brahmajyoti,* which is the impersonal effulgence of the Lord. Similarly, *praṇava,* or the *oṁkāra* transcendental sound used in the beginning of every Vedic hymn to address the Supreme Lord, also emanates from Him. Because the impersonalists are very much afraid of addressing the Supreme Lord Kṛṣṇa by His innumerable names, they prefer to vibrate the transcendental sound *oṁkāra.* But they do not realize that *oṁkāra* is the sound representation of Kṛṣṇa. The jurisdiction of Kṛṣṇa consciousness extends everywhere, and one who knows Kṛṣṇa consciousness is blessed. Those who do not know Kṛṣṇa are in illusion, and so knowledge of Kṛṣṇa is liberation, and ignorance of Him is bondage.

9. I am the original fragrance of the earth, and I am the light in fire. I am the life of all that lives, and I am the penances of all ascetics.

PURPORT

Everything in the material world has a certain flavor or fragrance, like the flavor and fragrance in a flower, or in the earth, water, fire or air. The uncontaminated flavor, the original flavor which permeates everything, is Kṛṣṇa. Similarly, everything has a particular original taste, and this taste can be changed by the mixture of chemicals. So everything original has some smell, some fragrance and some taste. Without fire we cannot run factories, we cannot cook, etc., and that fire is Kṛṣṇa. The heat in the fire is Kṛṣṇa. According to Vedic medicine, indigestion is due to a low temperature in the belly. So even for digestion, fire is required. In Kṛṣṇa consciousness we become aware that earth, water, fire, air and every active principle, all chemicals and all material elements are due to Kṛṣṇa. The duration of man's life is also due to Kṛṣṇa. Therefore, by the grace of Kṛṣṇa man can prolong his life or diminish it. So Kṛṣṇa consciousness is active in every sphere.

10. O son of Pṛthā, know that I am the original seed of all existences, the intelligence of the intelligent, and the prowess of all powerful men.

11. I am the strength of the strong, devoid of passion and desire. I am sex life which is not contrary to religious principles, O lord of the Bhāratas [Arjuna].

PURPORT

The strong man's strength should be applied to protect the weak, not for personal aggression. Similarly, sex life, according to religious principles (*dharma*), should be for the propagation of children, not otherwise. The responsibility of parents is then to make their offspring Kṛṣṇa conscious.

12. All states of being—goodness, passion or ignorance—are manifested by My energy. I am, in one sense, everything—but I am independent. I am not under the modes of this material nature.

13. Deluded by the three modes [goodness, passion and ignorance], the whole world does not know Me, who am above them and inexhaustible.

PURPORT

The whole world is enchanted by three modes of material nature. Those who are bewildered by these three modes cannot understand that transcendental to this material nature is the Supreme Lord, Kṛṣṇa. In this material world everyone is under the influence of these three *guṇas* and is thus bewildered. By nature, living entities have particular types of body and particular types of psychic and biological activity accordingly. There are four classes of men functioning in the three material modes of nature. Those who are purely in the mode of goodness are called *brāhmaṇas.* Those purely in the mode of passion are called *kṣatriyas.* Those in the modes of both passion and ignorance are called *vaiśyas.* Those completely in ignorance are called *śūdras.* And those who are less than that are animals or animal life. However, these designations are not permanent. I may be either a *brāhmaṇa, kṣatriya, vaiśya,* or whatever—in any case, this life is temporary. But although life is temporary and we do not know what we are going to be in the next life, still, by the spell of this illusory energy, we consider ourselves in the light of this bodily conception of life, and we thus think we are American, Indian, Russian or *brāhmaṇa,* Hindu, Muslim, etc. And if we become entangled with the modes of material nature, then we forget the Supreme Personality of Godhead, who is behind all these modes. So Lord Kṛṣṇa says that men deluded by these three modes of nature do not understand that behind the material background is the Supreme Godhead.

There are many different kinds of living entities—human beings, demigods, animals, etc.—and each and every one of them is under the influence of material nature, and all of them have forgotten the transcendent Personality of Godhead. Those who are in the modes of passion and ignorance, and even those who are in the mode of goodness, cannot go beyond the impersonal Brahman conception of the Absolute Truth. They are bewildered before the Supreme Lord in His supreme personal feature, possessing all beauty, opulence, knowledge, strength, fame and renunciation. When even those who are in goodness cannot understand, what hope is there for those in passion and ignorance? Kṛṣṇa consciousness is transcendental to all these three modes of material nature, and those who are truly established in Kṛṣṇa consciousness are actually liberated.

14. This divine energy of Mine, consisting of the three modes of material nature, is difficult to overcome. But those who have surrendered unto Me can easily cross beyond it.

15. Those miscreants who are grossly foolish, lowest among mankind, whose knowledge is stolen by illusion, and who are of the atheistic nature of demons, do not surrender unto Me.

PURPORT

It is said in *Bhagavad-gītā* that simply by surrendering oneself unto the lotus feet of the Supreme Personality, Kṛṣṇa, one can surmount the stringent laws of material nature. At this point a question arises: How is it that educated philosophers, scientists, businessmen, administrators and all the leaders of ordinary men do not surrender to the lotus feet of Śrī Kṛṣṇa, the all-powerful Personality of Godhead? *Mukti*, or liberation from the laws of material nature, is sought by the above-mentioned leaders in different ways and with great plans and perseverance for a great many years and births. But if that liberation is possible by simply surrendering unto the lotus feet of the Supreme Personality of Godhead, then why don't these intelligent and hardworking leaders adopt this simple method?

The *Gītā* answers this question very frankly. Those really learned leaders of society like Brahmā, Śiva, Kapila, the Kumāras, Manu, Vyāsa, Devala, Asita, Janaka, Prahlāda, Bali and later Madhvācārya, Rāmānujācārya, Śrī Caitanya and many others who are faithful philosophers, politicians, educators, scientists, etc., surrender to the lotus feet of the Supreme Person, the all-powerful authority. Those who are not actually philosophers, scientists, educators, administrators, etc., but who pose themselves as such for material gain, do not accept the plan or path of the

Supreme Lord. They have no idea of God; they simply manufacture their own worldly plans and consequently complicate the problems of material existence in their vain attempts to solve them. Because material energy (nature) is so powerful, it can resist the unauthorized plans of the atheists and baffle the knowledge of "planning commissions."

The atheistic plan-makers are described herein by the word *duṣkṛtina* or "miscreants." *Kṛtina* means those who have performed meritorious work. The atheistic plan-maker is sometimes very intelligent and meritorious also because any gigantic plan, good or bad, must take intelligence to execute. But because the atheist's brain is improperly utilized in its opposition to the plan of the Supreme Lord, the atheistic plan-makers are called *duṣkṛtina*, which indicates that their intelligence and efforts are misdirected.

In the *Gītā* it is clearly mentioned that material energy works fully under the direction of the Supreme Lord. It has no independent authority. It works as a shadow moves, in accordance with the movements of an object. But still material energy is very powerful, and the atheist, due to his godless temperament, cannot know how it works; nor can he know the plan of the Supreme Lord. Under illusion and the modes of passion and ignorance, all his plans are baffled, as in the cases of Hiraṇyakaśipu and Rāvaṇa, whose plans were smashed to dust although they were both materially learned as scientists, philosophers, administrators and educators. These *duṣkṛtinas*, or miscreants, are of four different patterns, as outlined below:

(1) The *mūḍhas* are those who are grossly foolish, like hardworking beasts of burden. They want to enjoy the fruits of their labor by themselves and so do not want to part with them for the Supreme. The typical example of the beast of burden is the ass. This humble beast is made to work very hard by his master. The ass does not really know for whom he works so hard day and night. He remains satisfied by filling his stomach with a bundle of grass, sleeping for a while under fear of being beaten by his master, and satisfying his sex appetite at the risk of being repeatedly kicked by the opposite party. The ass sings poetry and philosophy sometimes, but this braying only disturbs others. This is the position of the foolish fruitive worker who does not know for whom he should work. He does not know that *karma* (action) is meant for *yajña* (sacrifice).

Most often, those who work very hard day and night to clear the burden of self-created duties say that they have no time to hear of the immortality of the living being. To such *mūḍhas*, material gains, which are destructible, are life's all in all—despite the fact that the *mūḍhas* enjoy only a very small fraction of the fruit of labor. Sometimes they spend sleepless days and nights for fruitive gain, and although they may have ulcers or indigestion, they are satisfied with practically no food; they are simply absorbed in working hard day and night for the benefit of illusory masters. Ignorant of their real master, the foolish workers waste their valuable time serving mammon. Unfortunately, they never surrender to the supreme master of all masters, nor do they take time to hear of Him from the proper sources. The swine who eat the soil do not care to accept sweetmeats made of sugar and ghee. Similarly, the foolish worker will untiringly continue to hear of the sense-enjoyable tidings of the flickering mundane force that moves the material world.

(2) Another class of *duṣkṛtina* is called the *narādhama*, or the lowest of mankind. *Nara* means human being, and *adhama* means the lowest. Out of the 8,400,000 different species of living beings, there are 400,000 human species. Out of these there are innumerable lower forms of human life that are mostly uncivilized. Comparatively, there are only a very few classes of men who are actually civilized. The civilized human beings are those who have regulated principles of social, political and religious life. Those who are socially and politically developed but who have no religious principles must be considered *narādhamas*. Nor is religion without God religion, because the purpose of following religious principles is to know the supreme truth and man's relation with Him. In the *Gītā* the Personality of Godhead clearly states that there is no authority above Him and that He is the supreme truth. The civilized form of human life is meant for man's reviving the lost consciousness of his eternal relation with the supreme truth, the Personality of Godhead Śrī Kṛṣṇa, who is all-powerful. Whoever loses this chance is classified as a *narādhama*. We get information from revealed scriptures that when the baby is in the mother's womb (an extremely uncomfortable situation) he prays to God for deliverance and promises to worship Him alone as soon as he gets out. To pray to God when he is in difficulty is a natural instinct in every living being because he is eternally related with God. But after

his deliverance the child forgets the difficulties of birth and forgets his deliverer also, being influenced by *māyā*, the illusory energy.

It is the duty of the guardians of children to revive the divine consciousness dormant in them. The ten processes of reformatory ceremonies, as enjoined in the *Manu-smṛti*, which is the guide to religious principles, are meant for reviving God consciousness in the system of *varṇāśrama*. However, no process is strictly followed now in any part of the world, and therefore 99.9 percent of the population is *narādhama*.

Śrī Caitanya Mahāprabhu, in propagating the *bhāgavata-dharma*, or activities of the devotees, has recommended that people submissively hear the message of the Personality of Godhead. The essence of this message is *Bhagavad-gītā*. The lowest of human beings can be delivered by this submissive hearing process only, but unfortunately they even refuse to give an aural reception to these messages, and what to speak of surrendering to the will of the Supreme Lord? *Narādhamas*, or the lowest of mankind, will fully neglect the prime duty of the human being.

(3) The next class of *duṣkṛtina* is called *māyayāpahṛta-jñānāḥ*, or those persons whose erudite knowledge has been nullified by the influence of illusory material energy. They are mostly very learned fellows—great philosophers, poets, literati, scientists, etc.—but the illusory energy misguides them, and therefore they disobey the Supreme Lord. When the whole population becomes *narādhama*, naturally all their so-called education is made null and void by the all-powerful energy of physical nature. According to the standard of the *Gītā*, a learned man is he who sees on equal terms the learned *brāhmaṇa*, the dog, the cow, the elephant and the dog-eater. That is the vision of a true devotee.

(4) The last class of *duṣkṛtina* is called *āsuraṁ bhāvam āśritāḥ*, or those of demoniac principles. This class is openly atheistic. Some of them argue that the Supreme Lord can never descend upon this material world, but they are unable to give any tangible reasons as to why not. There are others who make Him subordinate to the impersonal feature, although the opposite is declared in the *Gītā*. Envious of the Supreme Personality of Godhead, the atheist will present a number of illicit incarnations manufactured in the factory of his brain. Such persons, whose very principle of life is to decry the Personality of Godhead, cannot surrender unto the lotus feet of Śrī Kṛṣṇa.

Śrī Yāmunācārya Ālabandāru of South India said, "O my Lord! You are unknowable to persons involved with atheistic principles, despite Your uncommon qualities, features and activities, despite Your personality's being strongly confirmed by all the revealed scriptures in the quality of goodness, and despite Your being acknowledged by the famous authorities renowned for their depth of knowledge in the transcendental science and situated in the godly qualities."

Therefore, (1) grossly foolish persons, (2) the lowest of mankind, (3) deluded speculators, and (4) the atheistic people, as above mentioned, never surrender unto the lotus feet of the Personality of Godhead in spite of all scriptural and authoritative advice.

16. O best among the Bhāratas [Arjuna], four kinds of pious men render devotional service unto Me—the distressed, the desirer of wealth, the inquisitive, and he who is searching for knowledge of the Absolute.

PURPORT

Unlike the miscreants, these are adherents of the regulative principles of the scriptures, the moral and social laws, and they are, more or less, devoted to the Supreme Lord. Out of these there are four classes of men: (1) those who are sometimes distressed, (2) those in need of money, (3) those who are sometimes inquisitive and (4) those who are sometimes searching after knowledge of the Absolute Truth. These persons come to the Supreme Lord for devotional service under different conditions. These are not pure devotees, for they have some aspiration to fulfill in exchange for devotional service. Pure devotional service is without aspiration and without desire for material profit. The *Bhakti-rasāmṛta-sindhu* defines pure devotion thus: "One should render transcendental loving service to the Supreme Lord Kṛṣṇa favorably and without desire for material profit or gain through fruitive activities or philosophical speculation. That is called pure devotional service."

When these four kinds of persons come to the Supreme Lord for devotional service and are completely purified by the association of a pure devotee, they also become pure devotees. So far as the miscreants are concerned, for them devotional service is very difficult because their lives are selfish, irregular and without spiritual goals. But even some of them, by chance, when they come in contact with a pure devotee, also become pure devotees.

Those who are always busy with fruitive activities come to the Lord in material distress and at that time associate with pure devotees and become, in their distress, devotees of the Lord. Those who are simply frustrated also sometimes come to associate with the pure devotees and become inquisitive to know about God. Similarly, when the dry philosophers are frustrated in every field of knowledge, they sometimes want to learn of God, and they come to the Supreme Lord to render devotional service. Thus they transcend knowledge of the impersonal Brahman and the localized Paramātmā and come to the personal conception of Godhead by the grace of the Supreme Lord or His pure devotee. On the whole, when the distressed, the inquisitive, the seeker of knowledge and those who are in need of money are free from all material desires, and when they fully understand that material remuneration has no value for spiritual improvement, then they become pure devotees. So long as such a purified stage is not attained, devotees in transcendental service to the Lord are tainted with fruitive activities, seeking after mundane knowledge, etc. One has to transcend all this before one can come to the stage of pure devotional service.

17. Of these, the wise one who is in full knowledge, in union with Me through pure devotional service, is the best. For I am very dear to him, and he is dear to Me.

18. All these devotees are undoubtedly magnanimous souls, but he who is situated in knowledge of Me I consider verily to dwell in Me. Being engaged in My transcendental service, he attains Me.

19. After many births and deaths, he who is actually in knowledge surrenders unto Me, knowing Me to be the cause of all causes and all that is. Such a great soul is very rare.

20. Those whose minds are distorted by material desires surrender unto the demigods and follow the particular rules and regulations of worship according to their own natures.

21. I am in everyone's heart as the Supersoul, and as soon as one desires to worship the demigods, I make his faith steady so that he can devote himself to some particular deity.

PURPORT

God has given independence to everyone; therefore, if a person desires to have material enjoyment and wants very sincerely to have such facilities from the material demigods, the Supreme Lord, as Supersoul in everyone's heart, understands and gives facilities to such persons. As the supreme father of all living entities, He does not interfere with their independence, but gives all facilities so that they can fulfill their material desires. Some may ask why the all-powerful God gives facilities to the living entities for enjoying this material world and so lets them fall into the trap of the illusory energy. The answer is that if the Supreme Lord as Supersoul did not give such facilities, then there would be no meaning to independence. Therefore, He gives everyone full independence—whatever one likes—but His ultimate instruction we find in *Bhagavad-gītā:* man should give up all other engagements and fully surrender unto Him. That will make him happy. Both the living entity and the demigods are subordinate to the will of the Supreme Personality of Godhead; therefore the living entity cannot worship the demigod by his own desire, nor can the demigod bestow any benediction without the supreme will. As it is said, not a blade of grass moves without the will of the Supreme Personality of Godhead. Generally, persons who are distressed in the material world go to the demigods, as they are advised in the Vedic literature. A person wanting some particular thing may worship such and such a demigod. For example, a diseased person is recommended to worship the sun-god, a person wanting education may worship the goddess of learning, Sarasvatī, and a person wanting a beautiful wife may worship the goddess Umā, the wife of Lord Śiva. In this way there are recommendations in the *śāstras* (Vedic scriptures) for different modes of worship of different demigods. And because a particular living entity wants to enjoy a particular material facility, the Lord inspires him with a strong desire to achieve that benediction from that particular demigod, and so he successfully receives the benediction. The particular mode of the devotional attitude of the living entity toward a particular type of demigod is also arranged by the Supreme Lord. The demigods cannot infuse the living entities with such an affinity, but because He is the Supreme Lord or the Supersoul who is present in the heart of all living entities, Kṛṣṇa gives impetus to man to worship certain demigods. The demigods are actually different parts of the universal body of the Supreme Lord; therefore, they have no independence. In the Vedic literature it is said: "The Supreme Personality of Godhead as Supersoul is also present within the heart of the demigod; therefore, He arranges through the demigod to fulfill the desire of the living entity. But both the demigod and the living entity are dependent on the supreme will. They are not independent."

22. Endowed with such a faith, he seeks favors of the demigod and obtains his desires. But in actuality these benefits are bestowed by Me alone.

23. Men of small intelligence worship the demigods, and their fruits are limited and temporary. Those who worship the demigods go to the planets of the demigods, but My devotees reach My supreme abode.

PURPORT

Some commentators on the *Gītā* say that one who worships a demigod can reach the Supreme Lord, but here it is clearly stated that the worshipers of demigods go to the different planetary systems where various demigods are situated, just as a worshiper of the sun achieves the sun or a worshiper of the demigod of the moon achieves the moon. Similarly, if anyone wants to worship a demigod like Indra, he can attain that particular god's planet. It is not that everyone, regardless of whatever demigod is worshiped, will reach the Supreme Personality of Godhead. That is denied here, for it is clearly stated that the worshipers of demigods go to different planets in the material world, but the devotee of the Supreme Lord goes directly to the supreme planet of the Personality of Godhead.

24. Unintelligent men, who know Me not, think that I have assumed this form and personality. Due to their small knowledge, they do not know My higher nature, which is changeless and supreme.

PURPORT

Those who are worshipers of demigods have been described as less-intelligent persons, and here the impersonalists are similarly described. Lord Kṛṣṇa in His personal form is speaking before Arjuna, and still, due to ignorance, they argue that the Supreme Lord ultimately has no form. Yāmunācārya, a great devotee of the Lord and spiritual master of Rāmānujācārya, has recited two very nice verses in this connection. He says, "My dear Lord, personalities and devotees like Vyāsadeva and Nārada know You to be the Personality of Godhead. By understanding different Vedic literatures, one can know Your characteristics, Your form and Your activities, and one can thus understand that You are the Supreme Personality of Godhead. But those who are in the modes of passion and ignorance, the demons, the nondevotees, cannot understand You. They are unable to understand You. However expert such nondevotees may be in discussing the *Vedas, Upaniṣads* and other Vedic literature, it is not possible for them to understand the Personality of Godhead."

25. I am never manifest to the foolish and unintelligent. For them I am covered by My eternal creative potency [*yogamāyā*], and so the deluded world knows Me not, who am unborn and infallible.

26. O Arjuna, as the Supreme Personality of Godhead, I know everything which has happened in the past, all that is happening in the present, and all things that are yet to come. I also know all living entities; but Me no one knows.

PURPORT

Here the question of personality and impersonality is clearly stated. If Kṛṣṇa, the form of the Supreme Personality of Godhead, is considered by the impersonalists to be *māyā*, to be material, then He would, like the living entity, change His body and forget everything in His past life. One with a material body cannot remember his past life, nor can he foretell his future life, nor can he predict the outcome of his present life; therefore, he cannot know what is happening in past, present and future. Unless one is liberated from material contamination, he cannot know past, present and future. Unlike the ordinary human being, Lord Kṛṣṇa clearly says that He completely knows what happened in the past, what is happening in the present, and what will happen in the future. In the Fourth Chapter, we have seen that Lord Kṛṣṇa remembers instructing Vivasvān, the sun-god, millions of years ago. Kṛṣṇa knows every living entity because He is situated in every living being's heart as the Supreme Soul. But despite His presence in every living being as Supersoul and His presence beyond the material sky as the Supreme Personality of Godhead, the less intelligent cannot realize Him as the Supreme Person. Certainly the transcendental body of Śrī Kṛṣṇa is not perishable. He is just like the sun, and *māyā* is like the cloud. In the material world we can see that there is the sun and there are clouds and different stars and planets. The clouds may cover all these in the sky temporarily, but this covering is only apparent to our limited vision. The sun, moon and stars are not actually covered. Similarly, *māyā* cannot cover the Supreme Lord. By His internal potency, He is unmanifested to the less-intelligent class of men. As stated in the third verse of this chapter, out of millions and millions of men, some try to become perfect in this human form of life, and out of thousands and thousands of such perfected men, hardly one can understand what Lord Kṛṣṇa is. Even if someone is perfected by realization of impersonal Brahman or localized Paramātmā, he cannot possibly understand the Supreme Personality of Godhead, Śrī Kṛṣṇa, without being in Kṛṣṇa consciousness.

27. O scion of Bharata [Arjuna], O conqueror of the foe, all living entities are born into delusion, overcome by the dualities of desire and hate.

28. Persons who have acted piously in previous lives and in this life, whose sinful actions are completely eradicated, and who are freed from the duality of delusion, engage themselves in My service with determination.

PURPORT

Those eligible for elevation to the transcendental position are mentioned in this verse. For those who are sinful, atheistic, foolish and deceitful, it is very difficult to transcend the duality of desire and hate. Only those who have passed their lives in practicing the regulative principles of religion, who have acted piously and have conquered sinful reactions, can accept devotional service and gradually rise to the pure knowledge of the Supreme Personality of Godhead. Then, gradually, they can meditate in trance on the Supreme Personality of Godhead. That is the process of being situated on the spiritual platform. This elevation is possible in Kṛṣṇa consciousness in the association of pure devotees who can deliver one from delusion. It is stated in the *Śrīmad-Bhāgavatam* that if one actually wants to be liberated he must render service to the devotees; but one who associates with materialistic people is on the path leading to the darkest region of existence. All the devotees of the Lord traverse this earth just to recover the conditioned souls from their delusion. The impersonalists do not know that to forget their constitutional position as subordinate to the Supreme Lord is the greatest violation of God's law, and unless one is reinstated in his own constitutional position it is not possible to understand the Supreme Personality or to be fully engaged in His transcendental loving service with determination.

29. Intelligent persons who are endeavoring for liberation from old age and death take refuge in Me in devotional service. They are actually Brahman because they entirely know everything about transcendental and fruitive activities.

PURPORT

Birth, death, old age and diseases affect this material body, but not the spiritual body. There is no birth, death, old age and disease in the spiritual body, so one who attains a spiritual body, becomes one of the associates of the Supreme Personality of Godhead, and engages in eternal devotional service, is really liberated. *Ahaṁ brahmāsmi:* I am spirit. It is said that one should understand that he is Brahman—spirit soul. This Brahman conception of life is also in devotional service, as described in this verse. The pure devotees are transcendentally situated on the Brahman platform and they know everything about transcendental and material activities.

30. Those who know Me as the Supreme Lord, as the governing principle of the material manifestation, who know Me as the one underlying all the demigods and as the one sustaining all sacrifices, can, with steadfast mind, understand and know Me even at the time of death.

PURPORT

Many subjects have been discussed in this chapter: the man in distress, the inquisitive man, the man in want of material necessities, knowledge of Brahman, knowledge of Paramātmā, liberation from birth, death and diseases, and worship of the Supreme Lord. However, he who is actually elevated in Kṛṣṇa consciousness does not care for the different processes. He simply directly engages himself in activities of Kṛṣṇa consciousness and thereby factually attains his constitutional position as eternal servitor of Lord Kṛṣṇa. In such a disposition he takes pleasure in hearing and glorifying the Supreme Lord in pure devotional service. He is convinced that by doing so, all his objectives will be fulfilled. This determined faith is called *dṛḍha-vrata*, and it is the beginning of *bhakti-yoga* or transcendental loving service. That is the verdict of all scriptures. This Seventh Chapter of the *Gītā* is the substance of that conviction.

Thus end the Bhaktivedanta purports to the Seventh Chapter of the *Śrīmad Bhagavad-gītā* in the matter of Knowledge of the Absolute.

CHAPTER EIGHT

Attaining the Supreme

1. Arjuna inquired: O my Lord, O Supreme Person, what is Brahman? What are fruitive activities? What is this material manifestation? And what are the demigods? Kindly explain this to me.

PURPORT

In this Eighth Chapter, Lord Kṛṣṇa answers different questions, beginning with, "What is Brahman?" The Lord also explains *karma-yoga*, devotional service and *yoga* principles, and devotional service in its pure form. The *Śrīmad-Bhāgavatam* explains that the Supreme Absolute Truth is known as Brahman, Paramātmā and Bhagavān. The living entity, the individual soul, is also called Brahman, or spirit. Arjuna also inquires about *ātmā*, which refers to body, soul and mind. According to the Vedic dictionary, *ātmā* refers to the mind, soul, body and senses also. Arjuna has addressed the Supreme Lord as Puruṣottama, which means that he was asking all his questions not simply to a friend but to the Supreme Personality of Godhead, knowing Him to be perfectly well informed. As Arjuna expected, the right answers will be received from the Supreme Personality of Godhead.

2. How does this Lord of sacrifice live in the body, and in which part does He live, O Madhusūdana? And how can those engaged in devotional service know You at the time of death?

PURPORT

Viṣṇu is the head of the primal demigods, including Brahmā and Śiva, and Indra is the head of the administrative demigods. Both Indra and Viṣṇu are worshiped. But Arjuna's inquiry is, "Who is actually the Lord of *yajña*, sacrifice, and how is the Lord of *yajña* residing within the body of the living entity?" Again, Arjuna addresses the Lord as Madhusūdana, the killer of the Madhu demon. Actually, the questions which have arisen in the mind of Arjuna regarding these six items should not have been there. These doubts are like demons, and Kṛṣṇa is expert in killing demons.

Whatever we do will be tested at the time of death, and so Arjuna is very anxious to know of those who are constantly engaged in Kṛṣṇa consciousness. What should be their position at that final moment? At the time of death all body functions become dislocated, and the mind is not in a proper condition. Thus disturbed by the bodily situation, one cannot even remember the Supreme Lord. A great devotee, Mahārāja Kulaśekhara, used to pray as follows: "My dear Lord, just now I am quite healthy, and it is better that I die immediately so that the swan of my mind can seek entrance at the stem of Your lotus feet." The allegory is that the swan, a bird of the water, takes pleasure in digging into the lotus flowers. Its sporting proclivity is to enter the lotus flower. Mahārāja Kulaśekhara said to the Lord, "My mind is not now in a disturbed condition, and I am quite healthy. If I die immediately, thinking of Your lotus feet, then I am sure that my performance of Your devotional service will become perfect. But if I have to wait for my natural death, then I do not know what will happen because at that time the bodily functions will be all dislocated, my throat will be choked up with cough, and I do not know whether I shall be able to chant Your name. Better let me die immediately." The question put forward by Arjuna is similar to this question: How can a person who is constantly Kṛṣṇa conscious fix his mind to Kṛṣṇa's lotus feet?

3. The Supreme Personality of Godhead replied: The indestructible, transcendental living entity is called Brahman, and his eternal nature is called the self. And action pertaining to the development of these material bodies is called *karma*, or fruitive activities.

PURPORT

Brahman is indestructible and eternally existing, and there is no change in its constitution. But beyond Brahman is Parabrahman, the Supreme Truth. Brahman means the living entity, and Parabrahman is the Supreme Personality of Godhead. The living entity's constitutional position is different from the position he takes in the material world. In the material world, in material consciousness, his nature is to lord it over nature, but when he is in his spiritual nature he is in Kṛṣṇa consciousness. A living entity is to be understood as pure when he is Kṛṣṇa conscious. But when the living entity is in material consciousness, then he has to take different kinds of bodies in this world, and that is called *karma*, or varied creation by the force of material consciousness.

4. The physical nature is known to be endlessly mutable. The universe is the cosmic form of the Supreme Lord, and I am that Lord represented as the Supersoul, dwelling in the heart of every embodied being.

5. Anyone who, at the end of life, quits his body remembering Me, attains immediately to My nature, and there is no doubt of this.

6. In whatever condition one quits his present body, in his next life he will attain to that state of being without fail.

7. Therefore, Arjuna, you should always think of Me, and at the same time you should continue your prescribed duty and fight. With your mind and activities always fixed on Me, and everything engaged in Me, you will attain to Me without doubt.

PURPORT

This instruction to Arjuna is very important for all men engaged in material activities. The Lord does not say that one should give up his prescribed duties or engagements. One can continue them and at the same time think of Kṛṣṇa by chanting Hare Kṛṣṇa. This will free one from material contamination, and will engage the mind and intelligence in Kṛṣṇa. By chanting Kṛṣṇa's names, one will be transferred to the supreme planet, Kṛṣṇaloka, without a doubt.

8. By practicing this remembrance without being deviated, thinking ever of the Supreme Godhead, one is sure to achieve the planet of the divine, the Supreme Personality, O son of Kuntī.

9. Think of the Supreme Person as one who knows everything, who is the oldest, who is the controller, who is smaller than the smallest, who is the maintainer of everything, who is beyond any material conception, who is inconceivable, and who is always a person. He is luminous like the sun, beyond this material nature, transcendental.

PURPORT

The process of thinking of the Supreme is mentioned in this verse. The foremost point is that He is not impersonal or void. One cannot meditate on something impersonal or void. That is very difficult. The process of thinking of Kṛṣṇa, however, is very easy, as is factually stated here. He is the oldest personality because He is the origin of everything; everything is born of Him. He is also the supreme controller of the universe, the maintainer and instructor of humanity. He is smaller than the smallest. The living entity is one ten-thousandth the tip of a hair in size, but the Lord is so inconceivably small that He enters into the heart of this particle. As the Supreme, He can enter the atom and into the heart of the smallest and control him as the Supersoul. Although so small, He is still all-pervading and maintains everything. By Him all these planetary systems are sustained. It is stated here that the Supreme Lord, by His inconceivable energy, is sustaining all these big planets and systems of galaxies. The word *acintya,* inconceivable, in this verse is very significant. God's energy is beyond our conception, beyond our thinking jurisdiction, and is therefore called inconceivable. Who can argue this point? He pervades this material nature and yet is beyond it. We cannot even comprehend this material world, which is insignificant compared to the spiritual world—so how can we comprehend what is beyond? *Acintya* means that which is beyond this world, that which our argument, logic and philosophical speculation cannot touch. Therefore, intelligent persons, avoiding useless argument and speculation, should accept what is stated in scriptures like the *Vedas*, the *Gītā*, and the *Śrīmad-Bhāgavatam* and follow the principles they set down. This will lead to understanding.

10. One who, at the time of death, fixes his life air between the eyebrows and in full devotion engages himself in remembering the Supreme Lord will certainly attain to the Supreme Personality of Godhead.

11. Learned persons and great sages in the renounced order enter into Brahman. Desiring such perfection, one practices celibacy. I shall now explain to you this process for attaining salvation.

12. The yogic situation is that of detachment from all sensual engagements. Closing all the doors of the senses and fixing the mind on the heart and the air of life on the top of the head, one establishes this situation.

13. After being situated in this *yoga* practice and vibrating the sacred syllable *om*, the supreme combination of letters, if one thinks of the Lord and thus quits his body, he will certainly reach the spiritual planets.

14. For one who is without deviation in remembering Me, I am easy to obtain, O son of Pṛthā, because of his constant engagement in devotional service.

15. After attaining Me, the great *mahātmās*, *yogīs* in devotion, never come back to this temporary world, so full of miseries, because they have attained the highest perfection.

PURPORT

The material world is full of miseries, specifically birth, death, old age and disease. It is also temporary. One who goes to the planet of Kṛṣṇa, called Goloka Vṛndāvana, has achieved the highest perfection, and naturally he does not wish to come back to this unhappy place. This spiritual planet is described in the Vedic literature. It is inexplicable, beyond our material vision, but it is the highest goal, the destination for great souls, who are known as *mahātmās.* They receive the transcendental message from realized devotees and thus gradually develop devotional service, Kṛṣṇa consciousness, and become so absorbed in transcendental loving service that they lose all desire for elevation to any material planets. Nor do they seek to be transferred to any spiritual planet. They want only Kṛṣṇa and Kṛṣṇa's association, nothing else. That is the highest perfection of life. This verse specifically mentions the personalist devotees of the Supreme Lord, Kṛṣṇa. These devotees in Kṛṣṇa consciousness achieve the highest perfection of life; in other words, they are the supreme souls.

16. From the highest planet in the material world down to the lowest, all are places of misery where repeated birth and death take place. But one who attains to My abode, O son of Kuntī, never takes birth again.

PURPORT

All *yogīs* are meant to attain this highest perfection of *bhakti,* and when it is said that the *yogīs* do not come again to this material world, it means that when they achieve devotional perfection in *bhakti-yoga,* or Kṛṣṇa consciousness, it is possible for them to go transcendentally into the spiritual world and never come back. Those who attain to the highest material planets, the planets of the demigods, will again be subjected to birth and death, old age and disease. Just as persons on this earth may be promoted to the higher planets, so persons on those higher planets, such as Brahmaloka, Candraloka or Indraloka, may be degraded to this earth. By the practice of certain sacrifices one can achieve Brahmaloka, but if, once there, one does not cultivate Kṛṣṇa consciousness, he again comes to this earthly sphere. Those who continue Kṛṣṇa consciousness, even on the higher planets, are gradually elevated still higher, and at the time of the devastation of this universe they are transferred to the spiritual world, to the Kṛṣṇaloka planet. It is said that when there is a devastation of this material universe, Brahmā, along with these devotees who are constantly engaged in Kṛṣṇa consciousness, is transferred to the spiritual world, to one of the spiritual planets.

17. By human calculation, a thousand ages taken together is the duration of Brahmā's one day. And such also is the duration of his night.

PURPORT

Brahmā lives for one hundred years. One thousand ages means 4,300,000 years, multiplied by 1,000. This is equal to twelve hours, the duration of Brahmā's one day, and his night is of the same duration. Thirty such days and nights make one month, and twelve such months equal one year. After one hundred such years, Brahmā also dies, according to the law of material nature. No one is free from this process of birth, death, old age and disease. Brahmā is also subjected to it. But the special facility for Brahmā is that, being directly engaged in the service of the Supreme Lord for the management of this universe, he at once gets liberation. It is to be noted that the perfect *sannyāsīs* are promoted to the Brahmaloka; but if Brahmā is himself subjected to death, what can be said of the *sannyāsīs* who are elevated to his planet? This duration of Brahmaloka is greater even than that of the sun and moon, or other worlds in the upper strata of planetary systems.

18. In the day of Brahmā all living entities come into being, and when the night falls all is annihilated.

PURPORT

Those who are less intelligent try to remain within this material world; they are elevated to some more advanced planets and then again come back to this earth. All of them, during the daytime of Brahmā, can exhibit their activities within this material world; but during the nighttime they are annihilated. During daytime they get their different kinds of body and material activities, and during nighttime they no longer have any form. They remain compact within the body of Viṣṇu and then again are manifested in the new daytime of Brahmā. In this way, they are manifested and again annihilated. Ultimately, when Brahmā's life is also finished, all is annihilated for millions upon millions of years, to be manifested again when Brahmā is born anew in another millennium. In this way, the living beings are captivated by the spell of the material world. But intelligent persons who take to Kṛṣṇa consciousness utilize this human form of life fully in devotional service to the Lord, chanting Hare Kṛṣṇa, Hare Kṛṣṇa, Kṛṣṇa Kṛṣṇa, Hare Hare/ Hare Rāma, Hare Rāma, Rāma Rāma, Hare Hare. Even in this life they transfer themselves to the planet of Kṛṣṇa and become eternally blissful and happy there.

19. Again and again the day comes, and this host of beings is active; and again the night falls, O Pārtha, and this host is helplessly dissolved.

20. There is another, eternal nature, which is transcendental to this manifested and nonmanifested matter. It is supreme and is never annihilated. When all in this world is annihilated, that part remains as it is.

21. That supreme status is called unmanifested and infallible, and it is the highest destination. When one goes there, one never returns. That is My supreme abode.

PURPORT

The supreme abode of the Personality of Godhead, Kṛṣṇa, is described in the *Brahma-saṁhitā* as the *cintāmaṇi-dhāma*. That abode of Lord Kṛṣṇa, known as Goloka Vṛndāvana, is full of palaces made of touchstone. There the trees are called desire trees, and the cows are called *surabhi*. The Lord is served by hundreds and thousands of goddesses of fortune, and He is called Govinda, the primal Lord and the cause of all causes. There the Lord plays His flute. His eyes are like lotus petals, and the color of His body is like a beautiful cloud. On His head is a peacock feather. So attractive is He that He excels thousands of cupids. Lord Kṛṣṇa gives only a little hint in the *Gītā* about His personal abode, which is the supermost planet in the spiritual kingdom.

22. The Supreme Personality of Godhead, than whom no one is greater, is attainable by unalloyed devotion, O Arjuna. Although there in His abode, still He is all-pervading, and everything is fixed within Him.

23. O best of the Bharatas, I shall now explain to you the different times at which, passing away from this world, one does or does not come back.

PURPORT

The unalloyed devotees of the Supreme Lord very easily and happily go back to Godhead, back home, but those who are not unalloyed devotees and who depend on different kinds of spiritual realization through *karma-yoga* or *jñāna-yoga* must have a suitable moment to leave this body. Then they can be assured whether they will be coming back or not. If the *yogī* is perfect, he can select the time and situation for passing out of this material world. But if the *yogī* is not so expert, then it will depend on his accidental passing away at a certain suitable time.

24. Those who know the Supreme Brahman pass away from this world during the influence of the fiery god, in the light, at an auspicious moment, during the fortnight of the moon and the six months when the sun travels in the north.

25. The mystic who passes away from this world during the smoke, the night, the moonless fortnight, or the six months when the sun passes to the south again comes back.

26. There are two ways of passing from this world, one in light and one in darkness. When one passes in light he does not come back, but when one passes in darkness he returns.

27. O Arjuna, the devotees who know these different paths are never bewildered. Therefore, be always fixed in devotion.

PURPORT

Kṛṣṇa is specifically advising Arjuna not to be disturbed by these different paths of departure from the material world. A devotee of the Supreme Lord Kṛṣṇa is advised not to bother about how to pass away, whether by arrangement or by accident. His duties should be always in Kṛṣṇa consciousness, chanting Hare Kṛṣṇa. A Kṛṣṇa conscious person should know that either of these ways, the light way or the dark way, is troublesome. The best way is to be always absorbed in Kṛṣṇa consciousness and to be dovetailed in His service. That will make for a safe departure from this material world, directly to the spiritual kingdom.

28. A person who accepts the path of devotional service is not bereft of any result of studying the *Vedas*, performing austere sacrifices, giving charity or pursuing philosophical and fruitive activities. And at the end he reaches the supreme abode.

Thus end the Bhaktivedanta purports to the Eighth Chapter of the *Śrīmad Bhagavad-gītā* in the matter of Attaining the Supreme.

CHAPTER NINE

The Most Confidential Knowledge

1. The Supreme Lord said: Because you are never envious of Me, O Arjuna, I shall give you this most secret wisdom, knowing which you will be relieved from the miseries of material existence.

PURPORT

As a devotee hears more and more about the Supreme Lord, he becomes enlightened. This hearing process is recommended in the *Śrīmad-Bhāgavatam:* "The messages of the Supreme Personality of Godhead are full of potencies, and these potencies can be realized if topics regarding the Supreme Godhead are discussed among devotees. This cannot be achieved by the association of mental speculators or academic scholars; it is realized knowledge." The Lord understands the mentality and sincerity of a particular living entity who is engaged in Kṛṣṇa consciousness, and He gives him the intelligence to understand the science of Kṛṣṇa in the association of devotees. Discussion of Kṛṣṇa is very potent, and if a fortunate person has such association and tries to assimilate the knowledge, then he will surely make advancement toward spiritual realization. Lord Kṛṣṇa, in order to encourage Arjuna to be elevated higher and higher in His potent service, is describing in this Ninth Chapter things more confidential than He has already disclosed.

2. This knowledge is the king of education, the most secret of all secrets. It is the purest knowledge, and because it gives direct perception of the self by realization, it is the perfection of religion. It is everlasting and joyfully performed.

3. Those who are not faithful on the path of devotional service, O killer of the enemies, cannot achieve Me. Therefore, they come back to birth and death in this material world.

4. In My unmanifested form I pervade all this creation. All things are resting in Me, but I am not in them.

PURPORT

The Supreme Personality of Godhead is not perceivable through the gross material senses. It is said that Lord Śrī Kṛṣṇa's name, fame and pastimes cannot be understood by the material senses. Only to one who is engaged in pure devotional service under proper guidance is He revealed. In the *Brahma-saṁhitā* it is stated that one can see the Supreme Personality of Godhead, Govinda, always within himself and outside if one has developed the transcendental loving attitude toward Him. Thus for people in general He is not visible. Here it is said that although He is all-pervading, everywhere present, still He is not conceivable to our material senses. But actually although we cannot see Him, everything is resting in Him. As we have discussed in the Seventh Chapter, the whole material cosmic manifestation is only a combination of His two different types of energies, the superior, spiritual energy and the inferior, material energy.

Now, one should not have concluded that because He is spread all over, the Lord has therefore lost His personal existence. To refute such arguments by those with a poor fund of knowledge, the Lord says, "I am everywhere, and everything is in Me, but still I am aloof." A crude example can be given in this manner. A king has his government, which is a manifestation of the king's energy. The different departments are nothing but the energies of the king, and each department is resting on the king's power, but still one cannot expect the king to be present in every department personally. Similarly, all the manifestations we see, and everything that exists in both this material world and in the spiritual world, are resting on the energy of the Supreme Personality of Godhead. The creation takes place by the diffusion of His different energies, and as stated in *Bhagavad-gītā,* He is everywhere present by His personal representation, this diffusion of energies.

5. Again, everything that is created does not rest on Me. Behold My mystic opulence! Although I am the maintainer of all living entities and although I am everywhere, still My Self is the very source of creation.

6. As in the great sky the wind is blowing everywhere, so all the cosmic manifestation is situated in Me.

PURPORT

For the ordinary person it is almost inconceivable how the huge material manifestation is resting in Him. But the Lord is giving an example which may help us to understand. The sky (space) is the biggest manifestation conceivable by us, and in that sky the air is the greatest manifestation of the cosmic world. So although the air is great, still it is situated within space; it is not beyond the sky. Similarly, all the manifold manifestations of wonderful things are going on by the simple supreme will of God, and all of them are subordinate to that supreme will. By His will everything is being created, everything is being maintained, and everything is being annihilated. Still, He is aloof from everything, as the sky is always aloof from the activities of the great air. In the *Upaniṣads* it is stated, "It is out of the fear of the Supreme Lord that the air is blowing." In the *Garga Upaniṣad* also it is stated, "By the supreme order, under the superintendence of the Supreme Personality of Godhead, the moon, the sun and other big planets are moving." In the *Brahma-saṁhitā* also this is stated. There is a description of the movement of the sun, and it is said that the sun is considered to be one of the eyes of the Supreme Lord and that it has immense potency to diffuse heat and light. Still, it is moving in its prescribed orbit by the order, by the supreme will, of Govinda. So from the Vedic literature we can find evidence that although this material manifestation appears to us very wonderful and great, still it is under the complete control of the Supreme Personality of Godhead, as will be explained in the later verses of this chapter.

7. O son of Kuntī, at the end of the millennium every material manifestation enters unto My nature, and at the beginning of another millennium, by My potency, I again create.

PURPORT

At the end of the millennium means at the death of Brahmā. Lord Brahmā lives for one hundred years, and his one day is calculated at 4,300,000,000 of our earthly years. His night is of the same duration. His month consists of thirty such days and nights, and his year of twelve such months. After one hundred such years, when Brahmā dies, the devastation or annihilation takes place, which means that the energy manifested by the Supreme Lord is again wound up in Him. Then again, when there is a necessity to manifest the cosmic world, it is done by His simple will: "Although I am one, I shall become many." This is the Vedic aphorism. He expands Himself in this material energy, and the whole cosmic manifestation again takes place.

8. The whole cosmic order is under Me. By My will it is manifested again and again, and by My will it is annihilated at the end.

9. O Dhanañjaya, all this work cannot bind Me. I am ever detached, seated as though neutral.

PURPORT

One should not think, in this connection, that the Supreme Personality of Godhead has no engagement. In His spiritual world He is always engaged. In the *Brahma-saṁhitā* it is stated: "He is always involved in His eternal, blissful, spiritual activities, but He has nothing to do with material activities." Material activities are being carried on by His different potencies. The Lord is always neutral in the material activities of the created world. This neutrality is explained here. Although He has control over every minute detail of matter, He is sitting as if neutral. The example can be given of a high court judge sitting on his bench. By his order so many things are happening: someone is being hanged, someone is being put into jail, someone is awarded a huge amount of wealth—but he is neutral. He has nothing to do with all that gain and loss. Similarly, the Lord is always neutral, although He has His hand in every sphere of activity. In the *Vedānta-sūtra* there is a code which says that He is not situated in the differential treatment of this material world. He is transcendental to this differential treatment. Nor is He attached to the creation and annihilation of this world. The living entities take their different forms as species of life according to their past deeds, and the Lord does not interfere with that.

10. This material nature is working under My direction, O son of Kuntī, producing all the moving and unmoving beings. By its rule this manifestation is created and annihilated again and again.

11. The foolish mock at Me, at My descending like a human being. They do not know My transcendental nature and My supreme dominion over all that be.

12. Those who are thus bewildered are attracted by demoniac and atheistic views. In that deluded condition, their hopes for liberation, their fruitive activities and their culture of knowledge are all defeated.

13. O son of Pṛthā, those who are not deluded, the great souls, are under the protection of the divine nature. They are fully engaged in devotional service because they know Me as the Supreme Personality of Godhead, original and inexhaustible.

14. They are always engaged in chanting My glories. Endeavoring with great determination, offering homage unto Me, they worship Me with devotion.

PURPORT

The *mahātmā*, or great soul, cannot be manufactured by rubber-stamping an ordinary man. His symptoms are described here. A *mahātmā* is always engaged in chanting the glories of the Supreme Lord Kṛṣṇa, the Personality of Godhead. He has no other business. When the question of glorification is there, one has to glorify the Supreme Lord, praising His holy name, His eternal form, His transcendental qualities and His uncommon pastimes. One has to describe all these things. One who is attached to the impersonal feature of the Supreme Lord, the *brahmajyoti*, is not described as *mahātmā* in the *Bhagavad-gītā*. He is described in a different way, as will appear in the next verse.

15. Others, who are engaged in the cultivation of knowledge, worship the Supreme Lord as the one without a second, as diverse in many and in the universal form.

16. But it is I who am the ritual, I the sacrifice, the offering to the ancestors, the healing herb, the transcendental chant; I am the butter and the fire and the offering.

17. I am the father, mother, maintainer and grandfather of all this universe. I am what is to be known, I am purity, and I am the syllable *om*. I am the *Ṛg*, *Sāma* and *Yajur* [*Vedas*].

18. I am the goal, the upholder, the master, the witness, the home, the shelter and the most dear friend. I am the creation and the annihilation, the basis of everything, the resting place and the eternal seed.

19. O Arjuna, I control heat, the rain and the drought. I am immortality, and I am death personified. Both being and nonbeing are in Me.

20. Those who study the *Vedas* and drink the *soma* juice worship Me indirectly, seeking the heavenly planets. They take birth on Indraloka, where they enjoy godly delights.

21. When they have thus enjoyed heavenly sense pleasure, they return to this mortal planet again. Thus through the Vedic principles they achieve only flickering happiness.

22. But those who devote themselves steadfastly to Me, meditating on My transcendental form, receive all bounties and securities from Me.

23. Whatever a man may sacrifice to other gods, O son of Kuntī, is really meant for Me alone, but it is offered without true understanding.

24. For I am the only enjoyer and the only object of sacrifice. They fall down who do not recognize My true transcendental nature.

25. Those who worship the demigods will take birth among the demigods, those who worship ghosts and spirits will take birth among such beings, and those who worship Me will live with Me.

26. If one offers Me with love and devotion a leaf, a flower, fruit, or water, I will accept it.

PURPORT

For the intelligent person, it is essential to be in Kṛṣṇa consciousness, engaged in the transcendental loving service of the Lord, in order to achieve a permanent, blissful abode for eternal happiness. The process of achieving such a marvelous result is very easy and can be attempted even by the poorest of the poor, without any kind of qualification. The only qualification required in this connection is to be a pure devotee of the Lord. It does not matter what one is or where one is situated. The process is so easy that even a leaf or a little water or fruit can be offered to the Supreme Lord in genuine love, and the Lord will be pleased to accept it. No one, therefore, can be barred from Kṛṣṇa consciousness, because it is so easy and universal. Who is such a fool that he does not want to be Kṛṣṇa conscious by this simple method and thus attain the highest perfectional life of eternity, bliss and knowledge? Kṛṣṇa wants only loving service and nothing more. Kṛṣṇa accepts even a little flower from His pure devotee. He does not want any kind of offering from a nondevotee. He is not in need of anything from anyone because He is self-sufficient, and yet He accepts the offering of His devotee in an exchange of love and affection. To develop Kṛṣṇa consciousness is the highest perfection of life. *Bhakti* is mentioned twice in this verse in order to declare more emphatically that *bhakti,* or devotional service, is the only means to approach Kṛṣṇa. No other condition, such as becoming a *brāhmaṇa,* a learned scholar, a very rich man or a great philosopher, can induce Kṛṣṇa to accept some offering. Without the basic principle of *bhakti,* nothing can induce the Lord to agree to accept anything from anyone. *Bhakti* is never casual. The process is eternal. It is direct action in service to the absolute whole.

Here Lord Kṛṣṇa, having established that He is the only enjoyer, the primeval Lord and the real object of all sacrificial offerings, reveals what types of sacrifices He desires. If one wishes to engage in devotional service to the Supreme in order to be purified and to reach the goal of life, the transcendental loving service of God, then he should find out what the Lord desires of him. One who loves Kṛṣṇa will give Him whatever He wants, but he should avoid offering anything which is undesirable or unasked for. Thus meat, fish and eggs should not be offered to Kṛṣṇa. If He desired such things as an offering, the Lord would have said so, but instead He clearly requests that a leaf, fruit, flowers and water be given to Him. And He says of this offering, "I will accept it." Therefore, we should understand that He will not accept meat, fish and eggs. Vegetables, grains, fruits, milk and water are the proper foods for human beings, as is here prescribed by Lord Kṛṣṇa Himself. Whatever else we may eat cannot be offered to Him, since He will not accept it. Thus we cannot be acting on the level of loving devotion if we offer such foods. In the Third Chapter, verse 13, Śrī Kṛṣṇa explains that only the remains of sacrifice are purified and fit for consumption by those who are seeking advancement in life and release from the clutches of material entanglement. Those who do not make an offering of their foodstuffs, He says in the same verse, are eating only sin. In other words, their every mouthful is simply deepening their involvement in the complexities of material nature. But to prepare nice, simple vegetable dishes and to offer them before the picture or Deity of Lord Kṛṣṇa, bowing down and praying for Him to accept such a humble offering, is to advance steadily in life, to purify the body, and to create fine brain tissues which will lead to clear thinking. Above all, the offering should be made with an attitude of love. Kṛṣṇa has no need of food, since He already possesses everything that is, but still He will accept the offering of one who desires to please Him in that way. So the important element, in preparation, in serving and in offering, is to act with love for Kṛṣṇa.

The impersonalist philosophers, who wish to maintain that the Absolute Truth is without senses, cannot comprehend this verse of *Bhagavad-gītā*. To them, either it is a metaphor, or else it is proof of the mundane character of Kṛṣṇa, the speaker of the *Gītā*. But in actuality Kṛṣṇa, the Supreme Godhead, has senses, and it is stated that His senses are interchangeable; in other words, one sense can perform the function of any other. This is what it means to say that Kṛṣṇa is absolute. Lacking senses, He could hardly be considered full in all opulences. In the Tenth Chapter, Kṛṣṇa will explain that He impregnates the living entities into the material nature by His glance. And so in this instance, Kṛṣṇa's hearing the devotee's words of love in offering foodstuffs is wholly identical with His eating and actually tasting. This point should be emphasized. Because of His absolute position, His hearing is wholly identical with His eating and tasting. Only the devotee, who accepts Kṛṣṇa as He describes Himself to be, without personal interpolations, can understand that the Supreme Absolute Truth can eat food and enjoy it.

27. O son of Kuntī, all that you do, all that you eat, all that you offer and give away, as well as all austerities that you may perform, should be done as an offering unto Me.

28. Thus you will be freed of all reactions to good and evil deeds, and by this principle of renunciation you will be liberated and come to Me.

29. I envy no one, nor am I partial to anyone. I am equal to all. But whoever renders service unto Me in devotion is a friend, is in Me, and I am a friend to him.

PURPORT

One may question here that if Kṛṣṇa is equal to everyone and no one is His special friend, then why does He take special interest in the devotees who are always engaged in His transcendental service? But this is not discrimination; it is natural. Any man in this material world may be very charitably disposed, but still he has a special interest in his own children. The Lord claims every living entity, in whatever form, as His son, and as such He provides everyone with a generous supply of the necessities of life. He is just like a cloud that pours rain all over, regardless of whether it falls on rock or land or water. But for the devotees the Lord has specific attention. Such devotees are mentioned here. They are always in Kṛṣṇa consciousness, and therefore they are always transcendentally situated in Kṛṣṇa. The very phrase Kṛṣṇa consciousness suggests that they are living transcendentalists, situated in Him. And the Lord is also in them. This is reciprocal. This is the nice explanation of the words "Anyone who surrenders unto Me, proportionately do I take care of him." This transcendental reciprocation exists because both the Lord and the devotee are conscious.

30. One who is engaged in devotional service, even if he commits the most abominable actions, is to be considered saintly because he is rightly situated.

PURPORT

In the *Śrīmad-Bhāgavatam* it is stated that if a person falls down but is wholeheartedly engaged in the transcendental service of the Supreme Lord, the Lord, being situated within his heart, purifies him and excuses him from that abomination. The material contamination is so strong that even a *yogī* fully engaged in the service of the Lord is sometimes ensnared; but Kṛṣṇa consciousness is so strong that such an occasional falldown is at once rectified.

31. Very shortly does he become righteous and attain to lasting peace. O son of Kuntī, declare it boldly that My devotee will never perish.

32. O son of Pṛthā, anyone who takes shelter in Me—even a woman, a merchant or one who is born in a low family—can approach the supreme destination.

33. How much greater then are the *brāhmaṇas*, the righteous, the devotees and saintly kings who in this temporary, miserable world engage in devotional service to the Lord.

34. Engage your mind always in thinking of Me, become My devotee, engage your body in My service, and surrender unto Me. Completely absorbed in Me, surely you will come to Me.

PURPORT

In this verse it is clearly indicated that Kṛṣṇa consciousness is the only means of being delivered from the clutches of the contamination of this material world. Sometimes unscrupulous commentators distort the meaning of what is clearly stated here: that all devotional service should be offered to the Supreme Personality of Godhead, Kṛṣṇa. Unfortunately, unscrupulous commentators divert the mind of the reader to some other thing which is not at all feasible. Such commentators do not know that there is no difference between Kṛṣṇa's mind and Kṛṣṇa. Kṛṣṇa is not an ordinary human being; He is Absolute Truth. His body, mind, and He Himself are one and absolute. But because they do not know this science of Kṛṣṇa, they hide Kṛṣṇa and divide His personality from His mind or from His body. This is sheer ignorance of the science of Kṛṣṇa, but some men make a profit out of misleading the people. There are some who are demoniac; they also think of Kṛṣṇa, but enviously, just like King Kaṁsa, Kṛṣṇa's uncle. Kaṁsa was always thinking of Kṛṣṇa as his enemy. He was ever in anxiety as to when Kṛṣṇa would come and kill him. That kind of thinking will not help us. One should be thinking of Kṛṣṇa in devotional love. That is *bhakti.* One should cultivate knowledge of Kṛṣṇa continuously. For favorable cultivation, one should learn from a bona fide teacher. Kṛṣṇa is the Supreme Personality of Godhead, and we have several times explained that His body is not material, but is eternal, blissful knowledge. This kind of talk about Kṛṣṇa will help one become a devotee.

Thus end the Bhaktivedanta purports to the Ninth Chapter of the *Śrīmad Bhagavad-gītā* in the matter of the Most Confidential Knowledge.

CHAPTER TEN

The Opulence of the Absolute

1. The Supreme Lord said: Again, O mighty-armed Arjuna, listen to My supreme word, which I shall impart to you for your benefit and which will give you great joy.

PURPORT

The great sage Parāśara Muni explains that one who is complete in the six opulences of full beauty, strength, fame, wealth, knowledge and renunciation is called *paramam,* or the Supreme Godhead. Kṛṣṇa displayed all these opulences while on this earth. Now Kṛṣṇa is about to impart knowledge to Arjuna about His opulences and work. Beginning with the Seventh Chapter, the Lord has been explaining His different energies and how they interact. In the previous chapter He clearly explained His different energies in order to establish firm devotion to Him. Now, He is explaining His various opulences in detail. As one hears about the Supreme God, one becomes fixed in devotional service, and therefore hearing of the Lord's opulences is important. Such discourses should best be held in a society of devotees who are anxious to advance in Kṛṣṇa consciousness.

2. Neither the hosts of demigods nor the great sages know My origin, for in every respect, I am the source of the demigods and the sages.

PURPORT

It is also stated in the *Brahma-saṁhitā* that Lord Kṛṣṇa is the Supreme Lord, the cause of all causes. The great sages and demigods cannot understand Kṛṣṇa or His name and personality, and certainly mundane scholars cannot begin to comprehend Him. No one can understand why the Supreme comes to earth as an ordinary human being and executes such wonderful and uncommon activities. Even the demigods and great sages have tried to understand Kṛṣṇa by mental speculation but have failed. They can speculate to the extent that imperfect senses will allow them, but they cannot really understand Him in this way. Here, Kṛṣṇa states that He is the eternal Supreme Godhead, and that one can understand Him by studying His words in the *Gītā* and the *Śrīmad-Bhāgavatam.* Those involved in the inferior energy of the Lord (matter) can begin to understand something of the impersonal Brahman, but one cannot conceive of the Personality of Godhead unless one is in the transcendental position. Because men cannot understand the Supreme Godhead, He descends out of His causeless mercy. The devotees of the Lord surrender unto Kṛṣṇa and are thus able to understand Him, but those who endlessly speculate remain ignorant of His true position.

3. He who knows Me as the unborn, as the beginningless, as the Supreme Lord of all the worlds—he, undeluded among men, is freed from all sins.

4-5. Intelligence, knowledge, freedom from doubt and delusion, forgiveness, truthfulness, self-control, calmness, pleasure and pain, birth, death, fear, fearlessness, nonviolence, equanimity, satisfaction, austerity, charity, fame and infamy are created by Me alone.

PURPORT

In this verse, intelligence means the power to analyze things in their proper perspective. Knowledge refers to understanding what is spirit and what is matter. This knowledge is not the ordinary knowledge acquired in universities, but transcendental knowledge. In modern education there is a paucity of spiritual knowledge—knowledge is unfortunately confined to materialism and bodily needs, and it is therefore incomplete. Spiritual knowledge is necessary in order for one to be free from doubt and delusion. Nothing should be accepted blindly; everything should be accepted with care and caution. One should practice tolerance and forgive the minor offenses of others. Truthfulness means that facts should not be misrepresented, but should be presented fully, for the benefit of others. Socially, people say that one should speak the truth only when it is palatable to others, but that is not truthfulness. One should always speak the truth, even though it may seem unpalatable at the time. Self-control means that the senses should not be utilized for unnecessary personal enjoyment. Sense indulgence is detrimental to spiritual development. Similarly, the mind should not engage in unnecessary thoughts, nor should it dwell on the objects of the senses. One should not spend one's time pondering over how to make money. One's thinking powers should be developed in association with those who are authorities on the scriptures, saintly persons and spiritual masters and men whose thinking is highly developed.

Pleasure, or happiness, should always be in that which is favorable for the cultivation of spiritual knowledge, or Kṛṣṇa consciousness. Similarly, that which is painful is that which is unfavorable for the cultivation of such knowledge. Whatever is favorable for the development of Kṛṣṇa consciousness should be accepted, and what is unfavorable should be rejected. Birth, as mentioned in this verse, is in reference to the body. As far as the soul is concerned, there is neither birth nor death. Birth and death apply to one's embodiment in the material world. Fear results from worrying over the future. A person in Kṛṣṇa consciousness has no fear because his activities assure him of going to the spiritual sky, back to Godhead. When one has no knowledge of the next life, then he is in anxiety. Fear is due to one's absorption in illusory energy, but when one is free from illusory energy and certain that he is not the material body, then he has nothing to fear. Therefore, if one is always situated in Kṛṣṇa consciousness, he does not fear, for his future is very bright. Nonviolence means that one should not do anything that will put others into misery or confusion. The human body is meant for spiritual realization, and anyone who does not further this end commits violence on the body. Equanimity refers to freedom from attachment and aversion. A person in Kṛṣṇa consciousness has nothing to reject and nothing to accept unless it is useful for prosecuting Kṛṣṇa consciousness. Satisfaction means that one should not be eager to acquire more and more material goods by unnecessary activity. One should be satisfied with whatever is obtained by the grace of the Supreme Lord. Austerity and penance refer to the Vedic rules and regulations, such as rising early and taking baths. Although some of these rules may be troublesome, one should practice them. The trouble that is suffered is called penance or austerity. As for charity, one should give up half of what he earns to a good cause, such as the advancement of Kṛṣṇa consciousness, or to those engaged in the cultivation or dissemination of spiritual knowledge. Real fame is attributed to one who is known to be a great devotee, and infamy is due to the lack of such devotion.

All these qualities are manifest throughout the universe in human society and in the society of the demigods. Kṛṣṇa gives man these qualities and attributes, but man develops them from within and advances in Kṛṣṇa consciousness accordingly. One who engages in Kṛṣṇa consciousness develops all the good qualities automatically. We should realize that all qualities, good or bad, have their origin in Kṛṣṇa. Nothing can be manifest in the material world which is not in Kṛṣṇa.

6. The seven great sages and before them the four other great sages and the Manus [progenitors of mankind] are born out of My mind, and all creatures in these planets descend from them.

PURPORT

Brahmā is the original creature born out of the energy of the Supreme Lord, and from Brahmā all the seven great sages, and before them the four Kumāras and the Manus, are manifest. These are all known as the patriarchs of living entities all over the universe. There are innumerable varieties of population on each planet, and all of them are born of these patriarchs. They in turn all descend from Brahmā, who is born out of the energy of Kṛṣṇa, the Supreme Godhead.

7. He who knows in truth this glory and power of Mine engages in unalloyed devotional service; of this there is not doubt.

8. I am the source of everything; from Me the entire creation flows. Knowing this, the wise worship Me with all their hearts.

9. Their thoughts dwell in Me, their lives are surrendered to Me, and they derive great satisfaction and bliss, enlightening one another and conversing about Me.

PURPORT

Pure devotees, whose characteristics are mentioned here, engage themselves fully in the transcendental loving service of the Lord. Their minds cannot be diverted from the lotus feet of Kṛṣṇa. Their talks are solely transcendental. Twenty-four hours daily, they glorify the pastimes of the Supreme Lord. Their hearts and souls are constantly submerged in Kṛṣṇa, and they take pleasure in discussing Him with other devotees. In the preliminary stage of devotional service they relish transcendental pleasure from the service itself, and in the mature stage they are situated in love of God and can relish the highest perfection exhibited by the Lord in His abode. Lord Caitanya likens transcendental devotional service to the sowing of a seed in the heart of the living entity. One travels throughout the universe before he is finally fortunate enough to meet a pure devotee who transmits the transcendental seed of devotional service. As one chants the *mahā-mantra,* the great chanting for deliverance—Hare Kṛṣṇa, Hare Kṛṣṇa, Kṛṣṇa Kṛṣṇa, Hare Hare/ Hare Rāma, Hare Rāma, Rāma Rāma, Hare Hare—this seed of devotional service fructifies, just as the seed of a tree fructifies with regular watering. The spiritual plant of devotional service grows and grows until it pierces the sky of the material universe and enters into the *brahmajyoti,* the effulgence in the spiritual sky. It finally grows until it reaches the highest spiritual planet, Goloka Vṛndāvana, the supreme planet of Kṛṣṇa. Ultimately, the plant takes shelter there under the lotus feet of Kṛṣṇa, where it gradually sprouts fruits and flowers. And the chanting and hearing, which is the watering process, continues. Once the plant has taken shelter of the Supreme Lord, it becomes fully absorbed in love of God and cannot live without His contact for a moment, as a fish cannot live without water. All this is explained in the *Caitanya-caritāmṛta.* The *Śrīmad-Bhāgavatam* is also rich with stories of the relationships between devotees and the Lord, and those relationships are fully described in that work. The realized souls take pleasure in hearing these stories.

10. To those who are constantly devoted and worship Me with love, I give the understanding by which they can come to Me.

11. Out of compassion for them, I, dwelling in their hearts, destroy with the shining lamp of knowledge the darkness born of ignorance.

PURPORT

When Lord Caitanya Mahāprabhu was in Benares and promulgating the chanting of Hare Kṛṣṇa, Hare Kṛṣṇa, Kṛṣṇa Kṛṣṇa, Hare Hare/ Hare Rāma, Hare Rāma, Rāma Rāma, Hare Hare, thousands of people were following Him. Prakāśānanda, a great scholar in Benares at the time, derided Lord Caitanya for being a sentimentalist. Typically, some philosophers criticize the devotees for sentimentalism and philosophical naiveté. But Lord Caitanya was a great scholar who taught the philosophy of devotion. But even if the spiritual master does not educate the devotee in spiritual knowledge, the Supreme Godhead will do so. Therefore, a person in pure Kṛṣṇa consciousness is not in ignorance. The Lord is telling Arjuna in this verse that there is no possibility of understanding the Supreme Absolute Truth simply by speculating, for it lies beyond man's reasoning powers. Man can speculate for millions of years, and if he is not a devoted lover of the Supreme Truth, his speculation will be in vain. But by devotional service the Supreme Truth, the Personality of Godhead, is pleased, and He reveals Himself to the heart of the pure devotee by His inconceivable potency. The pure devotee always has Kṛṣṇa within his heart, and therefore he is just like the sun, which dissipates the darkness of ignorance. This is special mercy rendered to the pure devotee by the Supreme Lord. Due to the contamination of material association through many millions of births, one's heart is always covered with the dust of materialism, but when one engages in devotional service and chants Hare Kṛṣṇa, the dust quickly clears, and one is elevated to the platform of pure knowledge. This platform can be reached only by devotional service, and not by speculation or argumentation. When the darkness of ignorance is removed, the Supreme Lord takes charge, and the devotee has no worries. This is the essence of the *Gītā's* teaching. By studying the *Gītā* one comes to surrender completely to the Supreme Lord and engages in His service. As the Lord takes charge, he becomes free.

12-13. Arjuna said: You are the Supreme Brahman, the ultimate, the supreme abode and purifier, the Absolute Truth and the eternal divine person. You are the primal God, transcendental and original, and You are the unborn and all-pervading beauty. All the great sages such as Nārada, Asita, Devala and Vyāsa proclaim this of You, and now You Yourself are declaring it to me.

14. O Kṛṣṇa, I totally accept as truth all that You have told me. Neither the gods nor demons, O Lord, know Thy personality.

15. Indeed, You alone know Yourself by Your own potencies, O origin of all, Lord of all beings, God of gods, O Supreme Person, Lord of the universe!

16. Please tell me in detail of Your divine powers, by which You pervade all these worlds and abide in them.

PURPORT

Arjuna has knowledge of Kṛṣṇa through Kṛṣṇa's grace, but here he is asking Kṛṣṇa to explain His all-pervading nature because there are others who do not understand it. The all-pervading nature is not the totality of the Divinity, it is sustained by His divine powers and energies. This question is being asked by Arjuna in order that the common people might understand in the future.

17. How should I meditate on You? In what various forms are You to be contemplated, O Blessed Lord?

18. Tell me again in detail, O Janārdana [Kṛṣṇa], of Your mighty potencies and glories, for I never tire of hearing Your ambrosial words.

19. The Blessed Lord said: Yes, I shall tell you of My splendorous manifestations, but only of those which are prominent, O Arjuna, for My opulence is limitless.

20. I am the Self, O conqueror of sleep, seated in the hearts of all creatures. I am the beginning, the middle and the end of all beings.

21. Of the Ādityas I am Viṣṇu, of lights I am the radiant sun, I am Marīci of the Maruts, and among the stars I am the moon.

PURPORT

There are twelve Ādityas, of which Kṛṣṇa is the principal. Among all the luminaries twinkling in the sky, the sun is the chief, and in the *Brahma-saṁhitā* the sun is accepted as the glowing effulgence of the Supreme Lord. Marīci is the controlling deity of the heavenly spaces.

22. Of the *Vedas* I am the *Sāma Veda,* of the demigods I am Indra, of the senses I am the mind, and in living beings I am consciousness.

23. Of all the Rudras I am Lord Śiva, of the Yakṣas and Rākṣasas I am the lord of wealth [Kuvera], of the Vasus I am fire [Agni], and of mountains I am Meru.

PURPORT

There are eleven Rudras, of whom Śaṅkara, Lord Śiva, is an incarnation of the Supreme Lord and is in charge of the mode of ignorance in the material universe. Kuvera is a master treasurer and a representative of the Supreme Lord. Meru is a mountain famed for its rich natural resources.

24. Of priests, O Arjuna, know Me to be the chief, Bṛhaspati, the lord of devotion. Of generals I am Skanda, the lord of war, and of bodies of water I am the ocean.

PURPORT

Indra is the chief demigod of all the heavenly planets and is known as the king of the heavens. Bṛhaspati is Indra's priest and is therefore the chief of all priests. Similarly Skanda and Lord Śiva are the chiefs of all military commanders. And of all bodies of water, the ocean is the greatest. These representations of Kṛṣṇa give only hints of His greatness.

25. Of the great sages I am Bhṛgu; of vibrations I am the transcendental *om.* Of sacrifices I am the chanting of the holy names [*japa*], and of immovable things I am the Himalayas.

PURPORT

Brahmā, the first living creature within the universe, created several sons for the propagation of various kinds of species. The most powerful among his sons is Bhṛgu, who is the greatest sage. Of all transcendental vibrations, *oṁ* (the *oṁkāra*) is the representation of Kṛṣṇa. Of all sacrifices, the chanting of Hare Kṛṣṇa, Hare Kṛṣṇa, Kṛṣṇa Kṛṣṇa, Hare Hare/ Hare Rāma, Hare Rāma, Rāma Rāma, Hare Hare is the purest representation of Kṛṣṇa. Whatever is sublime in the worlds is a representation of Kṛṣṇa. Therefore, the Himalayas, the greatest mountains, also represent Him. The mountain named Meru was mentioned in a previous verse, but Meru is movable. In contrast, the Himalayas are immovable and so are mentioned here.

26. Of all trees I am the holy fig tree, and among sages and demigods I am Nārada. Of the singers of the demigods [Gandharvas] I am Citraratha, and among perfected beings I am the sage Kapila.

PURPORT

The fig tree (*aśvattha*) is one of the most beautiful and tallest trees, and people in India often worship it as one of their daily morning rituals. Among the demigods they also worship Nārada, who is considered the greatest of demigods in the universe. Therefore, these are considered as representations of Kṛṣṇa. The Gandharva planets are filled with entities who sing beautifully, and among them the best singer is Citraratha. Kapila is considered an incarnation of Kṛṣṇa, and His philosophy is given in the *Śrīmad-Bhāgavatam.*

27. Of horses know Me to be Uccaiḥśravā, who rose out of the ocean, born of the elixir of immortality; of lordly elephants I am Airāvata, and among men I am the monarch.

PURPORT

The devotee demigods and the demons (*asuras*) once took a sea journey. On this journey, nectar and poison were produced, and Lord Śiva drank the poison. From the nectar were produced many entities, of which there was a nice horse named Uccaiḥśravā. This horse was a representation of Kṛṣṇa. Another animal produced from the nectar was an elephant named Airāvata, who was also a representation of Kṛṣṇa. These animals have special significance because they were produced from nectar. Kings are mentioned here because at one time they were appointed due to their godly qualifications and were truly superior men. Kings like Mahārāja Parīkṣit and Lord Rāma were highly righteous kings who always considered their subjects' welfare. In Vedic literature, the king is considered the representative of God. With the corruption of the principles of religion in the Age of Kali, monarchy has decayed and has been largely abolished. People were much happier, however, under a righteous and godly king.

28. Of weapons I am the thunderbolt; among cows I am the Surabhi, givers of abundant milk. Of procreators I am Kandarpa, the god of love, and of serpents I am Vāsuki, the chief.

PURPORT

The thunderbolt, indeed a mighty weapon, is a representation of Kṛṣṇa's power. In Kṛṣṇaloka, in the spiritual sky, there is a cow called the Surabhi cow, which can give a limitless supply of milk. In this supreme planet, the Lord is engaged in herding these Surabhi cows. Kandarpa is the god of love, the procreator. Of course, procreation is for begetting good children; otherwise it is considered sense gratification. When sex is not for sense gratification, it is a representation of Kṛṣṇa.

29. Of the celestial Nāga snakes I am Ananta; of the aquatic deities I am Varuṇa. Of departed ancestors I am Aryamā, and among the dispensers of law I am Yama, lord of death.

PURPORT

Among the many celestial Nāga snakes, Ananta is the greatest, as is Varuṇa among the aquatics. They both represent Kṛṣṇa. There is also a planet of trees presided over by Aryamā, who represents Kṛṣṇa. Yama dispenses punishment to miscreants who are sent to the hellish planets. Those who are very sinful in their earthly life have to undergo different kinds of punishment on hellish planets. This punishment, however, is not eternal.

30. Among the Daitya demons I am the devoted Prahlāda, among subduers I am time, among the beasts I am the lion, and among birds I am Garuḍa, the feathered carrier of Viṣṇu.

PURPORT

Diti and Aditi are two sisters. The sons of Aditi are called Ādityas, and the sons of Diti are called Daityas. All the Ādityas are devotees of the Lord, and all the Daityas are atheistic. Although Prahlāda was born in the family of the Daityas, he was a great devotee from his childhood. Because of his steadfast devotional service, he is considered to be a representative of Kṛṣṇa.

There are many subduing principles, but time wears down all things in the material universe and so represents Kṛṣṇa. Of animals, the lion is often considered the most powerful and ferocious. And of great birds, the greatest is Garuḍa, who carries Viṣṇu.

31. Of purifiers I am the wind, of the wielders of weapons I am Rāma, of fishes I am the shark, and of flowing rivers I am the Ganges.

PURPORT

Among aquatics, the shark is one of the biggest and is certainly the most dangerous to man. Of course, Rāma is the great warrior incarnation who is the subject of the epic *Rāmāyaṇa*, and the Ganges is the principal river of India.

32. Of all creations I am the beginning and the end, and also the middle, O Arjuna. Of all sciences I am the spiritual science of the self, and among logicians I am the conclusive truth.

33. Of letters I am the letter A, and among compounds I am the dual word. I am also inexhaustible time, and of creators I am Brahmā, whose manifold faces turn everywhere.

34. I am all-devouring death, and I am the generator of all things yet to be. Among women I am fame, fortune, speech, memory, intelligence, faithfulness and patience.

35. Of hymns I am the *Bṛhat-sāma* sung to the Lord Indra, and of poetry I am the Gāyatrī verse, sung daily by *brāhmaṇas.* Of months I am November and December, and of seasons I am flower-bearing spring.

PURPORT

Among the *Vedas,* the *Sāma Veda* is rich in beautiful songs to be played for the different demigods. One of these songs is the *Bṛhat-sāma,* which has an exquisite melody and which is sung at midnight.

In Sanskrit, there are definite rules that regulate poetry. The Gāyatrī verse is sung by the duly qualified *brāhmaṇas.* The *Śrīmad-Bhāgavatam* recommends the Gāyatrī verse as being especially good for God realization. One who can successfully chant this verse can enter into the Lord's transcendental position. To chant the Gāyatrī verse, one must be perfectly situated in the mode of goodness. The verse is considered a sound incarnation of Brahman. Brahmā is its initiator, and it is passed down by disciplic succession starting with him.

The months of November and December are considered the best of all months because in India grains are collected from the fields at this time and the people become very happy. Of course, spring is a season universally liked because it is neither too hot nor too cold, and the flowers and trees blossom and flourish. In Vṛndāvana, Kṛṣṇa's birthplace, there are many ceremonies at this time, celebrating Kṛṣṇa's pastimes. Spring, the best of all seasons, represents Kṛṣṇa.

36. I am also the gambling of cheats, and of the splendid I am the splendor. I am victory, I am adventure, and I am the good quality in all superior men.

PURPORT

There are many kinds of cheaters all over the universe. Of all cheating processes, gambling stands supreme and therefore represents Kṛṣṇa. As the Supreme, Kṛṣṇa can be more deceitful than any mere man. If Kṛṣṇa chooses to deceive a person, no one can surpass Him in deceit. His greatness is not simply onesided—it is all-sided. Among the victorious He is victory, and among the splendid He is splendor. Among the enterprising industrialists, He is the most enterprising. Among adventurers, He is the most adventurous, and among the strong, He is the strongest. Even as a child, no one could surpass Him in strength, for He lifted Govardhana Hill with one hand. Clearly, the Godhead excels in all things.

37. Of the descendants of Vṛṣṇi I am Vāsudeva, and of the Pāṇḍavas I am Arjuna. Of the sages I am Vyāsa, and among great thinkers I am Uśanā.

PURPORT

Vāsudeva is an immediate expansion of Kṛṣṇa. Arjuna is the most famous and valiant of the sons of Pāṇḍu; indeed, he is the best of men and therefore represents Kṛṣṇa. Among the *munis*, or learned men conversant in Vedic knowledge, Vyāsa is the greatest because he explained Vedic knowledge in many different ways for the common people in this Age of Kali to understand. Vyāsa is indeed a very opulent literary incarnation and therefore represents Kṛṣṇa. *Kavis* are those who are capable of thinking thoroughly on any subject. Among the *kavis*, Uśanā was the spiritual master of the demons; he was extremely intelligent and spiritual in every way and was a politician of great insight. Uśanā therefore represents another facet of Kṛṣṇa's opulence.

38. Among punishments I am the rod of chastisement, and of those who seek victory, I am morality. Of secret things I am silence, and of the wise I am wisdom.

PURPORT

There are many oppressing agents, of which the most important are those that cut down the miscreants. When miscreants are punished, the rod of chastisement represents Kṛṣṇa. Among the activities of hearing, thinking and meditating, silence is most important because by silence one can make spiritual progress very quickly. The wise man is he who can discriminate between matter and spirit, between God's superior and inferior natures. Such knowledge is Kṛṣṇa Himself.

39. Furthermore, O Arjuna, I am the generating seed of all existences. There is no being—moving or unmoving—that can exist without Me.

40. O mighty conqueror of enemies, there is no end to My divine manifestations. What I have spoken to you is but a mere indication of My infinite opulences.

41. Know that all beautiful, glorious, and mighty creations spring from but a spark of My splendor.

42. But what need is there, Arjuna, for all this detailed knowledge? With a single fragment of Myself I pervade and support this entire universe.

PURPORT

The Supreme Lord is represented throughout the entire material universe by His entering into all things as the Supersoul. The Lord here tells Arjuna that there is no point in understanding how things exist in separate grandeur. He should see all things as existing due to Kṛṣṇa's entering them as Supersoul. From Brahmā, the most gigantic material entity, on down to the smallest ant, all entities are existing because the Supreme Lord has entered and is sustaining each. Worship of demigods is discouraged because even the greatest demigods, such as Brahmā and Śiva, represent only a part of the Supreme Lord's opulence. The Supreme Lord is *asamaurdhva*, which means that no one is greater than or equal to Him. By studying the opulences of Kṛṣṇa, one can come to understand why one should worship Him. Pure devotees concentrate their minds in Kṛṣṇa consciousness, in full devotional service, and so they worship He who sustains the entire cosmic manifestation by one fraction of His divine yogic power.

Thus end the Bhaktivedanta purports to the Tenth Chapter of the *Śrīmad Bhagavad-gītā* in the matter of the Opulence of the Absolute.

CHAPTER ELEVEN

The Universal Form

1. Arjuna said: I have heard Your instruction on confidential spiritual matters, which You have so kindly delivered unto me, and my illusion is now gone.

PURPORT

This chapter shows that Kṛṣṇa is the cause of all causes. He is even the cause of the Mahā-Viṣṇu, from whom the material universes emanate. Kṛṣṇa is not an incarnation; He is the source of all incarnations. That has been completely explained in the last chapter. Now, as far as Arjuna is concerned, he says that his illusion is past. The illusion was this: Arjuna thought Kṛṣṇa a human being, a friend of his. But after the explanations in the Tenth Chapter, he is now convinced that Kṛṣṇa is the source of everything. So he is now very enlightened and is glad that he has such a great friend as Kṛṣṇa. But in spite of being thus convinced, he is also thinking that although he may accept Kṛṣṇa as the source of everything, others may not. So in order to aid his transcendental friends regarding Kṛṣṇa's divinity, he is requesting, in this chapter, to see the universal form. Actually, when one sees the universal form of Kṛṣṇa, one will be frightened. But Kṛṣṇa is so kind to Arjuna that after the display, He reverts to His original form. Arjuna agrees with what Kṛṣṇa has several times said. Kṛṣṇa is speaking to Arjuna for his benefit, and so Arjuna acknowledges that all this is happening to him by Kṛṣṇa's grace.

2. O lotus-eyed one, I have heard from You in detail about the appearance and disappearance of every living entity, as realized within the nature of Your inexhaustible glories.

3. O greatest of all beings, O supreme form, though I see here before me Your actual position, I yet wish to see how You have entered into this cosmic manifestation; I wish to see that form of Yours.

PURPORT

The Lord said that because He entered into the material universe by His personal representation, the cosmic manifestation has been made possible and is going on. Now, Arjuna is inspired by the statements of Kṛṣṇa, but to convince others in the future who may think Kṛṣṇa an ordinary person, he desires to see Him in His universal form, to see how He acts from within the universe, although He is apart from it. Arjuna's address to the Lord here is most significant. Since the Lord is the Supreme Personality of Godhead and is present within Arjuna himself, He knew the desire of Arjuna. Lord Kṛṣṇa could understand that Arjuna had no special desire to see Him in His universal form because he was completely satisfied by the personal form of Kṛṣṇa. He could understand that Arjuna wanted to see the universal form only for future guidance, for in the future there would be so many imposters who would pose themselves as incarnations of God. People should therefore be careful; before accepting such nonsense, one should try to see the universal form of such a misrepresentation of God.

4. If You think that I am able to see Your cosmic form, O my Lord, O master of all mystic power, then kindly show me that universal self.

PURPORT

It is said that no one can see, hear, understand or perceive the Supreme Lord Kṛṣṇa by material research. But if one is engaged in loving transcendental service to the Lord, then one can see the Lord by revelation.

Every living entity is only a spiritual spark. Therefore, it is not possible to see or to understand the Supreme Lord. Arjuna, as a devotee, does not depend on his speculative strength; he admits his inability, acknowledging his position. He could understand that for a living entity it is not possible to understand the unlimited infinite. If the infinite reveals Himself, then it is possible to understand the nature of the infinite by the mercy of the infinite. The name Yogeśvara, "master of all mystic power," is also very significant because the Lord has inconceivable power. If He likes, he can reveal Himself—although He is unlimited—by His grace. Therefore, Arjuna pleads for the inconceivable grace of Kṛṣṇa. He did not give Kṛṣṇa orders. Kṛṣṇa is not obliged to reveal Himself to anyone, unless one surrenders fully in Kṛṣṇa consciousness and engages in devotional service. So this revelation is not possible for persons who depend on the strength of their mental speculations.

5. The Supreme Personality of Godhead said: My dear Arjuna, O son of Pṛthā, see now My opulences—hundreds of thousands of varied divine forms, multicolored like the sea.

PURPORT

Arjuna wanted to see Kṛṣṇa in His universal form, which, although transcendental, is suitable only for the cosmic manifestation and is subject to the temporary time of this material nature. As the material nature is manifested and not manifested, so is this form of Kṛṣṇa, which is not eternally situated in the spiritual sky, as other forms are.

6. O best of the Bharatas, see here the different manifestations of Ādityas, Rudras and all the demigods. Behold the many things which none has ever seen or heard before.

7. Whatever you want to see can be seen in this body all at once. This universal form can show you all that you now desire, as well as whatever you may want in the future. Everything is here completely.

8. But you cannot see Me with your present eyes. Therefore I give you divine eyes, so that you can behold My mystic opulence.

PURPORT

The pure devotee does not like to see Kṛṣṇa in any other form except in His form with two hands, and therefore a devotee has to see the universal form by the grace of the Lord, not with the mind but with spiritual eyes. To see the universal form of Kṛṣṇa, Arjuna is told not to change his mind, but to change his vision. The universal form of Kṛṣṇa is not very important; that will be clear in the succeeding verses. But still, because Arjuna wanted to see it, the Lord offered him the particular vision to see that form. Devotees who are correctly in a transcendental relationship with Kṛṣṇa are attracted by loving features, not by a godless display of opulence. The playmates of Kṛṣṇa, the friends of Kṛṣṇa and the parents of Kṛṣṇa never desire Kṛṣṇa to show His opulences. They are so immersed in pure love that they do not even know that Kṛṣṇa is the Supreme Personality of Godhead. In their loving exchange they forget that Kṛṣṇa is the Supreme Lord. In the *Śrīmad-Bhāgavatam* it is stated that the boys who are playing with Kṛṣṇa are all highly pious souls, so that after many, many births they are now able to play with Him. Such boys do not know that Kṛṣṇa is the Supreme Personality of Godhead. They take Him as a personal friend and are playing. The fact is that the devotee is not concerned to see the *viśva-rūpa*, the universal form. Arjuna wanted to see this *viśva-rūpa* not for himself but to establish Kṛṣṇa's position, so that in future history people could understand that Kṛṣṇa not only theoretically presented Himself as the Supreme, but actually revealed Himself as the Supreme. And it is confirmed by Arjuna, who is the beginning of the *paramparā*, the chain of disciplic succession.

9. Sañjaya said: O King, speaking thus, the Supreme, the Lord of all mystic power, the Personality of Godhead, displayed His universal form to Arjuna.

10-11. Arjuna saw in that universal form unlimited mouths and unlimited eyes. It was all wondrous. The form was decorated with divine, dazzling ornaments and arrayed in many garbs. He was garlanded gloriously, and there were many scents smeared over His body. All was magnificent, all-expanding, unlimited. This was seen by Arjuna.

12. If hundreds of thousands of suns rose at once into the sky, they might resemble the effulgence of the Supreme Person in that universal form.

13. At that time Arjuna could see in the universal form of the Lord the unlimited expansions of the universe situated in one place although divided into many, many thousands.

PURPORT

The Sanskrit word *tatra* ("there") is very significant. It means that both Arjuna and Kṛṣṇa were sitting on the chariot. Although Arjuna was visualizing the universal form of the Lord when both of them were seated on the chariot, others who were present on the battlefield could not see. This is because of the eyes of Arjuna. Arjuna saw in the body of Kṛṣṇa many thousands of universes, with many planets. Some of them are made of earth, some of them are made of gold, some of them are made of jewels, some of them are very great, and some of them are not so great. Arjuna could see all these varieties while sitting on his chariot. No one else could understand what was going on between Arjuna and Kṛṣṇa.

14. At that time, bewildered and astonished, his hairs standing on end, Arjuna began to pray with folded hands, offering obeisances to the Supreme Personality of Godhead.

15. Arjuna said: My dear Lord, Kṛṣṇa, I see in Your body all the demigods and different kinds of living entities, assembled together. I see Brahmā sitting on the lotus flower, as well as Lord Śiva and many sages and divine snakes.

16. O Lord of the universe, I see in Your universal body many, many forms—arms, bellies, mouths, eyes—expanded without limit. There is no end, there is no beginning, and there is no middle to all this.

17. Your form is very hard to see on account of its glowing effulgence, which is fiery and immeasurable like the sun.

18. You are the supreme primal objective; You are the best in all the universes; You are inexhaustible, and You are the oldest. You are the maintainer of religion, the eternal Personality of Godhead.

19. You are the origin, without beginning, middle or end. You have numberless arms, and the sun and moon are among Your great, unlimited eyes. By Your own radiance You are heating this entire universe.

20. Although You are one, You are spread throughout the sky and the planets and in all space between. O great one, as I see this terrible form, all the planetary systems are perplexed.

21. All the demigods surrender unto You, entering into You. Very much afraid, with folded hands, they are praying the Vedic hymns.

22. The different manifestations of Lord Śiva, the Ādityas, the Vasus, the Sādhyas, the Viśvadevas, the two Aśvins, the Maruts, the forefathers and the Gandharvas, the Yakṣas, *asuras* and all perfected demigods are seeing You in wonder.

23. O mighty-armed one, all the planets with their demigods are perturbed at seeing Your many faces, eyes, arms, bellies and legs and Your terrible teeth. And as they are perturbed, so am I.

24. O all-pervading Viṣṇu, I am unable to keep the equilibrium of my mind! Seeing Your radiant color filling the skies and seeing Your mouths and eyes, I am afraid.

25. O Lord of lords, O refuge of the worlds, please be gracious toward me! I cannot keep my balance seeing thus Your blazing, deathlike faces and awful teeth. I am bewildered in all directions.

26-27. All the sons of Dhṛtarāṣṭra, along with their allied kings, and Bhīṣma, Droṇa and Karṇa and all our soldiers are rushing into Your mouths, their heads smashed by Your fearful teeth. And some I see being crushed between Your teeth as well.

PURPORT

In the previous verses the Lord said, "I shall show you other things also, which you may be interested to see." Now Arjuna is seeing that the enemies—Bhīṣma, Droṇa, Karṇa and all the sons of Dhṛtarāṣṭra—are being smashed with their soldiers, and Arjuna sees that his soldiers are also being smashed. This indicates that after the death of all the persons assembled at Kurukṣetra, Arjuna will be victorious. It is also mentioned that Bhīṣma, who is supposed to be unconquerable by Arjuna, will be smashed. So also Karṇa. Not only will the great warriors of the other party like Bhīṣma be smashed; some of the great warriors on the side of Arjuna will also fall.

28. As the rivers flow down to the ocean, so all these great warriors enter into Your blazing mouths and perish.

29. I see all people entering with full speed into Your mouths, as moths hurry into a blazing fire.

30. O Viṣṇu, I see You devouring all people in Your blazing mouths and covering all the universe by Your immeasurable rays. Scorching the worlds, You are manifest.

31. O Lord of lords, so fierce of form, please tell me who You are. I offer my obeisances unto You; please be gracious to me. I do not know what Your mission is, and I desire to hear of this.

32. The Supreme Personality of Godhead said: Time I am, the destroyer of the worlds, and I have come to engage all people. Except for you [the Pāṇḍavas], all soldiers on both sides here will be slain.

PURPORT

Although Arjuna knew that Kṛṣṇa was his friend and the Supreme Personality of Godhead, still he was puzzled by the various forms exhibited to him by Kṛṣṇa. Therefore, he asked about the actual mission of this devastating force. The Vedic literature says that the Supreme Truth destroys everything, even Brahmā. This form of the Supreme Lord is the all-devouring giant. Here Kṛṣṇa presents Himself in that form of time, and He expresses His determination that except for the Pāṇḍavas everyone present on the battlefield should be devoured by Him. Now, Arjuna was not in favor of the fight, and he thought it better not to fight; then there would be no frustration. In reply, the Lord said that even if he did not fight, the plan was already made, and so every one of them would be destroyed. If he stopped fighting they would die in another way. Death cannot be checked, even if he did not fight. When the time has come for destruction, any manifestation may be vanquished by the desire of the Supreme Lord. That is the law of nature.

33. Therefore, get up and prepare to fight. After conquering your enemies you will enjoy the flourishing kingdom. They are already put to death by My arrangement, and you, O Savyasācin, can be but an instrument in the fight.

34. The Blessed Lord said: All the great warriors—Droṇa, Bhīṣma, Jayadratha, Karṇa—are already destroyed. Simply fight, and you will vanquish your enemies.

35. Sañjaya said to Dhṛtarāṣṭra: O King, after hearing all these words from the Supreme Personality of Godhead, Arjuna trembled, fearfully offered obeisances with folded hands and began, falteringly, to speak as follows.

36. O master of the senses, the world becomes joyful hearing Your name, and thus do all become attached to You. The demons are afraid and flee here and there, while the perfect beings offer You their respectful homage. All this is rightly done.

PURPORT

After hearing from Kṛṣṇa about the preconceived decision regarding the Battle of Kurukṣetra, Arjuna was enlightened. He now says that everything done by Kṛṣṇa is quite fitting. Arjuna confirmed that Kṛṣṇa as the maintainer and the object of worship of the devotees and Kṛṣṇa as the destroyer of the undesirables is in each case equally good. He understood that while the Battle of Kurukṣetra was being concluded, present in outer space were many demigods and *siddhas* and the intelligentsia of different planets. They were observing the fight because Kṛṣṇa was present there. So when he saw the universal form of the Lord killing the undesirables, they took pleasure in it. But others, the demons and atheists, could not bear it when the Lord was praised. Out of their natural fear of the devastating form of the Supreme Personality of Godhead, they fled. This kind of treatment to the devotees and the atheists by the Supreme Person is praised by Arjuna. The devotee glorifies the Lord because he knows that whatever is done by the Supreme is good for all.

37. O great one, who stands above even Brahmā, You are the original master. Why should they not offer their homage up to You, O limitless one? O refuge of the universe, You are the invincible source, the cause of all causes, transcendental to this material manifestation.

38. You are the original personality, the Godhead. You are the only sanctuary of this manifested cosmic world. Knowing everything, You are all that is knowable. You are above the material modes. O limitless form! This whole cosmic manifestation is pervaded by You.

PURPORT

Everything, even the pure effulgence, or Brahman, rests on the Supreme Personality of Godhead, Kṛṣṇa. He is the knower of everything that is happening in this world, and if knowledge has any end, He is that end. Therefore, He is the known and the knowable. He is the object of knowledge because He is all-pervading. Because He is the cause dwelling in the spiritual world, He is transcendental, and He is chief personality in the transcendental world.

39. You are air, fire, water and the moon! You are the supreme controller and the grandfather. Thus I offer my respectful obeisances unto You a thousand times, and again and yet again!

PURPORT

The Lord is addressed here as the air because the air is the most important representation of all the demigods, being all-pervading. He is addressed as the grandfather because He is the father even of Brahmā, the first living creature of this universe.

40. I offer my respects from the front, from behind and from all sides! O unbounded power, You are the master of limitless might! You are all-pervading, and thus You are everything!

41. I have in the past addressed You, "O Kṛṣṇa," "O Yādava," "O my friend," without knowing Your glories. Please forgive whatever I may have done in madness or in love.

42. I have dishonored You many times while in relaxation, while lying on the same bed or eating together; sometimes alone, and sometimes in front of many friends. Please excuse me for all the many offenses I have committed against You.

PURPORT

Kṛṣṇa is now manifested before Arjuna in the universal form, but Arjuna cannot forget his friendly relationship with the Supreme Lord. Therefore, he is asking pardon and requesting Him to excuse him. He is admitting that formerly he did not know that Kṛṣṇa could assume such a form, although it was explained. Arjuna did not know how many times he might have dishonored Him by addressing Him, "O my friend," "O Kṛṣṇa," "O Yādava," etc., without knowing His opulence. But Kṛṣṇa is so kind and merciful that in spite of such opulence, He played with Arjuna as a friend. That is the transcendental loving reciprocation between the devotee and the Lord. The relationship with the living entity and Kṛṣṇa is fixed eternally. It cannot be forgotten, as we can see from the behavior of Arjuna, for although he saw such opulence in the universal form, he could not forget his relationship of friendliness.

43. You are the father of this complete cosmic manifestation, the worshipable chief, the spiritual master. No one is equal to You, nor can anyone be one with You. Within the three worlds, You are immeasurable.

44. You are the Supreme Lord, to be worshiped by every living being. Thus I fall down to offer You my respects, and I ask Your mercy. As a

father tolerates the impudence of his son, or a friend tolerates the impertinence of a friend, or a wife tolerates the familiarity of her partner, so should You tolerate those wrongs that I may have done to You.

45. After seeing this universal form, which I have never seen before, I am gladdened, but at the same time my mind is disturbed with fear. Therefore, please reveal again Your form as the Personality of Godhead to grace me, O Lord of lords, O sanctuary of the universe.

46. O universal Lord, I wish to see You in Your four-handed form, with helmeted head and with club, wheel, conch and lotus flower in Your hands. I long to see You in that form.

PURPORT

The Lord is eternally situated in hundreds and thousands of forms, and principal among these are Rāma, Nṛsiṁha, Nārāyaṇa, and so on. Arjuna knew that Kṛṣṇa is the original Personality of Godhead; but since He had assumed His temporary *viśva-rūpa*, the universal form, now Arjuna's inquisitiveness increased, and he also wanted to see the form of Nārāyaṇa. This confirms without any doubt the statement of the *Śrīmad-Bhāgavatam* that Kṛṣṇa is the original Personality of Godhead and that all other features originate from Him. It is also clearly stated there that He is not different from His plenary expansions. He is God in any of His innumerable forms, and all those forms are fresh, just like a young man. That is the feature of the Supreme Personality of Godhead. One who thus knows Kṛṣṇa becomes at once free from all contamination of the material world.

47. The Supreme Personality of Godhead said: My dear Arjuna, happily do I show you this universal form within the material world by My internal potency. No one before you has ever seen this unlimited and glaringly effulgent form.

PURPORT

No one had seen the universal form of the Lord before Arjuna, but when the form was shown to him, devotees on the heavenly planets and in outer space also were fortunate enough to behold it. They had not seen it before, but because of Arjuna they were now able to see it. Someone has commented that this form had been previously shown to Duryodhana when Kṛṣṇa went to him negotiating for peace. Unfortunately, Duryodhana did not accept the peace offer, but at that time Kṛṣṇa manifested some of His universal forms. They were different, however, from the one shown here to Arjuna. It is clearly mentioned that no one has seen it before.

48. O best of the Kuru warriors, no one before you has seen this universal form of Mine, for neither by studying the *Veda,* nor by performing sacrifices, nor by charities or similar activities can this form be seen. Only you have seen this.

49. Your mind has been perturbed at seeing this horrible feature of Mine. Now let it be finished. My devotee, be free from all disturbance. With a peaceful mind you can see My form as you have desired.

50. Sañjaya said to Dhṛtarāṣṭra: The Supreme Personality of Godhead, Kṛṣṇa, while speaking thus to Arjuna, displayed His real four-handed form, and at last He showed His two-handed form, thus encouraging the fearful Arjuna.

PURPORT

When Kṛṣṇa appeared in this world as the son of Vasudeva and Devakī, He first of all showed His four-handed Nārāyaṇa form; then, requested by His parents, He transformed Himself and became just like an ordinary child. Similarly, Kṛṣṇa knew that Arjuna was not interested in seeing a four-handed form of Kṛṣṇa, but since he asked to see this form, Kṛṣṇa showed him this form, and then Kṛṣṇa showed Himself in His two-handed form. The Sanskrit word *saumya-vapuḥ* in this verse is very significant. *Saumya-vapuḥ* means a very beautiful form or the most beautiful form. When He was present, everyone was attracted by Kṛṣṇa. Because Kṛṣṇa is the director of the universe, He washed the fear out of Arjuna, His devotee, and showed Him again His beautiful form as Kṛṣṇa. It has been stated that only a person whose eyes are smeared with the ointment of love can see the beautiful form of Śrī Kṛṣṇa.

51. When Arjuna thus saw Kṛṣṇa in His original form, he said: Seeing this humanlike form, so very beautiful, I am now settled in mind and am restored to my original nature.

52. The Supreme Personality of Godhead said: My dear Arjuna, the form you are seeing now is very difficult to behold. Even the demigods are ever seeking the opportunity to see this form, which is so dear.

PURPORT

In the forty-eighth verse of this chapter, when the Lord concluded the manifestation of His universal form, He informed Arjuna that this form is not visible by dint of so many activities, penances, charities, sacrifices, etc. Now here it is said that although one may be able to see the universal form of Kṛṣṇa by adding a little tinge of devotional service to various pious activities, still, beyond that universal form, the form of Kṛṣṇa with two hands is yet more difficult to see, even for demigods like Brahmā and Lord Śiva. We have evidence in the *Śrīmad-Bhāgavatam* that when Kṛṣṇa was in the womb of His mother, Devakī, all the demigods from heaven came to see the marvel of Kṛṣṇa, and they offered nice prayers to the Lord, although He was not at that time visible to them. They waited to see Kṛṣṇa. Therefore, the foolish person may mock at Him, thinking Him an ordinary man, and may offer respect not to Him but to the impersonal "something" within Him, but these are nonsensical postures. Kṛṣṇa is desired to be seen by demigods like Brahmā and Śiva. They long to see Him in this two-handed form. In *Bhagavad-gītā* it is elsewhere confirmed that He is not visible to the foolish who deride Him. Now, the reason for mocking at Kṛṣṇa's form may be stated as follows. Kṛṣṇa's body is completely spiritual, full of bliss and eternal. His body is never like our material body. But for those who are making a cultural phenomenon of Kṛṣṇa by studying *Bhagavad-gītā* or similar Vedic scriptures, He is a problem. This problem has three methods of approach: by the transcendental process, by the material process, and by the speculative process. According to the material process, Kṛṣṇa is considered a great historical personality or a very learned philosopher, not an ordinary man, but even though He was so powerful, He had to accept a material body. The Absolute Truth is impersonal, and therefore from the impersonal feature He assumed a personal feature, attached to material nature. This is the materialistic calculation of the Supreme Lord. The next calculation is speculative. Those in search of knowledge also sometimes speculate on Kṛṣṇa and consider Him less important than the universal form. They think that the universal form Kṛṣṇa manifested to Arjuna is more important than His personal form. According to them, the personal form of the Supreme is something like imagination. Otherwise, in the ultimate issue, the Absolute Truth is not a person. But the transcendental process is described in *Bhagavad-gītā*, Second Chapter: to hear about Kṛṣṇa from authorities. That is the actual Vedic process. Those who are in the Vedic line hear about Kṛṣṇa from authority, and through repeatedly hearing about Him, Kṛṣṇa becomes dear. Because, as we have several times discussed, Kṛṣṇa is covered by the *yogamāyā* potency, He is not to be seen by, or revealed to, anyone and everyone. Only those to whom He reveals Himself can see Him. This is confirmed in Vedic literature. The Absolute Truth can actually be understood by one who is a surrendered soul. This transcendentalist, by continuous Kṛṣṇa consciousness in devotional service to Kṛṣṇa, has his spiritual eyes opened and sees Kṛṣṇa through revelation. Such a revelation is not available even to the demigods; even for them it is difficult to understand Kṛṣṇa. And among the demigods, those who are advanced always hope to see Kṛṣṇa in His two-hand form. The conclusion is that although to see the universal form of Kṛṣṇa is very, very difficult and not possible for anyone and everyone, it is still more difficult to understand His personal form as Śyāmasundara.

53. The form which you are seeing with your transcendental eyes cannot be understood simply by studying the *Veda*, nor by undergoing serious penances, nor by charity, nor by worship. Not by these means can one see Me as I am.

54. My dear Arjuna, only by undivided devotional service can I be understood as I am, standing before you, and can thus be seen directly. Only in this way can you enter into the mysteries of My understanding.

55. My dear Arjuna, anyone who is engaged in My pure devotional service, freed from the contaminations of previous activities and from men-

tal speculation, and who is friendly to every living entity, certainly comes to Me.

PURPORT

Anyone who wants to approach the supreme of all the Personalities of Godhead, on the Kṛṣṇaloka planet in the spiritual sky, and be intimately connected with the Supreme Personality, Kṛṣṇa, must take this formula, as is stated by the Supreme Himself. Therefore, this verse is considered to be the essence of *Bhagavad-gītā. Bhagavad-gītā* is a book directed to the conditioned souls, who are engaged in the material world with the purpose of lording it over nature and who do not know of the real, spiritual life. *Bhagavad-gītā* is meant to show how one can understand his spiritual existence and his eternal relationship with the supreme spiritual personality and to teach one how to go back home, back to Godhead. Now here is the verse which clearly explains the process by which one can attain success in his spiritual activity: devotional service. So far as work is concerned, one should transfer his energy entirely to Kṛṣṇa conscious activities. No work should be done by any man except in relationship to Kṛṣṇa. This is called *kṛṣṇa-karma.* People may be engaged in many different activities, but one should not be attached to the result of the activity; it should be done only for Him. For example, one may be engaged in business. Just to transform that business activity into Kṛṣṇa consciousness, one has to do business for Kṛṣṇa. If Kṛṣṇa is the proprietor of the business, then Kṛṣṇa should enjoy the profit of the business. If a businessman is in possession of thousands and thousands of dollars, and if he has to offer it to Kṛṣṇa, he can do it. This is work for Kṛṣṇa. Instead of constructing a big building for his sense gratification, he can construct a nice temple for Kṛṣṇa. He can install the Deity of Kṛṣṇa and arrange for the Deity's service, as mentioned in the authorized books of devotional service. These are all *kṛṣṇa-karma.* One should not be attached to the result of his work; the result should be offered to Kṛṣṇa, and one should accept as *prasāda,* food, the remnants of nice offerings to Kṛṣṇa. If, however, one is not able to construct a temple for Kṛṣṇa, one can engage himself in cleansing the temple of Kṛṣṇa; that is also *kṛṣṇa-karma.* One can cultivate a garden. Anyone who has land—in India, at least, any poor man has a certain amount of land—can utilize that for Kṛṣṇa by growing flowers to offer to Kṛṣṇa. He can sow *tulasī* plants because *tulasī* leaves are very important, and Kṛṣṇa has recommended this in *Bhagavad-gītā*. Kṛṣṇa desires that one offer Him either a leaf, a flower, or a little water—and He is satisfied. This leaf especially refers to *tulasī*. So one can sow *tulasī* seeds and pour water on the plant. Thus, even the poorest man can be engaged in the service of Kṛṣṇa. These are some examples of how one can engage in working for Kṛṣṇa.

A devotee of Kṛṣṇa is friendly to everyone. Therefore, it is said here that he has no enemy. How is this? A devotee situated in Kṛṣṇa consciousness knows that only devotional service to Kṛṣṇa can relieve a person from all the problems of life. He has personal experience of this, and therefore he wants to introduce this system, Kṛṣṇa consciousness, into human society. There are many examples in history of devotees of the Lord who have risked their lives for the spreading of God consciousness. The favorite example is Lord Jesus Christ. He was crucified by the nondevotees, but he sacrificed his life only for spreading God consciousness. Of course, it would be superficial to understand that he was killed. Similarly, in India also there are many examples, such as Haridāsa Ṭhākura. Why such risk? Because they wanted to spread Kṛṣṇa consciousness, and it is difficult. A Kṛṣṇa conscious person knows that if a man is suffering, it is due to his forgetfulness of his eternal relationship with Kṛṣṇa. Therefore, the highest benefit one can render to human society is to relieve one's neighbor from all material problems. In such a way, a pure devotee is engaged in the service of the Lord. Now, we can imagine how merciful Kṛṣṇa is to those engaged in His service, risking everything for Him. Therefore, it is sure and certain that such persons must reach the supreme planet after leaving this body.

In summary, the universal form of Kṛṣṇa, which is a temporary manifestation, and the form of time, which devours everything, and even the form of Viṣṇu, four-handed, have all been exhibited by Kṛṣṇa. Thus Kṛṣṇa is the origin of all these manifestations. It is not that Kṛṣṇa is a manifestation of the original *viśva-rūpa*, or Viṣṇu. Kṛṣṇa is the origin of all other forms. There are hundreds and thousands of Viṣṇus, but for a devotee no form of Kṛṣṇa is important except the original form, two-handed Śyāmasundara. In the *Brahma-saṁhitā* it is stated that those who are attached to the Śyāmasundara form of Kṛṣṇa by love and devotion can see Him always within the heart and cannot see anything else. One should understand, therefore, that the purport of this Eleventh Chapter is that the form of Kṛṣṇa is essential and supreme.

Thus end the Bhaktivedanta purports to the Eleventh Chapter of the *Śrīmad Bhagavad-gītā* in the matter of the Universal Form.

CHAPTER TWELVE

Devotional Service

1. Arjuna inquired: Of those who are properly engaged in Your devotional service and those who worship the impersonal Brahman, the unmanifested, which is considered to be more perfect?

PURPORT

Kṛṣṇa has now explained about the personal, the impersonal and the universal and has described all kinds of devotees and *yogīs*. Generally, the transcendentalists can be divided into two classes. One is the impersonalist, and the other is the personalist. The personalist devotee engages himself with all energy in the service of the Supreme Lord. The impersonalist also engages himself, not directly in the service of Kṛṣṇa but in meditation on the impersonal Brahman, the unmanifested.

We find in this chapter that of the different processes for realization of the Absolute Truth, *bhakti-yoga*, devotional service, is the highest. If one at all desires to have the association of the Supreme Personality of Godhead, then he must take to devotional service.

In the Second Chapter of *Bhagavad-gītā*, it was explained by the Supreme Lord that a living entity is not the material body; he is a spiritual spark. And the Absolute Truth is the spiritual whole. Now, qualitative equality of the spiritual whole and the spiritual spark exists.

In the Seventh Chapter of *Bhagavad-gītā* it was said that if the living entity, being part and parcel of the supreme whole, transfers his attention fully and only to the supreme whole, Kṛṣṇa, he is the most perfect of all *yogīs*. Then again in the Eighth Chapter it was said that anyone who thinks of Kṛṣṇa at the time of quitting his body is at once transferred to the spiritual sky, to the abode of Kṛṣṇa. And at the end of the Sixth Chapter the Lord clearly said that of all *yogīs*, one who always thinks of Kṛṣṇa within himself is considered the most perfect. So in practically every chapter the conclusion has been that one should be attached to the personal form of Kṛṣṇa, for that is the highest spiritual realization.

Nevertheless, there are those who are not attached to the personal form of Kṛṣṇa. They are so firmly detached that even in the preparation of commentaries to *Bhagavad-gītā*, they want to distract other people from Kṛṣṇa and transfer all devotion to the impersonal *brahmajyoti*. They prefer to meditate on the impersonal form of the Absolute Truth, which is beyond the reach of the senses and is not manifest.

And so, factually, there are two classes of transcendentalists. Now Arjuna is trying to settle the question of which process is easier and which of the classes is most perfect. In other words, he is clarifying his own position because he is attached to the personal form of Kṛṣṇa. He is not attached to the impersonal Brahman, and so he wants to know whether his position is secure. The impersonal manifestation, either in this material world or in the spiritual world of the Supreme Lord, is a problem for meditation. Practically no one is able to conceive perfectly of the impersonal feature of the Absolute Truth. Therefore, Arjuna wants to say, "What is the use of such a waste of time?" Arjuna experienced in the Eleventh Chapter that to be attached to the personal form of Kṛṣṇa is best because he could thus understand all other forms at the same time and there was no disturbance to his love for Kṛṣṇa. This important question asked of Kṛṣṇa by Arjuna will clarify the distinction between the impersonal and personal conceptions of the Absolute Truth.

2. The Supreme Personality of Godhead said: He whose mind is fixed on My personal form, always engaged in worshiping Me with great and transcendental faith, is considered by Me to be most perfect.

3-4. But those who fully worship the unmanifested, that which lies beyond the perception of the senses, the all-pervading, inconceivable, fixed, and immovable—the impersonal conception of the Absolute Truth—by controlling the various senses and being equally disposed everywhere, such persons, engaged in the welfare of all, at last achieve Me.

5. For those whose minds are attached to the unmanifested, impersonal feature of the Supreme, advancement is very troublesome. To make progress in that unmanifested discipline is always difficult for those who are embodied.

PURPORT

The group of transcendentalists who follow the path of the inconceivable, unmanifested, impersonal feature of the Supreme Lord are called *jñāna-yogīs,* and persons who are in full Kṛṣṇa consciousness, engaged in devotional service to the Lord, are called *bhakti-yogīs.* Now, here the difference between *jñāna-yoga* and *bhakti-yoga* is definitely expressed. The process of *jñāna-yoga,* although ultimately bringing one to the same goal, is very troublesome, whereas the path of *bhakti-yoga,* the process of direct service to the Supreme Personality of Godhead, is easier and is natural for the embodied soul. The individual soul is embodied since time immemorial. It is very difficult for him to simply theoretically understand that he is not the body. Therefore, the *bhakti-yogī* accepts the Deity of Kṛṣṇa as worshipable because there is some bodily conception fixed in the mind, which can thus be applied. Of course, worship of the Supreme Personality of Godhead in His form within the temple is not idol worship. There is evidence in the Vedic literature that worship may be *saguṇa* and *nirguṇa*—of the Supreme possessing or not possessing attributes. Worship of the Deity in the temple is *saguṇa* worship, in which the Lord is represented by material qualities. But the form of the Lord, even when represented by the material qualities such as stone, wood or oil paint, is not actually material. That is the absolute nature of the Supreme Lord.

A crude example may be given here. We may find some mailboxes on the street, and if we post our letters in those boxes, they will naturally go to their destination without difficulty. But any old box, or an imitation we may find somewhere, which is not authorized by the post office, will not do the work. Similarly, God has an authorized representation in the Deity form, which is called *arcā-vigraha.* This *arcā-vigraha* is an incarnation of the Supreme Lord. God will accept service through that form. The Lord is omnipotent and all-powerful; therefore, by His incarnation as *arcā-vigraha* He can accept the services of the devotee, just to make it convenient for the man in conditioned life.

So for a devotee there is no difficulty in approaching the Supreme immediately and directly, whereas for those who are following the impersonal way to spiritual realization, the path is difficult. They have to understand the unmanifested representation of the Supreme through such Vedic literature as the *Upaniṣads*, and they have to learn the language, understand the nonperceptual feelings, and realize all these processes. This is not very easy for a common man. A person in Kṛṣṇa consciousness, engaged in devotional service, simply by the guidance of the bona fide spiritual master, simply by offering regulative obeisances unto the Deity, simply by hearing the glories of the Lord, and simply by eating the remnants of foodstuffs offered to the Lord, realizes the Supreme Personality of Godhead very easily. There is no doubt that the impersonalists are unnecessarily taking a troublesome path, with the risk of not realizing the Absolute Truth at the ultimate end. But the personalist, without any risk, trouble or difficulty, approaches the Supreme Personality directly. A similar passage appears in *Śrīmad-Bhāgavatam*, where it is said that if ultimately one has to surrender unto the Supreme Personality of Godhead (this surrendering process is called *bhakti*), but instead one takes the trouble to understand what is Brahman and what is not Brahman, spending his whole life in that way, the result is simply troublesome. Therefore, it is advised here that one should not take up this troublesome path of self-realization because there is uncertainty in the ultimate result.

A living entity is eternally an individual soul, and if he wants to merge into the spiritual whole, he may accomplish the realization of the eternal and knowledgeable aspects of his original nature, but the blissful portion is not realized. By the grace of some devotee, such a transcendentalist, highly learned in the process of *jñāna-yoga*, may come to the point of *bhakti-yoga*, or devotional service. At that time, long practice in impersonalism also becomes a source of trouble because he cannot give up the idea. Therefore, an embodied soul is always in difficulty with the unmanifest, at the time of practice and at the time of realization. Every living soul is partially independent, and one should know certainly that this unmanifested realization is against the nature of his spiritual, blissful self. One should not take up this process. For every individual living entity the process of Kṛṣṇa consciousness, in which one fully engages in devotional service, is the best way. If one wants to ignore this devotional service, there is the danger of turning to atheism. In the modern age, when impersonal philosophy has received so much stress, people are turning to atheism in great numbers. Therefore, this process of centering attention on the unmanifested, the inconceivable, which is beyond the approach of the senses, as already expressed in this verse, should never be encouraged at any time, especially in this age. It is not advised by Lord Kṛṣṇa.

6-7. For one who worships Me, giving up all his activities unto Me and being devoted to Me without deviation, engaged in devotional service and always meditating upon Me, who has fixed his mind upon Me, O son of Pṛthā, for him I am the swift deliverer from the ocean of birth and death.

8. Just fix your mind upon Me, the Supreme Personality of Godhead, and engage all your intelligence in Me. Thus you will live in Me always, without a doubt.

9. My dear Arjuna, O winner of wealth, if you cannot fix your mind upon Me without deviation, then follow the regulated principles of *bhakti-yoga*. In this way you will develop a desire to attain to Me.

PURPORT

In this verse, two different processes of *bhakti-yoga* are indicated. The first applies to one who has actually developed an attachment for Kṛṣṇa, the Supreme Personality of Godhead, by transcendental love. And the other is for one who has not developed an attachment for the Supreme Person by transcendental love. For this second class there are different prescribed rules and regulations, which they can follow to be ultimately elevated to the stage of attachment.

Bhakti-yoga means purification of the senses. At the present moment in material existence the senses are always impure, being engaged in sense gratification. But by the practice of *bhakti-yoga*, these senses can become purified, and in the purified state the senses become directly connected with the Supreme Lord. In this material existence, I may be engaged in some service to some master, but I don't really lovingly serve my master. I serve to get some money. And the master also is not in love; he takes service from me and pays me. So there is no question of love. But for spiritual life we have to be elevated to the pure stage of love. That stage of love can be achieved by practice of devotional service, performed with the present senses.

This love of God is now in a dormant state in everyone's heart. And, there, love of God is manifested in different ways, but it is contaminated by the material association. Now the material association has to be purified, and that dormant, natural love for Kṛṣṇa has to be revived. That is the whole process.

10. If you cannot practice the regulations of *bhakti-yoga*, then just try to work for Me, because by working for Me you will come to the perfect stage.

PURPORT

One who is not able even to practice the regulated principles of *bhakti-yoga* under the guidance of a spiritual master can still be drawn to this perfectional stage by working for the Supreme Lord. How to do this work has already been explained in the fifty-fifth verse of the Eleventh Chapter. One should be sympathetic to the propagation of Kṛṣṇa consciousness. There are many devotees engaged in the propagation of Kṛṣṇa consciousness, and they require help. So even if one cannot directly practice the regulated principles of *bhakti-yoga*, he can try to help such work. Every endeavor requires land, capital, organization and labor. Just as, in business, one requires a place to stay, some capital to use, some labor and some organization to expand, so the same is required in the service of Kṛṣṇa. The only difference is that in materialism one works for sense gratification. The same work, however, can be performed for the satisfaction of Kṛṣṇa. That is spiritual activity. If one has sufficient money, he can help in building an office or temple for propagating Kṛṣṇa consciousness. Or he can help with publication work. There are various fields of activity, and one should be interested in such activities. If one cannot sacrifice the result of such activities, the same person can still sacrifice some percentage to propagate Kṛṣṇa consciousness. This voluntary service to the cause of Kṛṣṇa consciousness will help one to rise to a higher state of love for God, whereupon one becomes perfect.

11. If, however, you are unable to work in Kṛṣṇa consciousness, then try to act giving up all the results of your work, and be self-situated.

PURPORT

If there are impediments to accepting Kṛṣṇa consciousness, one may try to give up the results of his actions. In that respect, social service, community service, national service, sacrifice for the country and so on may be accepted so that someday he may come to the stage of pure devotional service to the Supreme Lord. In *Bhagavad-gītā* we find it stated that to try to serve the supreme cause, although not knowing that it is Kṛṣṇa who is the cause of all causes, will bring one ultimately to the goal.

12. If you cannot take to this practice, then engage yourself in the cultivation of knowledge. Better than knowledge, however, is meditation, and better than meditation is renunciation of the fruits of action, for by such renunciation one may have peace of mind.

PURPORT

To reach the Supreme Personality of Godhead, the highest goal, there are two processes. One is by gradual development, and the other is direct. Devotional service in Kṛṣṇa consciousness is the direct method, and the other method is to first renounce the result of one's activities, then come to the stage of knowledge, then come to the stage of meditation, then come to the stage of understanding the Supersoul, and then come to the stage of knowing the Supreme Person. One may take the step-by-step process or the direct path. But the direct process is not possible for everyone, and so the indirect method is also useful. It is better, however, to accept the direct process of chanting the holy name of Lord Kṛṣṇa.

13-14. One who is not envious but is a kindly friend to all creatures, who does not think himself a proprietor, who is free from false ego and equal both in happiness and distress, who is always satisfied and engaged in devotional service with determination, and whose mind and intelligence are fixed upon Me—he is very dear to Me.

15. He for whom no one is put into difficulty and who is not disturbed by anxiety, who is steady in happiness and distress, is very dear to Me.

16. A devotee who is not dependent on the ordinary course of activities, who is pure, expert, without cares, free from all pains and not striving for some result is very dear to Me.

17. One who does not grasp either pleasure or grief, who neither laments nor desires, and who renounces both auspicious and inauspicious things, is very dear to Me.

18-19. One who is equal to friends and enemies, who is equipoised in honor and dishonor, heat and cold, happiness and distress, fame and infamy, who is always free from contamination, always silent, and satisfied with anything, who doesn't care for any residence, who is fixed in knowledge and engaged in devotional service, is very dear to Me.

PURPORT

A devotee is free from all bad association. Sometimes one is praised and sometimes defamed; that is the nature of human society. But a devotee is always transcendental to such artificial reputation and defamation, distress or happiness. He is very patient, and he does not speak except on the topics of Kṛṣṇa. Therefore, he is called silent. Silent does not mean that one should not speak at all. Silent means one should not speak nonsense. One should speak only of the essential, and the most essential speech for the devotee is to speak for the Supreme Lord. A devotee is happy in all conditions. Sometimes he may get very luxurious foodstuffs, and sometimes he may not, but he is satisfied. He does not care for any residential facility. He may sometimes live underneath a tree, and he may sometimes live in a very palatial building; neither of them has any special attraction for him. He is called fixed because he is fixed in his determination and knowledge. We may find some repetition in the descriptions of the qualifications of a devotee, but that is meant to emphasize that a devotee must acquire all these qualities. Without good qualifications one cannot be a pure devotee. And, again, there is no good qualification in a person who is not a devotee. Therefore, one who wants to be recognized as a devotee must develop these qualifications. Of course, he does not extraneously endeavor to acquire each one, but his engagement in Kṛṣṇa consciousness and devotional service automatically helps him to develop these symptoms.

20. He who follows this imperishable path of devotional service and completely engages himself with faith, making Me the supreme goal, is very, very dear to Me.

PURPORT

Regarding the question of who is better—one engaged in the pursuit of the impersonal Brahman or one engaged in the personal service of the Supreme Personality of Godhead—the Lord replied quite explicitly, saying that there is no doubt that devotional service to the Personality of Godhead is the best of all processes for spiritual realization. The impersonal conception of the Supreme Absolute Truth, as described in this chapter to dispel the doubts of Arjuna, is recommended only up to the time when one can surrender himself for self-realization. In other words, as long as one does not have the chance for association with a pure devotee, the impersonal conception may be good.

Thus end the Bhaktivedanta purports to the Twelfth Chapter of the *Śrīmad Bhagavad-gītā* in the matter of Devotional Service.

CHAPTER THIRTEEN

Nature, the Enjoyer, and Consciousness

1-2. Arjuna said: O my dear Kṛṣṇa, I wish to know about *prakṛti* [nature], *puruṣa* [the enjoyer], and the field and the knower of the field, and of knowledge and the end of knowledge. Then the Lord said: This body, O son of Kuntī, is called the field, and one who knows this body is called the knower of the field.

PURPORT

Arjuna was inquisitive about *prakṛti* (nature), *puruṣa* (the enjoyer), *kṣetra* (the field), *kṣetrajña* (its knower), and about knowledge and the object of knowledge. When he inquired about all these, Kṛṣṇa said that this body is called the field and that one who knows this body is called the knower of the field. This body is the field of activity for the conditioned soul. The conditioned soul is entrapped in material existence, attempting to lord it over the material nature, and so, according to his capacity to lord it over the material nature, he gets a field of activity. That field of activity is this body. And what is this body? This body is made of senses. The conditioned soul wants to enjoy sense gratification, and according to his capacity to enjoy sense gratification, he is offered a body, or field of activity. Therefore, the body is called *kṣetra*, or the field of activity for the conditioned soul. Now the person who does not identify himself with this body is called *kṣetrajña*, the knower of the field. It is not very difficult to understand the difference between the field and its knower, the body and the knower of the body. Any person can consider that from his childhood to old age he has undergone so many changes of body and yet is still one person remaining. Then the difference between the knower of the field of activities and the actual field of activities becomes clear.

In the first six chapters of *Bhagavad-gītā*, the knower of the body, the living entity, is very nicely described, and the position needed to understand the Supreme Lord is also described. The middle six chapters of the *Gītā* describe the Supreme Personality of Godhead and the relationship between the individual soul and the Supersoul in regard to devotional service. The superior position of the Supreme Personality of Godhead and the subordinate position of the individual soul are definitely described in these chapters. The living entities are subordinate under all circumstances, but in their forgetfulness they are suffering. When enlightened by pious activities, they approach the Supreme Lord in different capacities—as the distressed, those in want of money, the inquisitive, and those in search of knowledge. Now, starting with the Thirteenth Chapter, how the living entity comes into contact with material nature and how he is delivered by the Supreme Lord through different methods of fruitive activity, cultivation of knowledge and the discharge of devotional service will be nicely explained. Although the living entity is completely different from his material body, he somehow becomes related to it. This will also be explained.

3. O scion of Bharata, you should understand that I am also the knower in all bodies, and to understand this body and its owner is called knowledge. That is My opinion.

PURPORT

The Lord says that He is also the knower of the field of activities in every individual body. I may be knower of my body, but I am not in knowledge of other bodies. The Supreme Personality of Godhead, however, who is present as Supersoul in my body, knows everything about my body and about other bodies as well. He knows all the different bodies of all the various species of life. A citizen may know everything about his patch of land, but the king knows not only his palace, but all the properties possessed by the individual citizens. Similarly, one may be the proprietor of his individual body, but the Supreme Lord is the proprietor of all bodies. The king is the original proprietor of the kingdom, and the citizen is the secondary proprietor. Similarly, the Supreme Lord is the supreme proprietor of all bodies.

The body consists of senses. The Supreme Lord is called Hṛṣīkeśa, which means the controller of the senses. He is the original controller of the senses, just as the king is the original controller of all the activities of the state; the citizens are secondary controllers. Therefore when the Lord says, "I am also the knower," this means that He is the superknower; the individual soul knows only his particular body. Now, the distinction between the field of activities, the owner of those activities and the supreme owner of activities is described as follows. Perfect knowledge of the constitution of the body, the individual soul and the Supersoul, understood in terms of the Vedic literature, is called knowledge. That is the opinion of Kṛṣṇa. One should not misunderstand the soul and the Supersoul to be one.

4. Now please hear My brief description of this field of activity, and how it is constituted, what its changes are, whence it is produced, who that knower of the field of activities is, and what his influences are.

5. That knowledge of the field of activities and of the knower of activities is described by various sages in various Vedic writings—especially in the *Vedānta-sūtra*—and is presented with all reasoning as to cause and effect.

PURPORT

The Supreme Personality of Godhead, Kṛṣṇa, is the highest authority in explaining this knowledge. Still, as a matter of course, learned scholars and standard authorities always give evidence from previous authorities. Kṛṣṇa is explaining this most controversial point regarding the duality and nonduality of the soul and the Supersoul by referring to the scriptures, the *Vedānta*, which is accepted as an authority. We are all transcendental, although we are in material bodies. Now we have fallen into the ways of the three modes of material nature according to our different *karma*. As such, some of us are on higher levels and some on lower ones.

This higher or lower nature of the individual is due to ignorance, and it is being manifested in an infinite number of living entities. But the Supersoul, which is infallible, is free from contamination by the three qualities of nature and is therefore transcendental.

In the original *Vedas*, a distinction between the soul, the Supersoul and the body is made, especially in the *Kaṭha Upaniṣad.* There is a manifestation of the Supreme Lord's energy known as *annamaya,* dependence upon food for existence. This is a materialistic realization of the Supreme. Then, in *prāṇamaya,* after realizing the Supreme Absolute Truth in food, one can realize the Absolute Truth in the living symptoms or life forms. In *jñānamaya,* realization extends beyond the living symptoms to the point of thinking, feeling and willing. Then there is Brahman realization, *vijñānamaya,* in which the living entity's mind and life symptoms are distinguished from the living entity himself. The next and supreme stage is *ānandamaya,* realization of the all-blissful nature. Thus there are five stages of Brahman realization, which are called *brahma-puccham.* Out of these the first three—*annamaya, prāṇamaya* and *jñānamaya*—pertain to the fields of activities of the living entities. Transcendental to all these fields of activities is the Supreme Lord, who is called *ānandamaya.* The *Vedanta-sūtra* also describes the Supreme by saying, *ānandamayo 'bhyāsāt:* the Supreme Personality of Godhead is by nature full of joy. To enjoy His transcendental bliss, He expands into *vijñānamaya, jñānamaya, prāṇamaya* and *annamaya.* In the field of activities the living entity is considered the enjoyer, and different from him is the *ānandamaya.* This means that if the living entity decides to enjoy by dovetailing himself with the *ānandamaya,* he becomes perfect. This is the real picture of the Supreme Lord as the supreme knower of the field, the living entity as the subordinate knower, and the nature of the field of activities.

6-7. The five great elements, false ego, intelligence, the unmanifested, the ten senses, the mind, the five sense objects, desire, hatred, happiness, distress, the aggregate, the life symptoms, and convictions—all these are considered, in summary, to be the field of activities and its interactions.

8-12. Humility, pridelessness, nonviolence, tolerance, simplicity, approaching a bona fide spiritual master, cleanliness, steadfastness and self-control; renunciation of the objects of sense gratification, absence of false ego, perception of the evil of birth, death, old age and disease; non-attachment to children, wife, home and so on, and equilibrium of the mind; devotion to the service of the Lord, the aspiration to live in a solitary place, detachment from the general mass of people; accepting the importance of self-realization, and philosophical search for the Absolute Truth—all these are an aggregate called knowledge, and besides this whatever there may be is ignorance.

PURPORT

This process of knowledge is sometimes misunderstood by less intelligent men to be the interactions of the field of activity. But actually this is the real process of knowledge. If one accepts this process, then the possibility of approaching the Absolute Truth exists. This is not the interaction of the twenty-four elements, as described before. This is actually the means to get out of the entanglement of those elements. The embodied soul is entrapped by the body, which is a casing made of the twenty-four elements, and the process of knowledge as described here is the means to get out of it. Of all the descriptions of the process of knowledge, the most important point is described in the first line of the tenth verse: the process of knowledge terminates in unalloyed devotional service to the Lord. If one does not approach, or is not able to approach, the transcendental service of the Lord, then the other nineteen items are of no particular value. But if one takes to devotional service in full Kṛṣṇa consciousness, the other nineteen items automatically develop within him. The principle of accepting a spiritual master, as mentioned in the eighth verse, is essential. Even for one who takes to devotional service, it is most important. The beginning of transcendental life is to accept a bona fide spiritual master. The Supreme Personality of Godhead, Śrī Kṛṣṇa, clearly states here that this process of knowledge is the actual path. Anything speculated beyond this is nonsense.

As for the knowledge outlined here, the items may be analyzed as follows. Humility means that one should not be anxious to have the satisfaction of being honored by others. The material conception of life makes us very eager to receive honor from others, but from the point of view of a man in perfect knowledge, who knows that he is not this body, anything pertaining to this body, including honor and dishonor, is useless. One should not hanker after this material deception. People are very anxious to be famous for their religion, and consequently it is sometimes found that without understanding the principles of religion, one enters into some group which is not actually following religious principles and then wants to advertise himself as a religious mentor. As for actual advancement in spiritual science, one should have a test to see how far he is progressing. He can judge by these items.

Nonviolence is generally taken to mean not killing or destroying the body, but actually nonviolence means not putting others into distress. People in general are trapped by ignorance in the material concept of life, and they perpetually suffer material pains. So if one does not elevate people to spiritual knowledge, one is practicing violence. One should try his best to distribute real knowledge to the people, so that they may become enlightened and leave this material entanglement. That is nonviolence.

Tolerance means one should be practiced to bear insults and dishonor from others. If one is engaged in the advancement of spiritual knowledge, there will be many insults and much dishonor from others. This is expected because material nature is so constituted. Even a boy like Prahlāda, who although only five years old was engaged in the cultivation of spiritual knowledge, was endangered when his father became antagonistic to his devotion. The father wanted to kill him in so many ways, but Prahlāda tolerated him. So there may be many impediments to advancement in spiritual knowledge, but we should be tolerant and continue our progress with determination.

Simplicity means that without diplomacy one should be so straightforward that he can disclose the real truth even to an enemy. As for acceptance of the spiritual master, that is essential, because without the instruction of a bona fide spiritual master, one cannot progress in spiritual science. One should approach the spiritual master with all humility and offer him all services so that he will be pleased to bestow his blessings upon the disciple. Because a bona fide spiritual master is a representative of Kṛṣṇa, if he bestows any blessings upon his disciple, that will make the disciple immediately advanced without the disciple's following the regulative principles. Or, the regulative principles will be easier for one who has served the spiritual master without reservation.

Cleanliness is essential for making advancement in spiritual life. There are two kinds of cleanliness: external and internal. External cleanliness means taking a bath and washing the body, but for internal cleanliness one must think of Kṛṣṇa always and chant Hare Kṛṣṇa, Hare Kṛṣṇa, Kṛṣṇa Kṛṣṇa, Hare Hare/ Hare Rāma, Hare Rāma, Rāma Rāma, Hare Hare. This process cleans the accumulated dust of past *karma* from the mind.

Steadfastness means that one should be very determined to make progress in spiritual life. Without such determination one cannot make any tangible progress. And self-control means that one should not accept anything detrimental to the path of spiritual progress. One should become accustomed to rejecting anything against the path of spiritual progress. Next comes the question of renunciation. The senses are so strong that they are always anxious to have sense gratification. One should not cater to these demands, which are unnecessary. The senses should be gratified only to keep the body fit so that one can discharge his duty in advancing in spiritual life. The most important and uncontrollable sense is the tongue. If one can control the tongue, then there is every possibility of controlling the other senses. The function of the tongue is to taste and to vibrate. Therefore, by systematic regulation, the tongue should always be engaged in tasting the remnants of foods offered to Kṛṣṇa and chanting Hare Kṛṣṇa. As far as the eyes are concerned, they should not be allowed to see anything but the beautiful form of Kṛṣṇa. That will control the eyes. Similarly, the ears should be engaged in hearing about Kṛṣṇa and the nose smelling flowers offered to Kṛṣṇa. This is devotional service, and it is understood here that the *Bhagavad-gītā* is simply meant to expand the science of devotional service. Devotional service is the main and sole objective. Unintelligent commentators try to divert the mind of the reader to other subjects, but there is no other subject in the *Bhagavad-gītā* than devotional service.

False ego means accepting this body as oneself. When one understands that he is not this body and is spirit soul, he comes to his real ego. Ego is there. False ego is condemned, but not real ego. In the Vedic literature it is said, *ahaṁ brahmāsmi:* I am Brahman, I am spirit. This "I am," this sense of self, also exists in the liberated stage of self-realization. This sense of "I am" is ego, but when the sense of "I am" is applied to this false body, it is false ego. When the sense of self is applied to reality, that is real ego. There are some philosophers who say we should give up our ego. But we cannot give up our ego, because ego means identity. We ought, of course, to give up the false identification with the body. One should also try to understand the distress of accepting birth, death, old age and disease.

As for detachment from children, wife, and home, it is not meant that one should have no feeling for these. They are natural objects of affection, but when they are not favorable to spiritual progress, then we should not be attached to them. The best process for making the home nice is to live in Kṛṣṇa consciousness. If one is in full Kṛṣṇa consciousness, he can make his home very happy because this process of Kṛṣṇa consciousness is very easy. One need only chant Hare Kṛṣṇa, Hare Kṛṣṇa, Kṛṣṇa Kṛṣṇa, Hare Hare/ Hare Rāma, Hare Rāma, Rāma Rāma, Hare Hare, accept the remnants of foods offered to Kṛṣṇa, have some discussion on books like *Bhagavad-gītā* and *Śrīmad-Bhāgavatam*, and engage oneself in Deity worship. These four things will make one happy, and one should train the members of his family in this way. The family members can sit down morning and evening and chant together Hare Kṛṣṇa, Hare Kṛṣṇa, Kṛṣṇa Kṛṣṇa, Hare Hare/ Hare Rāma, Hare Rāma, Rāma Rāma, Hare Hare. If one can mold his family life in such a nice way for developing Kṛṣṇa consciousness by following these four principles, then there is no need to change from family life to renounced life. But if it is not congenial, not favorable for spiritual advancement, then family life should be abandoned. In all cases, one should be detached from the happiness and distress of family life because this world can never be fully happy or fully miserable. Happiness and distress are concomitant factors of material life.

13. I shall now explain to you the knowable, knowing which you will taste the eternal. This is beginningless and subordinate to Me. It is called Brahman, the spirit, and it lies beyond the cause and effect of this material world.

14. Everywhere are His hands and legs, His eyes and faces, and He hears everything. In this way the Supersoul exists.

15. The Supersoul is the original source of all senses, yet He is without senses. He is unattached, although He is the maintainer of all living beings. He transcends the modes of nature, and at the same time is the master of all modes of material nature.

PURPORT

The Supreme Lord, although the source of all the senses of the living entities, does not have material senses like they have. Actually, the individual souls have spiritual senses, but in conditioned life they are covered by the material elements, and therefore the sense activities are exhibited through matter. The Supreme Lord's senses are not covered. His senses are transcendental and are therefore called *nirguṇa*. *Guṇa* means the material modes, but His senses have no material covering. It should be understood that His senses are not exactly like ours. Although He is the source of all our sensual activities, He has transcendental senses, which are not contaminated by matter.

16. The Supreme Truth exists both internally and externally, in the moving and the nonmoving. He is beyond the power of the material senses to see or to know. Although far, far away, He is also near to all.

17. Although the Supersoul appears to be divided, He is never divided. He is situated as one. Although He is the maintainer of every living entity, it is to be understood that He devours and develops.

18. He is the source of light in all luminous objects. He is beyond the darkness of matter and is unmanifested. He is knowledge, He is the object of knowledge, and He is the goal of knowledge. He is situated in everyone's heart.

19. Thus the field of activities [the body], knowledge, and the knowable have been summarily described by Me. Only My devotees can understand this thoroughly and thus attain to My nature.

20. The material nature and the living entities should be understood to have no beginning. The transformations and modes of matter are produced of the material nature.

21. Nature is said to be the cause of all material activities and effects, whereas the living entity is the cause of the various sufferings and enjoyments in this world.

22. The living entity in material nature thus follows the ways of life, enjoying the three modes of nature. This is due to his association with that material nature. Thus he meets with good and evil among the various species.

PURPORT

This verse of the *Gītā* is very important for an understanding of how the living entities transmigrate from one body to another. It was explained in the Second Chapter that the living entity is transmigrating from one body to another just as though changing his dress. This change of dress is due to his attachment to material existence. As long as he is captivated by this false manifestation, he has to continue going from one body to another. Due to his desire to lord it over the material nature, he is put into such undesirable circumstances. Under the influence of material desire, the entity is born sometimes as a demigod, sometimes as a man, sometimes as a beast, as a bird, as a worm, as an aquatic, as a saintly man, as a bug and so on. Nevertheless, under the influence of material nature, one thinks himself the master of his circumstances.

How he is put into such different bodies is explained here. It is due to association with the different qualities or modes of nature. One has to rise, therefore, above the three material modes and be situated in the transcendental position. That is called Kṛṣṇa consciousness. Unless one is situated in Kṛṣṇa consciousness, his material consciousness will oblige him to transfer from one body to another. He has had material desires since time immemorial, but now he has to change his conceptions. That change can be effected only if one hears from authoritative sources. The best example is here: Arjuna is hearing the science of God from Kṛṣṇa. The living entity, if he submits to this hearing process, will lose his long-cherished desire to lord it over the material nature, and gradually he will come to enjoy spiritual happiness.

23. In this body there is another, a transcendental enjoyer, who is the Lord, the supreme proprietor, who exists as overseer and permitter, and who is known as the Supersoul.

24. One who understands this philosophy of the material nature, the living entity, and the interaction of the modes of nature is sure to attain liberation. He will not take birth here again, regardless of his position.

25. That Supersoul is perceived by some through meditation, by some through the cultivation of knowledge, and by others through working without fruitive desire.

26. Again, there are those not conversant in spiritual knowledge who, by hearing from others, begin to worship the Supreme Person. Because of their tendency to hear from authorities, they also transcend the path of birth and death.

PURPORT

This verse is particularly applicable to modern society because in modern society there is practically no education in spiritual matters. Some people may appear atheistic, agnostic or philosophical, but actually there is no knowledge of philosophy. As for the common man, if he is a good soul there is a chance for advancement simply by hearing. This hearing process is very important. Lord Caitanya, who preached Kṛṣṇa consciousness in the modern world, gave great stress to hearing because if the common man simply hears from authoritative sources, he can progress. Hearing the transcendental vibration Hare Kṛṣṇa, Hare Kṛṣṇa, Kṛṣṇa Kṛṣṇa, Hare Hare/ Hare Rāma, Hare Rāma, Rāma Rāma, Hare Hare is most beneficial. Lord Caitanya has said that in this age one does not require to change his position, but he should give up the endeavor to understand the Absolute Truth by speculative reasoning. One should learn to become a servant of those who are in knowledge of the Supreme Lord. If one is fortunate enough to take shelter of the guidance of a pure devotee, hear from him about self-realization, and follow in the footsteps of such an authority, he will gradually be elevated to the position of a pure devotee.

27. O chief of the Bhāratas, whatever you see in existence, whether moving or unmoving, is only a combination of the field of activities and the knower of the field.

28. One who sees the Supersoul accompanying the individual soul in all bodies and understands that neither the soul nor the Supersoul is ever destroyed actually sees.

PURPORT

After the destruction of the body, both the soul and the Supersoul exist, and they go on eternally in many various moving and unmoving forms. Here the Sanskrit word *parameśvara* is sometimes translated as "the individual soul" because the soul is the master of the body and he transfers to another form after the destruction of the body. But there are others who interpret this *parameśvara* as Supersoul. In either case, both the Supersoul and the individual soul continue. They are not destroyed. One who can see in this way can actually see what is happening.

29. One who sees the Supersoul in every living being and equal everywhere does not degrade himself by his mind. Thus he approaches the transcendental destination.

30. One who can see that all activities are done by the body, which is created of material nature, and that he himself does nothing, actually sees.

31. When a sensible man ceases to see different identities due to different material bodies, he attains to the Brahman conception. Thus he sees that beings are expanded everywhere.

32. Those with the vision of eternity can see that the soul is transcendental, eternal, and beyond the modes of nature. In spite of his contact with the material body, O Arjuna, he is not doing anything, nor is he entangled.

33. Because of its subtle nature, the sky, although all-pervading, does not mix with anything. Similarly, the soul, situated in Brahman vision, does not mix with the body, though situated in that body.

34. O son of Bharata, as the sun alone illuminates all this universe, so does the living entity, one within the body, illuminate the entire body by consciousness.

PURPORT

There are various theories regarding consciousness. Here *Bhagavad-gītā* gives the example of the sun and the sunshine. As the sun is situated in one place but is illuminating the whole universe, so a small particle of spirit soul, although situated in the heart of this body, is illuminating the whole body by consciousness. Therefore, consciousness is the proof of the presence of the soul, as the sunshine is the proof of the presence of the sun. When the soul is present in the body, there is consciousness all over the body, and as soon as the soul has passed from the body, there is no more consciousness. This can be easily understood by any intelligent man. Therefore, consciousness is not a product of combinations of matter. It is the symptom of the living entity. Although qualitatively one with the supreme consciousness, the consciousness of the living entity is not supreme because the consciousness of one particular body does not share that of another body. But the Supersoul, which is situated in all bodies as the friend of the individual soul, is conscious of all bodies. That is the difference between supreme consciousness and individual consciousness.

35. One who knowingly sees this difference between the body and owner of the body and can understand the process of liberation from this bondage attains to the supreme goal.

PURPORT

The purport of this Thirteenth Chapter is that one should know the distinction between the body, the owner of the body, and the Supersoul. One should also recognize the process of liberation, as described in verses eight through twelve. Then one can attain the supreme destination.

A faithful person should at first have some good association in which to hear of God. By such good association, one gradually becomes enlightened and thus accepts the spiritual master in order to be guided for advancement in spiritual science. By such association and instruction, under the guidance of the spiritual master, he can distinguish between matter and spirit, and that becomes the stepping-stone for further spiritual realization. By various instructions, the spiritual master teaches his students to be free from the material concept of life, just as in *Bhagavad-gītā* we find Kṛṣṇa instructing Arjuna.

One can understand that this body is matter; it can be analyzed, with its twenty-four elements. The body is a gross manifestation. Its subtle manifestation consists of mental and psychological effects. The symptoms of life are interactions of these bodily features. But over and above this, there is the soul, and there is also the Supersoul. The soul and the Supersoul are two. This material world is working because of the conjunction of the soul and the twenty-four material elements. One who can see the constitution of the whole material manifestation in this combination of the soul and material elements and also see the situation of the Supreme Soul becomes eligible for transfer to the spiritual world. These things are meant for contemplation and for realization. One should have a serious understanding of this chapter, with the help of the spiritual master.

Thus end the Bhaktivedanta purports to the Thirteenth Chapter of the *Śrīmad Bhagavad-gītā* in the matter of Nature, the Enjoyer, and Consciousness.

Plate 36 Seeing the universal form of the Lord, Arjuna began to pray with folded hands. *(pp.180–183)*

Plate 37 The Supreme Personality of Godhead, Śrī Kṛṣṇa, displayed His real four-armed form to Arjuna, and at last showed him His two-armed form. *(p.188)*

Plate 38 Kṛṣṇa delivers His unalloyed devotee from the ocean of birth and death.
(p.199)

Plate 39 The Supersoul is the original source of all senses. He is unattached, although He is the maintainer of all living beings. He transcends the modes of nature, and at the same time He is the master of all modes of material nature. *(p.213)*

late 40 The three modes of nature are the cause of all material activities.
p.223–224)

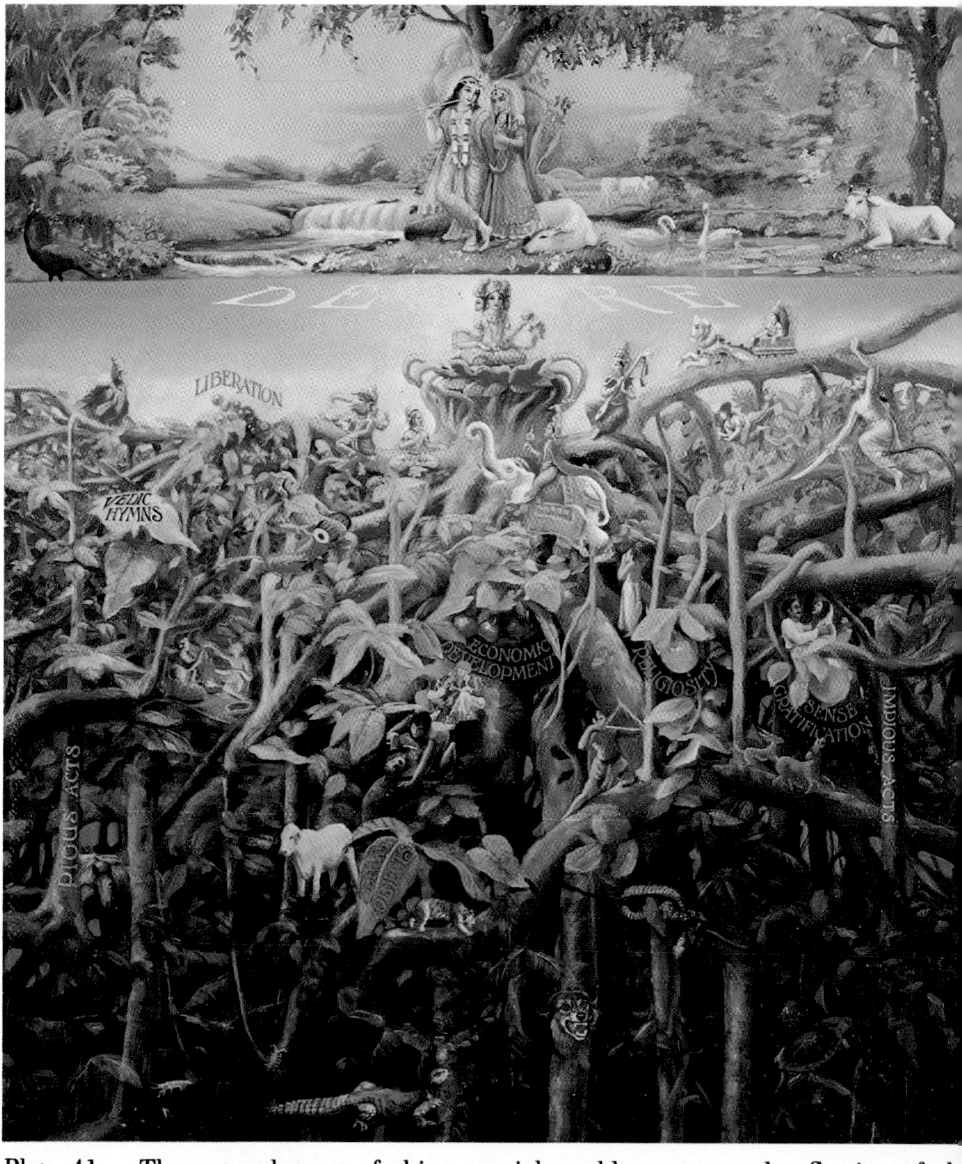

Plate 41 The entanglement of this material world, a perverted reflection of th spiritual world, is compared to a banyan tree. *(pp.227–228)*

Plate 42 The spiritual and material worlds. *(p.230)*

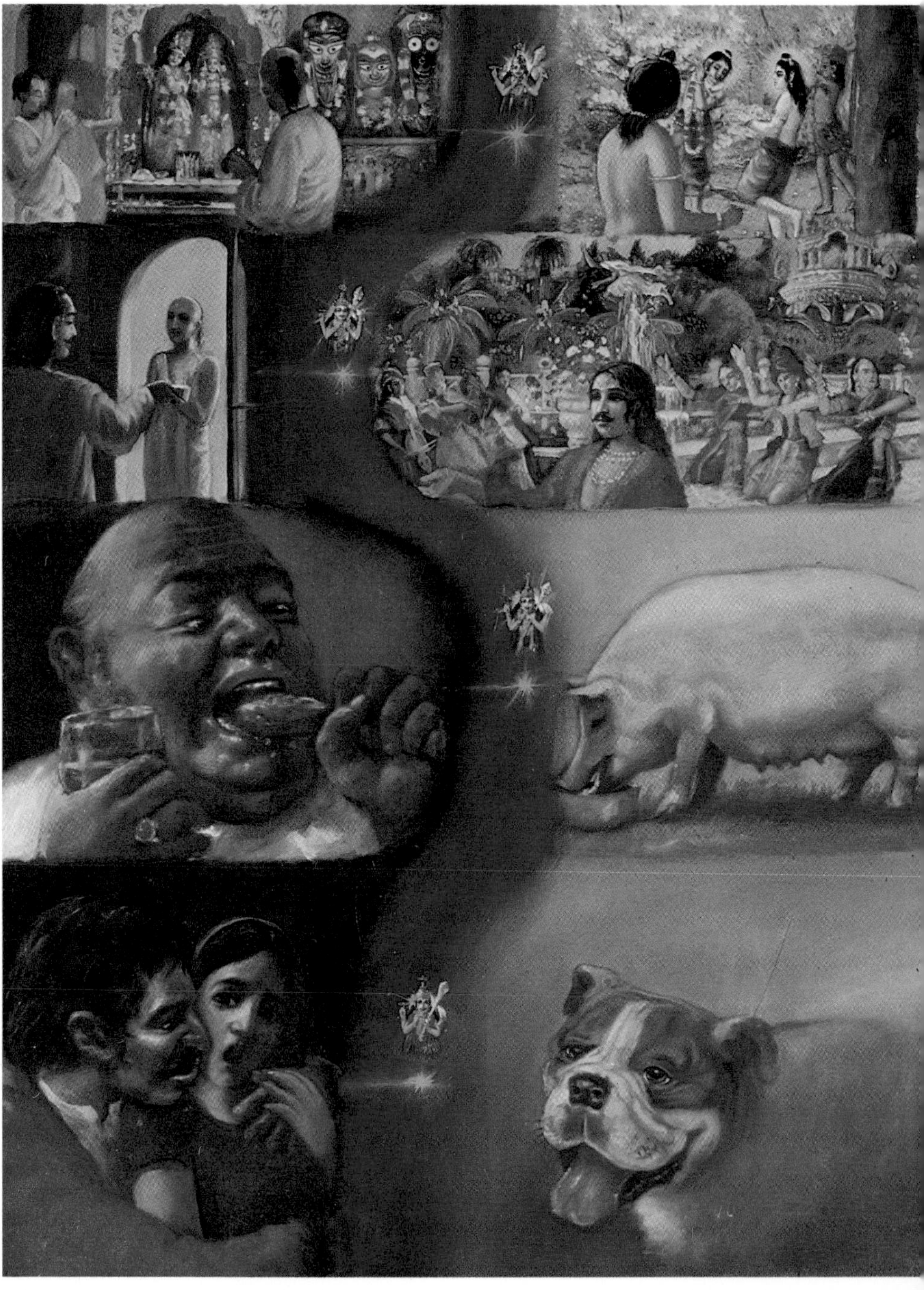

Plate 43 At the time of death the consciousness created by the living being will carry him to the next body. *(pp.230–231)*

Plate 44 The transcendental qualities lead to liberation, whereas the demoniac qualities lead to bondage. *(p.236)*

Plate 45 The demoniac, taking shelter of insatiable lust, pride and false prestige, and being thus illusioned, are always sworn to unclean work, attracted by the impermanent. *(pp.238–240)*

Plate 46 Those who are in the mode of goodness worship the demigods, those in the mode of passion worship the demons, and those in the mode of darkness worship the dead and the ghosts. *(pp.246–247)*

Plate 47 Foods in the three modes of nature. ("You are what you eat.") *(pp.248–249)*

Plate 48 The place of action, the senses, the performer, the endeavor, and the Supersoul—these are the five factors of action. *(p.258)*

Plate 49 By worship of the Lord, man can, in the performance of his own duty, become perfect. (*pp.263–264*)

late 50 "Always think of Me and become My devotee. Worship Me and offer your omage unto Me." (p.270)

Plate 51 Wherever there is Kṛṣṇa, the master of all mystics, and wherever there Arjuna, the supreme archer, there will also certainly be opulence, victory, extr ordinary power, and morality. *(pp.273–274)*

CHAPTER FOURTEEN

The Three Modes of Material Nature

1. The Supreme Personality of Godhead said: Again, I shall declare to you this supreme wisdom, the best of all knowledge, knowing which all the sages have attained to supreme perfection.

PURPORT

From the Seventh Chapter to the end of the Twelfth Chapter, Lord Kṛṣṇa has revealed the Absolute Truth, the Supreme Personality of Godhead. Now, the Lord Himself is further enlightening Arjuna. If one understands this chapter through the process of philosophical speculation, he will come to an understanding of devotional service. In the Thirteenth Chapter, it was clearly explained that by developing knowledge with an attitude of humility, one may be freed from material entanglement. It has also been explained that it is due to association with the modes of nature that the living entity is entangled in this world. Now, in this chapter, the Supreme Personality will explain what those modes of nature are, how they act, how they bind, and how they give liberation. The knowledge explained in this chapter is said by the Supreme Lord to be better than the knowledge given so far in other chapters. By understanding this knowledge, various great sages have attained perfection and transferred to the spiritual world.

2. By becoming fixed in this knowledge, one can attain to the transcendental nature, like My own, and not to be born at the time of creation or disturbed at the time of dissolution.

PURPORT

The particular meaning of this verse is that after acquiring perfect transcendental knowledge, one acquires qualitative equality with the Supreme Personality of Godhead, becoming free from the repetition of birth and death. One does not, however, lose his identity as an individual soul. It is understood from Vedic literature that the liberated souls who have reached the transcendental planets of the spiritual sky always look to the lotus feet of the Supreme Lord, being engaged in His transcendental loving service. Even after liberation, such devotees do not lose their individual identities.

3. The total material substance, called Brahman, is the source of birth, and in that Brahman I create pregnancy. Thus come the possibilities for the births of all living beings.

PURPORT

The scorpion lays its eggs in piles of rice, and sometimes it is said that the scorpion is born out of rice. But the rice is not the cause of the scorpion. Actually the eggs were laid by the mother. Similarly, material nature is not the cause of birth of the living entities. The seeds are given by the Supreme Personality of Godhead, and they only seem to come out as products of material nature. Thus every living entity, according to his past activities, has a different body, created by this material nature, so that he can enjoy or suffer according to those deeds. The Lord is the cause of all the manifestations of living entities in this material world.

4. It should be understood that all species of life, O son of Kuntī, are made possible by birth in this material nature, and that I am the seedgiving father.

5. Material nature consists of the three modes—goodness, passion and ignorance. When the living entity comes in contact with nature, he becomes conditioned by these modes.

6. O sinless one, the mode of goodness, being purer than the others, is illuminating, and it frees one from all sinful reactions. Those situated in that mode develop knowledge and become conditioned by the sense of happiness.

PURPORT

The difficulty here is that when a living entity is situated in the mode of goodness, he becomes conditioned to feeling that he is advanced in knowledge and is better than others. The best examples are the scientist and the philosopher. Each is very proud of his knowledge, and because he generally improves his living conditions, he feels a sort of material happiness. This sense of advanced happiness in conditioned life binds him to the mode of goodness of material nature. As such, he is attracted toward working in the mode of goodness, and as long as he has an attraction for working in that way, he has to take some type of body in the modes of nature. There is no likelihood of liberation or of being transferred to the spiritual world. He may repeatedly become a philosopher, a scientist or a poet and repeatedly be involved in the same disadvantages of birth and death. But due to the illusion of the material energy, he thinks that sort of life is nice.

7. The mode of passion is born of unlimited desires and longings, O son of Kuntī, and because of this, one is bound to material, fruitive activities.

PURPORT

The mode of passion is exemplified in the attraction between man and woman. Woman has an attraction for man, and man has an attraction for woman. And when the mode of passion is increased, one develops the hankering for material enjoyment. For sense gratification, a man in the mode of passion wants some honor in society or in his nation, and he wants to have a happy family, with nice children, a wife, and a house. These are the products of the development of the mode of passion. As long as one hankers after these things, he has to work very hard. Therefore it is clearly stated here that he becomes associated with the fruits of his activities and thus becomes bound by such activities. The whole material world is more or less in the mode of passion. Modern civilization is considered to be advanced in the standards of this mode.

although formerly the advanced condition was considered to be in the mode of goodness. Since there is no liberation even in the mode of goodness, what can be said of those entangled in passion?

8. O son of Bharata, the delusion of all living entities is the mode of ignorance. The results of this mode are madness, indolence and sleep, which bind the conditioned soul.

PURPORT

This mode of ignorance is just the opposite of the mode of goodness. In the mode of goodness, by development of knowledge, one can understand what is what. But everyone under the spell of the mode of ignorance becomes mad, and a madman cannot understand what is what. Instead of making advancement, one becomes degraded. For example, everyone can see that his grandfather has died, and therefore he will die; man is mortal. The children that he has fathered will also die. So death is sure. Still, people are madly accumulating money and working very hard all day and night, not caring for the eternal spirit. This is madness. In their madness, they are very reluctant to make advancement in spiritual understanding. Such people are very lazy. When they are invited to associate for spiritual understanding, they are not much interested. They are not even active like the man conducted by the mode of passion. Thus another symptom of one embedded in the mode of ignorance is that he sleeps more than required. Six hours of sleep is sufficient, but a man in the mode of ignorance sleeps at least ten or twelve hours a day. Such a man appears to be always dejected and is addicted to intoxicants and sleeping.

9. The mode of goodness conditions one to happiness, passion conditions him to the fruits of action, and ignorance to madness.

10. Sometimes the mode of passion becomes prominent, defeating the mode of goodness, O son of Bharata, and sometimes the mode of goodness defeats passion. Again, sometimes the mode of ignorance defeats goodness and passion. In this way, there is ever a competition for supremacy.

11. The manifestation of the mode of goodness can be experienced when all the gates of one's body are illuminated by knowledge.

PURPORT

There are nine gates in the body: two eyes, two ears, two nostrils, the mouth, the genital and the anus. In the mode of goodness, one can see things in the right perspective and can properly hear and taste. One becomes cleansed inside and outside. At every gate there is the development of the symptoms of happiness, and that is the position of goodness.

12. O chief of the Bhāratas, when there is an increase in the mode of passion, the symptoms of great attachment, uncontrollable desire, hankering and intense endeavor develop.

13. O son of Kuru, when there is an increase in the mode of ignorance, madness, illusion, inertia and darkness are manifested.

14. When one dies in the mode of goodness, he attains to the pure higher planets.

15. One who dies in the mode of passion takes birth among those engaged in fruitive activities, and one who dies in the mode of ignorance takes birth in the animal kingdom.

PURPORT

Some people have the impression that when the soul reaches the platform of human life, he never goes down again. This is incorrect. According to this verse, if one develops the mode of ignorance, after his death he is degraded to the animal form of life. From there one has to again elevate himself by the evolutionary process to come to the human form of life. Therefore, those who are actually serious about human life should take to the mode of goodness.

16. By acting in the mode of goodness, one becomes purified. Works done in the mode of passion result in distress, and actions performed in the mode of ignorance result in foolishness.

17. From the mode of goodness real knowledge develops; from the mode of passion, greed develops; and from the mode of ignorance, foolishness, madness and illusion develop.

18. Those situated in the mode of goodness gradually go upward to the higher planets; those in the mode of passion live on the earthly planets; and those in ignorance go down to the hellish worlds.

19. When you see that there is nothing beyond these modes of nature in all activities and that the Supreme Lord is transcendental to these modes, then you can know My spiritual nature.

PURPORT

One can transcend all these activities of the modes of material nature simply by understanding them properly by learning from the proper souls. The real spiritual master is Kṛṣṇa, and He is imparting this spiritual knowledge to Arjuna. Similarly, it is from those who are fully Kṛṣṇa conscious that one has to learn this science of the real situation of activities in terms of the modes of nature. Otherwise, his life is very wrong. By the instruction of a bona fide spiritual master, a living entity can know of his spiritual position, his material body, his senses, how he is entrapped and how he is under the spell of the material modes of nature. He is helpless, being in the grip of these modes. But when he can see his real position, then he can attain to the transcendental platform, having the scope for spiritual life. Actually, the living entity is not the performer of different activities. He is forced to act because he is situated in a particular type of body, conducted by some particular mode of material nature. Unless one has the help of spiritual authority, he cannot understand what position he is actually in. But with the association of a bona fide spiritual master, he can see his real position, and by such an understanding he can become fixed in full Kṛṣṇa consciousness. A man in Kṛṣṇa consciousness is not controlled by the spell of the material modes of nature. It has already been stated in the Seventh Chapter that one who has surrendered to Kṛṣṇa is relieved from the activities of material nature. Therefore for one who is able to see things as they are, the influence of material nature slowly ceases.

20. When the embodied being is able to transcend these three qualities, he can become free from birth, death, old age and their distresses and can enjoy nectar even in this life.

21. Arjuna inquired: O my dear Lord, by what symptoms is one known who is transcendental to those qualities? What is his behavior? And how does he transcend the modes of nature?

22-25. The Supreme Personality of Godhead said: He who neither hates nor desires the development of the three qualities of illumination, attachment and delusion, who is transcendentally situated, remaining neutral through all the reactions of the modes, thinking that they may work but that he is transcendental; he who looks equally upon happiness and distress, upon a pebble, a stone or a piece of gold, who is equal toward the desirable and the undesirable, who is steady and well situated in defamation or in adoration; he who receives honor and dishonor equally, who treats friend and enemy alike and who is not engaged in material activities—he is said to have transcended the three modes of nature.

26. One who is engaged in full devotional service, unfailing in all circumstances, at once transcends the modes of material nature and thus comes to the level of Brahman.

27. And I am the basis of the impersonal Brahman, which is immortal, imperishable and eternal and which is the constitutional position of ultimate happiness.

PURPORT

Brahman is the beginning of transcendental realization; Paramātmā, the Supersoul, is the middle, the second stage of transcendental realization; and the Supreme Personality of Godhead is the ultimate realization of the Absolute Truth. Therefore, both Paramātmā and the impersonal Brahman are within the Supreme Person. It is explained in the Seventh Chapter that material nature is the manifestation of the inferior energy of the Supreme Lord. Impregnating the inferior, material nature with fragments of the superior nature is the spiritual touch. When a living entity conditioned by material nature begins the cultivation of spiritual knowledge, he elevates himself from the position of material existence and gradually rises up to the Brahman conception of the Supreme. This attainment of the Brahman conception of life is the first stage in self-realization. At this stage the Brahman-realized person is transcendental to the material position, but he is not actually perfect in realization. If he wants, he can continue to stay in the Brahman position and then gradually rise to the Paramātmā realization, and then to realization of the Supreme Personality of Godhead. There are many examples of this in Vedic literature. The four Kumāras were situated first in the impersonal Brahman conception of truth, but then they gradually rose to the platform of devotional service.

One who cannot elevate himself from the impersonal conception of Brahman to the higher stage of the personal conception of God runs the risk of falling down. In the *Śrīmad-Bhāgavatam* it is stated that a person may rise to the stage of impersonal Brahman, but, without going further, with no information of the Supreme Person, his intelligence is not perfectly clear. Therefore, in spite of being raised to the Brahman platform, there is the chance of falling down if one is not engaged in the devotional service of the Lord. When one understands the Personality of Godhead, the reservoir of pleasure, Kṛṣṇa, he actually becomes transcendentally blissful. The Supreme Lord is full in six opulences, and when a devotee approaches Him, there is reciprocation with these opulences. The servant of the king enjoys on an almost equal level with the king. Therefore imperishable happiness and eternal life accompany devotional service. All conceptions of Brahman, eternity and imperishability are included in devotional service. They are all subordinate for a person engaged in the devotional service of the Lord.

Thus end the Bhaktivedanta purports to the Fourteenth Chapter of the *Śrīmad Bhagavad-gītā* in the matter of the Three Modes of Material Nature.

CHAPTER FIFTEEN

The Yoga of the Supreme Person

1. The Supreme Lord said: There is a banyan tree which has its roots upward and its branches down and whose leaves are the Vedic hymns. One who knows this tree is the knower of the *Vedas.*

PURPORT

After discussing the importance of *bhakti-yoga,* one may question, What about the *Vedas?* It will be explained in this chapter that the purpose of Vedic study is to understand Kṛṣṇa. Therefore, one who is in Kṛṣṇa consciousness, engaged in devotional service, is already in knowledge of the *Vedas.* The entanglement of this material world is compared here to a banyan tree. For one who is engaged in fruitive activities, there is no end to the banyan tree. He wanders from one branch to another, to another, to another. The tree of this material world has no end, and one who is attached to this tree has no possibility of liberation. The Vedic hymns, meant for elevating oneself, are called the leaves of this tree. This tree's roots are upward because they begin from where Brahmā is located, which is the topmost planet of this universe. One should understand this indestructible tree of illusion, and then one can break away from it. This should be understood. In the previous chapters it has been explained that there are many processes to get out of material entanglement. And, up to the Thirteenth Chapter, we have seen that devotional service to the Supreme Lord is the best way. Now, the basic principle of devotional service is detachment from material activities and attachment to the transcendental service of the Lord. The root of this material existence is upward. This means that it begins from the total material substance, from the topmost planet of the universe. From there the whole universe is expanded, with so many branches, representing the various planetary systems. The fruits are the results of the living entities' activities. They include religion, economic development, sense gratification and liberation. One should have a thorough understanding of this imperishable tree.

Now, we have no ready experience in this world of a tree situated with its branches down and its roots upward, but there is such a thing. That tree can be found when we go to a reservoir of water. We can see that the trees on the bank are reflected upon the water—branches down, roots up. In other words, the tree of this material world is only a reflection of the real tree. The real tree is the spiritual world. The reflection of the real tree is situated on desire, as the tree's reflection is situated on water. One who wants to get out of this material existence must know this tree thoroughly, through analytical study. Then he can cut off the relationship with it.

2. The branches of this tree extend downward and upward, nourished by the three modes of material nature. The twigs are the objects of the senses, and this tree also has roots going down, bound to the fruitive actions of human society.

3. The real form of this tree cannot be perceived in this world. No one can understand where it ends, where it begins, or where its foundation is. Using the weapon of detachment one must cut down this banyan tree with determination.

4. Thereafter, one must seek that situation from which, having gone, one never comes back. One must surrender to that Supreme Personality of Godhead from whom everything has begun and is extending since time immemorial.

5. One who is free from illusion, false prestige and false association, who understands the eternal, who is done with material lust, who is freed from the duality of happiness and distress, and who knows how to surrender unto the Supreme Person attains to that eternal kingdom.

PURPORT

The surrendering process is described here very nicely. The qualification is that one should be out of the illusion of false prestige. The conditioned soul is puffed up, thinking himself the Lord of material nature. It is therefore very difficult for him to surrender unto the Supreme Personality of Godhead. One should know, by the cultivation of real knowledge, that he is not the lord of the material nature; the Supreme Personality of Godhead is the Lord. For one who is always expecting some honor in this material world, it is not possible to surrender to the Supreme Person. This false prestige is due to illusion. One comes here for some time and then goes away, living here only briefly, but still he has the foolish notion that he is the lord of the world. He thus makes all things complicated, and he is always in trouble. The whole world moves under this impression. People are considering that the land, this earth, belongs to human society, and they have divided the land according to their mental concoction, under the false impression that they are the proprietors. One has to get out of this false notion that human society is the proprietor of this world. When one is freed from such a false notion, he becomes free from all false associations caused by familial, social and national affections. These faulty associations bind one to this material world. After this stage, one has to develop spiritual knowledge. One has to cultivate knowledge of what is actually his own and what is actually not his own. And when one has understanding of things as they are, he becomes free from all conceptions of happiness and distress. He comes into full knowledge; then it is possible to surrender to the Supreme Personality of Godhead.

6. That abode of Mine is not illumined by the sun or moon, nor by electricity. One who reaches it never comes back to this material world.

PURPORT

The description of the spiritual world and of the abode of the Supreme Personality of Godhead, Kṛṣṇa—which is known as Kṛṣṇaloka, Goloka Vṛndāvana—is described here. In the spiritual sky there is no need of sunshine, moonshine or electricity, because all the planets there are self-luminous. We have only one planet in this universe, the sun, which is self-luminous, but all the planets in the spiritual sky are self-luminous. The shining effulgence of all those self-luminous planets (called Vaikuṇṭhas) is the shining sky known as the *brahmajyoti.* Actually, the effulgence is emanating from the planet of Kṛṣṇa, Goloka Vṛndāvana. Part of that shining effulgence is covered by this *mahat-tattva,* the material world. Other than this, the major portion of that shining sky is full of spiritual planets, which are called Vaikuṇṭhas, one of which is Goloka Vṛndāvana. As long as a living entity is in this dark material world, he is in conditional life, but as soon as he reaches the spiritual sky by cutting through the false, perverted tree of this world, he becomes liberated. Then there is no chance of his coming back here.

7. The living entities in this conditional world are My fragmental parts, and they are eternal. But due to conditioned life, they are struggling very hard with the six senses, which include the mind.

PURPORT

In this verse, the identity of the living being is clearly mentioned. The living entities are fragmental parts and parcels of the Supreme Lord—eternally. They do not assume individuality in conditioned life and become one with the Supreme Lord in the liberated state. Each is eternally fragmented.

8. The living entity in the material world carries his different conceptions of life as the air carries aromas. Thus he takes one kind of body and again quits it to take another.

PURPORT

Here the living entity is described as *īśvara,* the controller of his own body. If he likes, he can change his body to a higher grade, and if he likes, he can move to a lower class. Minute independence is there. The change of his body depends on him. The process is that at the time of death, the consciousness he has created will carry him on to the next type of body. If he has made his consciousness like that of a cat or dog, he is sure to change from his human body to a cat's or a dog's body. If he has fixed his consciousness on godly qualities, he will change into the form of a demigod. And if he changes his consciousness into Kṛṣṇa consciousness, he will be transferred to Kṛṣṇaloka in the spiritual world and be with Kṛṣṇa.

9. The living entity, thus taking another gross body, obtains a particular type of ear, tongue, nose, and sense of touch, centered about the mind. He thus enjoys a particular set of sense objects.

PURPORT

Consciousness is originally pure, like water. But if we mix water with a certain color, it changes. Similarly, consciousness is pure, for the spirit soul is pure, but consciousness is changed according to the association of the material qualities. Real consciousness is Kṛṣṇa consciousness. When, therefore, one is situated in Kṛṣṇa consciousness, he is in his pure life. Otherwise, if his consciousness is adulterated by some type of material mentality, in the next life he gets a corresponding body.

10. The foolish cannot understand how a living entity can quit his body, or what sort of body he enjoys under the spell of the modes of nature. But one whose eyes are trained in knowledge can see this.

11. The endeavoring transcendentalist, who is situated in self-realization, can see all this clearly. But those who are not situated in self-realization, though they may try, cannot see what is taking place.

12. The splendor of the sun, which dissipates the darkness of this universe, is due to Me. And the splendor of the moon and the splendor of fire are also from Me.

13. I enter into each planet, and by My energy these stay in orbit. I become the moon and thereby supply the juice of life to all vegetables.

PURPORT

It is due to the Supreme Personality of Godhead that the moon nourishes all vegetables. Due to the moon's influence, the vegetables become delicious. Without the moonshine, vegetables can neither grow nor taste succulent. Human society is working, living comfortably and enjoying food due to the supply from the Supreme Lord. Otherwise, mankind could not survive. Everything becomes palatable by the agency of the Supreme Lord through the influence of the moon.

14. I am the fire of digestion in every living body, and I am the air of life, outgoing and incoming, by which I digest the four kinds of foods.

15. I am seated in everyone's heart, and from Me come remembrance, knowledge and forgetfulness. By all the *Vedas*, I am to be known. I am the compiler of *Vedānta*, and I know the *Vedas* as they are.

16. There are two classes of beings, the fallible and the infallible. In the material world every entity is called fallible, and in the spiritual world every entity is called infallible.

PURPORT

Here the Lord is giving, in summary, the contents of the *Vedānta-sūtra*. He says that the living entities, who are innumerable, can be divided into two classes—the fallible and the infallible. The living entities are eternally separated parts and parcels of the Supreme Personality of Godhead. When they are in contact with the material world, they are called *jīva-bhūtāḥ*, and the Sanskrit words given here, *sarvāṇi bhūtāni*, mean that they are fallible. Those who are in oneness with the Supreme Personality of Godhead, however, are called infallible. Oneness means not that they have no individuality, but that there is no disunity. They are all agreeable to the purpose of the Lord.

17. Besides these two, there is the greatest living personality, the Lord Himself, who has entered into these worlds and is maintaining them.

18. Because I am transcendental, beyond both the fallible and the infallible, and because I am the greatest, I am celebrated both in the world and in the *Vedas* as that Supreme Person.

19. Anyone who knows Me as the Supreme Personality of Godhead, without doubting, is to be understood as the knower of everything, and he therefore engages himself in full devotional service, O son of Bharata.

PURPORT

There are many philosophical speculations about the constitutional position of the living entities and the Supreme Absolute Truth. Now, in this verse, the Supreme Personality of Godhead clearly explains that anyone who knows Lord Kṛṣṇa as the Supreme Person is actually the knower of everything. The difference between a perfect knower and an imperfect knower is that the imperfect knower simply goes on speculating about the Absolute Truth, but the perfect knower, without wasting his valuable time, engages directly in Kṛṣṇa consciousness, the devotional service of the Supreme Lord. Throughout the whole of *Bhagavad-gītā*, this fact is being stressed at every step. And yet there remain so many stubborn commentators on *Bhagavad-gītā* who unnecessarily try to make the Supreme Absolute Truth and the living entities one and the same.

20. This is the most confidential part of the Vedic scriptures, O sinless one, disclosed now by Me. Anyone who understands this will become wise, and his endeavors will know perfection.

PURPORT

The Lord clearly explains here that this is the substance of all revealed scriptures. One should understand this as it is given by the Supreme Personality of Godhead. Thus one will become intelligent and perfect in transcendental knowledge. In other words, by understanding this philosophy of the Supreme Personality of Godhead and engaging oneself in His transcendental service, everyone can become freed from all contaminations of the modes of material nature. Devotional service is a process of spiritual understanding. Whenever such devotional service exists, material contamination cannot coexist. Devotional service to the Lord and the Lord Himself are one and the same because they are spiritual, manifesting the internal energy of the Supreme Lord.

The Lord is said to be the sun, and ignorance is called darkness. Where sun is present, there is no question of darkness. Therefore, whenever devotional service is present under the proper guidance of a bona fide spiritual master, there is no question of ignorance.

Thus end the Bhaktivedanta purports to the Fifteenth Chapter of the *Śrīmad Bhagavad-gītā* in the matter of the *Yoga* of the Supreme Person.

CHAPTER SIXTEEN

The Divine and Demoniac Natures

1-3. The Supreme Personality of Godhead said: Fearlessness, purification of one's existence, cultivation of spiritual knowledge, charity, sense control, performance of sacrifice, study of the *Vedas*, austerity, simplicity, nonviolence, truthfulness, freedom from anger, renunciation, peacefulness, aversion to faultfinding, compassion toward every living entity, freedom from greed, gentleness, shyness, determination, vigor, forgiveness, fortitude, cleanliness, and freedom from both envy and the passion for honor—these are the transcendental qualities, born of the godly atmosphere, O son of Bharata.

PURPORT

In the beginning of the Fifteenth Chapter, the banyan tree of this material world was explained. The extra roots coming out of it were compared to the activities of the living entities, some auspicious, some inauspicious. In the Ninth Chapter, also, the *devas*, or godly, and the *asuras*, the ungodly, or demons, were explained. Now, according to Vedic rites, activities in the mode of goodness are considered auspicious for progress on the path of liberation, and such activities are known as *daiva-prakṛti*, transcendental by nature. Those who are situated in the transcendental nature are making progress on the path of liberation. For those who are acting in the modes of passion and ignorance, on the other hand, there is no possibility of liberation. Either they will have to remain in this material world as human beings, or they will descend among the species of animals or other, even lower forms of life. In this Sixteenth Chapter the Lord explains the transcendental nature and its attendant qualities, as well as the demoniac nature and its qualities. He also explains the advantages and disadvantages of these qualities.

4. Those who are born with demoniac qualities exhibit pride, arrogance, false prestige, anger, harshness and ignorance, O son of Pṛthā.

PURPORT

In this verse, the royal road to hell is described. The demoniac want to make a show of religion and advancement in spiritual science, although they do not follow the principles. They are always arrogant, proud of possessing some type of education or wealth. Desiring to be worshiped by others, they demand respect, although they do not command respect. Over trifles they grow very angry, and they speak harshly, not gently. They do not know what should be done and what should not be done. They do everything whimsically, according to their own desire, and they do not recognize any authority. These demoniac qualities are taken by them from the beginning of their bodies in the wombs of their mothers, and as they grow they manifest all these inauspicious qualities.

5. The transcendental assets lead to liberation, whereas the demoniac assets are meant for bondage. But do not worry, O son of Pāṇḍu, for you are born with transcendental qualities.

6. O son of Pṛthā, in this world there are two kinds of created beings. One is called divine and the other demoniac. I have already explained to you at length the divine qualities; now I shall describe the demoniac.

7. Those who are of demoniac quality do not know what is to be done and what is not to be done. They are unclean, they do not know how to behave, nor is there any truth in them.

8. They say that this world is unreal, that there is no foundation and that there is no God in control. It is produced of sex desire and has no other cause than lust.

PURPORT

The demoniac conclude that the creation of the world is a phantasmagoria. There is no cause or effect, no controller, no purpose: everything is unreal. As the will-o'-the-wisp is caused by certain atmospheric changes, so this cosmic manifestation is due to chance material actions and reactions. That is their conclusion. They do not think that the world was created by God for a certain purpose. They have their own theory: that the world has come about in its own way and that there is no reason to believe that there could be a God behind it. For them there is no difference between spirit and matter, and they do not accept the Supreme Spirit. Everything is matter only, and the whole cosmos is supposed to be a mass of ignorance. According to them, everything is void, and whatever manifestation exists is due to our ignorance in perception. They take it for granted that all manifestation of diversity is a display of ignorance. Just as in a dream we may create so many things which actually have no existence, so when we are awakened we shall see that everything is simply a dream. But factually, although the demons say that life is a dream, they are very expert in enjoying this dream. And so instead of getting knowledge, they become more and more implicated in their dreamland.

9. Following such conclusions, the demoniac, lost to themselves and without intelligence, engage in unbeneficial, horrible works meant to destroy the world.

PURPORT

The demoniac are engaged in activities that will lead the world to destruction. The Lord states here that they are less intelligent. The materialists, who have no concept of God, think that they are advancing. But according to the *Bhagavad-gītā*, they are unintelligent and devoid of all sense. They try to enjoy this material world to the utmost limit and therefore always engage in inventing something for sense gratification. Such materialistic inventions are considered the advancement of human civilization, but the result is that the people are growing more and more violent and more and more cruel, cruel to animals and cruel to other human beings. They have no idea of how to behave toward one another. Animal killing is very prominent among demoniac people.

Such people are considered the enemies of the world because ultimately they invent or create something that will bring destruction to all. Indirectly, this verse points to the invention of nuclear weapons, for which the whole world is today very proud. At any moment war may take place, and these atomic weapons may create havoc. Such things are created solely for the destruction of the world, and this is indicated in *Bhagavad-gītā*. Due to godlessness, such weapons are invented in human society; they are not meant for the peace and prosperity of the world.

10. Taking shelter of insatiable lust, pride and false prestige and being thus illusioned, the demoniac are always sworn to unclean work, attracted by the impermanent.

11. Their belief is that to gratify the senses until the end of life is the prime necessity of human civilization. Thus there is no measurement for their anxiety.

PURPORT

The demoniac accept that the enjoyment of the senses is the ultimate goal of life, and this concept they maintain until death. They do not believe in life after death, and they do not believe there are different grades of bodies, according to one's *karma*, or activities in this world. Their plans for life are never finished; they go on preparing plan after plan, all of which are never finished. We have personal experience of a person of such demoniac mentality, who, even at the point of death, was requesting the physician to prolong his life for four years more because his plans were not yet complete. Such foolish people do not know that a physician cannot prolong life even for a moment. When the notice is there, there is no consideration of the man's desire. The laws of nature allow not even a second beyond what one is destined to enjoy.

12. Being bound by hundreds and thousands of desires, by lust and anger, they secure money by illegal means for sense gratification.

13-15. The demoniac person thinks: "So much wealth do I have today, and I will gain more according to my schemes. So much is mine now, and it will increase in the future, more and more. He is my enemy, and I have killed him, and my other enemy will also be killed. I am the Lord of everything, I am the enjoyer, I am perfect, powerful and happy. I am the richest man, surrounded by aristocratic relatives. There is none so powerful and happy as I am. I shall perform sacrifices, I shall give some charity, and thus I shall rejoice." In this way, such persons are deluded by ignorance.

16. Thus perplexed by various anxieties and bound by a network of illusions, one becomes too strongly attached to sense enjoyment and falls down into hell.

PURPORT

The demoniac man has no limit to his desire to acquire money. For that reason, he does not mind acting in any sinful way. Thus he deals on the black market for illegal gratification. He is enamored by the possessions he already has, such as land, family, house and bank balance, and he is always thinking of improving them. He believes in his own strength, and he has no knowledge that whatever he is gaining is due to his past good deeds. He is given the opportunity to accumulate such things, but he has no conception of the past causes. He simply thinks that all his mass of wealth is due to his own endeavor. A demoniac person believes in the strength of his personal work, not in the law of *karma*. According to the law of *karma*, a man takes his birth in a high family or becomes rich, very well educated, or very beautiful because of good work in the past. The demoniac thinks that all these things are accidental and due to the strength of one's personal ability. He does not sense any arrangement behind the varieties of people, beauty and education. Anyone who comes into competition with such a demoniac man is his enemy. There are many demoniac people, and each is enemy to the others. This enmity becomes more and more deep—between persons, then between families, then between societies, and at last between nations. Therefore there is constant strife, war, and enmity all over the world.

Each demoniac person thinks that he can live at the sacrifice of all others. Generally, a demoniac person thinks of himself as the Supreme

God, and demoniac preachers instruct their followers: "Why are you seeking God elsewhere? You are all yourselves God! Whatever you like you can do. Don't believe in God. Throw God away. God is dead." These are their preachings.

The best example of a demoniac man was Rāvaṇa, whose history is in the narrative of the *Rāmāyaṇa.* He offered a program to the people by which he would prepare a staircase so that anyone could reach the heavenly planets without performing sacrifices such as those prescribed in the *Vedas.* Similarly, in the present age, such demoniac men are striving to reach the higher planetary systems by mechanical arrangements. These are examples of the bewilderment of the demoniac. The result is that without their knowledge they are gliding toward hell. Here the Sanskrit word *moha-jāla* is very significant. *Jāla* means net; like fishes caught in a net, they have no way to come out.

17. Self-complacent and always impudent, deluded by wealth and false prestige, they sometimes perform sacrifices in name only, without following any rules or regulations.

18. Bewildered by false ego, strength, pride, lust and anger, the demon becomes envious of the Supreme Personality of Godhead, who is situated in his own body and in others, and blasphemes against the real religion.

PURPORT

A demoniac person, being always against the existence of God's supremacy, does not like to believe in the scriptures. He is envious of both the scriptures and the existence of the Supreme Personality of Godhead because of his so-called prestige and his accumulation of wealth and strength. He does not know that the present life is a preparation for the next life. Not knowing this, he is actually envious of his own self, as well as of others. He commits violence on other bodies and on his own. He does not care for the supreme control of the Personality of Godhead because he has no knowledge. Being envious of the scriptures and the Supreme Personality of Godhead, he puts forward false logic against the existence of God and refutes the scriptural authority. He thinks himself independent and powerful in every action. He thinks that since no one can equal him in strength, power or wealth, he can therefore act in any way and no one can stop him. If there is any enemy who might check the advancement of his sensual activities, he will plan to cut him down by his own power.

19. Because they are envious and mischievous, the lowest of men, I ever put them back into the ocean of material existence, into various demoniac species of life.

PURPORT

In this verse it is clearly indicated that to put a particular individual soul in a particular body is the prerogative of the supreme will. The demoniac person may not agree to accept the supremacy of the Lord, and it is a fact that he may act according to his own whims, but his next birth will depend upon the decision of the Supreme Personality of Godhead and not on himself. In the *Śrīmad-Bhāgavatam*, Third Canto, it is stated that an individual soul, after his death, is put into the womb of a mother where he gets a particular type of body under the supervision of superior power. Therefore in material existence we find so many species of life—animals, men and so on. This is all arranged by that superior power; it is not accidental. As for the demoniac, it is clearly said here that they are perpetually put into the wombs of demons and thus they continue to be envious, the lowest of mankind. Such demoniac species of life are held to be always full of lust, always violent and hateful and always unclean.

20. Gaining repeated birth among the species of demoniac life, such persons can never approach Me. Gradually they sink down to the most abominable position of existence.

PURPORT

It is known that God is all-merciful, but here we find that God is never merciful to the demoniac. It is clearly stated that the demoniac people, life after life, are put into the wombs of similar demons. Not achieving the mercy of the Supreme Lord, they go down and down so that at last they achieve bodies like those of cats, dogs and hogs. It is clearly stated that such demons have practically no chance of receiving the mercy of

God at any stage of later life. In the *Vedas* also it is stated that such persons gradually go down to become dogs and hogs. It may be argued that God should not be advertised as all-merciful, since He is not merciful to such demons. In answer to this question, in the *Vedānta-sūtra* we find that the Supreme Lord has no hatred or favor for anyone. To put the *asuras*, the demons, into the lowest status of life is simply another feature of His mercy. Sometimes the *asuras* are killed by the Supreme Lord. This killing is also good for them, for in Vedic literature we find that anyone killed by the Supreme Lord is liberated. There are instances in history of many *asuras*—Rāvaṇa, Kaṁsa, Hiraṇyakaśipu—to whom the Lord appeared in various incarnations just to kill them. Therefore, God's mercy is shown to the *asuras* if they are fortunate enough to be killed by Him.

21. There are three gates leading down to hell—lust, anger and greed. Every sane man should give these up, for they lead to the degradation of the soul.

22. One who is freed from these gates to hell, O son of Kuntī, performs acts conducive to his self-realization and thus gradually attains to the supreme destination.

PURPORT

One should be very careful of these three enemies to human life: lust, anger and greed. The more a person is freed from lust, anger and greed, the more his existence becomes pure. Then he can follow the rules and regulations enjoined in the Vedic literature. By following the regulative principles of human life, one gradually raises himself to the platform of spiritual realization. If one is so fortunate, by such practice, to rise to the platform of Kṛṣṇa consciousness, then success is guaranteed for him. In the Vedic literature, the ways of action and reaction are prescribed just to bring one to the stage of purification. The whole method is based on giving up lust, greed and anger. By cultivating knowledge of how to do this, one is elevated to the highest position of self-realization; this self-realization is perfect in devotional service. In devotional service, the liberation of the conditioned soul is guaranteed. Therefore, according to the Vedic system, there are instituted the four orders of life and the four social statuses, called the spiritual order system and the caste system. There are different rules and regulations for different castes or divisions of society, and if a person is able to follow them, he will be automatically raised to the highest platform of spiritual realization. Then he can have liberation without a doubt.

23. One who acts whimsically, not caring for the regulations of the scriptures, can never attain perfection, nor happiness, nor the supreme destination.

24. One should understand what is duty and what is not duty by the regulations of the scriptures. Knowing such rules and regulations, one should act so that he may gradually be elevated.

PURPORT

As stated in the Fifteenth Chapter, all the rules and regulations of the *Vedas* are meant for knowing Kṛṣṇa. If one understands Kṛṣṇa from the *Bhagavad-gītā* and becomes situated in Kṛṣṇa consciousness, engaging himself in devotional service, he has reached the highest perfection of knowledge offered by the Vedic literature. Lord Caitanya Mahāprabhu made this process very easy: He asked people simply to chant Hare Kṛṣṇa, Hare Kṛṣṇa, Kṛṣṇa Kṛṣṇa, Hare Hare/ Hare Rāma, Hare Rāma, Rāma Rāma, Hare Hare and to engage in the devotional service of the Lord and eat the remnants of food offered to the Deity. One who is directly engaged in all these devotional activities should be understood to have studied all the Vedic literature and to have come to the conclusion perfectly. Of course, for ordinary persons who are not Kṛṣṇa conscious or engaged in devotional service, what is to be done and what is not to be done must be decided by the injunctions of the *Vedas*. One should act accordingly, without argument. That is called following the principles of *śāstra*, or scriptures. *Śāstra* is free from the four principal defects visible in the conditioned soul: imperfect senses, the propensity for cheating, certainty of committing mistakes, and certainty of being illusioned. These four principal defects in conditioned life disqualify one from putting forth rules and regulations. Therefore, the rules and regulations as described in the *śāstra*—being above these defects—are accepted without alteration by all great saints, *ācāryas* and great souls.

In India especially there are many parties of spiritual understanding, generally classified as two: the impersonalist and the personalist. Both of them, however, lead their lives according to the principles of the *Vedas*. Without following the principles of the scriptures, one cannot elevate himself to the perfectional stage.

In human society, aversion to the principles of understanding the Supreme Personality of Godhead is the cause of all falldowns. That is the greatest offense of human life. Therefore, *māyā*, the material energy of the Supreme Personality of Godhead, is always giving us trouble in the shape of the threefold miseries. This material energy is constituted of the three modes of material nature. One has to raise himself at least to the mode of goodness before the path to understanding the Supreme Lord can be open. Without raising oneself to the standard of the mode of goodness, one remains in ignorance and passion, which cause one to become gradually demoniac. Those in the modes of passion and ignorance deride the scriptures, deride the holy men, and deride the proper understanding of the Supreme Personality of Godhead. They disobey the instructions of the spiritual master, and they do not care for the regulations of the scriptures. In spite of hearing the glories of devotional service, they are not attracted to it, and therefore they manufacture their own way of elevation. These are some of the defects of human society that lead to the demoniac condition of life. If, however, one is able to be guided by a proper and bona fide spiritual master, who can lead one to the path of elevation to the highest stage, then his life becomes successful.

Thus end the Bhaktivedanta purports to the Sixteenth Chapter of the *Śrīmad Bhagavad-gītā* in the matter of the Divine and Demoniac Natures.

CHAPTER SEVENTEEN

The Divisions of Faith

1. Arjuna inquired: What is the situation of one who does not follow the principles of scripture but worships according to his own imagination? Is he in goodness, in passion or in ignorance?

PURPORT

In the Fourth Chapter, thirty-ninth verse, it is said that a person faithful to a particular type of worship gradually becomes elevated to the stage of knowledge and thus attains the highest perfection of peace and prosperity. In the Sixteenth Chapter, it was concluded that one who does not follow the principles laid down in the scriptures is called an *asura*, demon, and one who follows the scriptural injunctions faithfully is called a *deva*, or demigod. Now, if one follows with faith some rules not mentioned in the scriptural injunctions, what is his position?

2. The Supreme Personality of Godhead answered: According to the modes of nature acquired by the embodied soul, there are three kinds of faith—faith in goodness, in passion, and in ignorance.

3. According to one's existence under the various modes of nature, one evolves a particular kind of faith. The living being is said to be of a particular faith according to the modes he has acquired.

PURPORT

Everyone has a particular type of faith, regardless of what he is. But his faith is considered good, passionate or ignorant according to the nature he has acquired. Therefore, according to his particular type of faith, he associates with certain persons. Now the real fact is that every living being, as stated in the Fifteenth Chapter, is originally the fragmental part and parcel of the Supreme Lord. Therefore, he is originally transcendental to all the modes of material nature. But when he forgets his relationship with the Supreme Personality of Godhead and comes into contact with this material nature in conditional life, he generates his own position by association with the different varieties of material nature. The resultant artificial faith and existence are only material. Although one may be conducted by some impression or conception of life, originally he is *nirguṇa,* or transcendental. Therefore, one has to become cleansed of the material contamination that he has acquired in order to get back his relationship with the Supreme Lord. That is the only path without fear: Kṛṣṇa consciousness. If one is situated in Kṛṣṇa consciousness, then his elevation to the perfectional stage is guaranteed.

4. Men in the mode of goodness worship the demigods, those in the mode of passion worship the demons, and those in the mode of darkness worship the dead and ghosts.

PURPORT

In this verse the Supreme Personality of Godhead is describing different kinds of worshipers according to their external activities. According to scriptural injunction, only the Supreme Personality of Godhead is worshipable, but those who are not very conversant with, or faithful to, the scriptural injunctions worship different objects, according to their specific situations in the modes of material nature. Those who are in goodness generally worship the demigods. The demigods include Brahmā and Śiva, and others such as Indra, Candra, and the sun-god. There are various demigods. Those in goodness may worship a particular demigod for a particular purpose. Similarly, those who are in the mode of passion worship the demons. We remember that in the Second World War, a man in Calcutta was worshiping Hitler because thanks to that war he had amassed a large amount of wealth by dealing in the black market. Similarly, those in the modes of passion and ignorance generally select an ordinary man to be God. They think that anyone can be worshiped as God and that the same results will be obtained.

Now, it is clearly stated here that those who are in the mode of passion worship and create such gods, and those who are in the mode of ignorance, in darkness, worship dead spirits. Sometimes we find that people worship at the tomb of a dead man. Sexual service is also calculated to be in the mode of darkness. Similarly, in remote villages in India there are worshipers of ghosts. We have seen in India that the lower-class people sometimes go to the forest when they have knowledge that a ghost lives in some tree, and they worship that tree and offer sacrifices. These different kinds of worship are not actually God worship. God worship is for persons who are transcendentally situated in pure goodness. In the *Śrīmad-Bhāgavatam* it is said that when one is on the plane of purified goodness, one worships Vāsudeva, Kṛṣṇa.

The impersonalists are supposed to be situated in the mode of goodness, and they worship five kinds of demigods. They worship the impersonal Viṣṇu, the Viṣṇu form in the material world, which is known as philosophized Viṣṇu. Viṣṇu is the expansion of the Supreme Personality of Godhead, but the impersonalists, because they do not ultimately believe in the Supreme Person, imagine that the Viṣṇu form is another aspect of the impersonal Brahman; similarly, they imagine that Brahmā is the impersonal form, in the material nature, of passion. Thus they sometimes describe five kinds of gods worshipable at the start, but because they think that the actual truth is impersonal Brahman, they dispose of all worshipable objects at the ultimate end. However, the different qualities of the material modes of nature can be purified through the association of persons who are in the modes of transcendental nature.

5. There are those who undergo severe penances and austerities not mentioned in the scriptural injunctions; this they do out of pride, egoism, lust and attachment because they are impelled by passion.

6. Those who parch the material elements of this body, and the Supersoul within it, are to be known as demons.

7. There are differences in eating, in forms of sacrifice and in austerity and charity as well, according to the three modes of material nature. Now hear of these.

8. Foods in the mode of goodness increase the duration of life, purify existence, give strength, and increase health, happiness and satisfaction. Such foods are juicy and fatty. They are very conducive to the healthy condition of the body.

9. Food that is too bitter, too sour, too salty, too pungent, too dry or too hot causes distress, misery and disease. Such food is very dear to those in the mode of passion.

10. Foods prepared more than three hours before being eaten, which are tasteless, juiceless and decomposed, which have a bad smell, and which consist of remnants and untouchable things are very dear to those in the mode of darkness.

PURPORT

The purpose of food is to increase the duration of life, purify the mind and aid bodily strength. This is its only purpose. In the past, great authorities selected those foods that best aid health and increase life's duration, such as milk products, sugar, rice, wheat, fruits and vegetables. These foods are very dear to those in the mode of goodness. Some other foods, such as baked corn and molasses, while not very palatable in themselves, can be made pleasant when mixed with milk or other foods. They are then in the mode of goodness. All these foods are pure by nature. They are quite distinct from untouchable things like meat and liquor. Fatty food, as mentioned in the eighth verse, has no connection with animal fat obtained by slaughter. Animal fat is available in the form of milk, which is the most wonderful of all foods. Milk, butter, cheese and similar products give animal fat in a form that rules out any need for the killing of innocent creatures. It is only through brute mentality that this killing goes on. The civilized method of obtaining needed fat is by milk. Slaughter is the way of subhumans. Protein is amply available through peanuts, split peas, dahl, whole wheat and so on.

Foods in the mode of passion, which are bitter, too salty or too hot, cause misery by producing mucus in the stomach, leading to disease. Foods in the mode of darkness are essentially those that are not fresh. Any food cooked more than three hours before it is to be eaten (except *prasāda*, food offered to the Lord) is considered to be in the mode of darkness. Because they are decomposing, foods in the mode of darkness frequently emanate a bad smell, which often attracts people in these modes but repulses those in the mode of goodness.

Remnants of food may be eaten only when they are part of a meal that was first offered to the Supreme Lord or first eaten by saintly persons, especially the spiritual master.

11. The performance of sacrifice in terms of the directions of the scriptures, as a matter of duty and with no desire for material results, is said to be in the mode of goodness.

12. Any sacrifice performed with pride and for some material benefit, O chief of the Bhāratas, should be known to be in the mode of passion.

13. Any sacrifice performed without direction from scriptural injunctions, without Vedic hymns, without priestly remuneration and without faith must be considered to be in the mode of darkness.

14. Austerity of the body consists of offering worship to the Supreme Lord, to *brāhmaṇas*, to the spiritual master and to superiors like the father and mother. Cleanliness, simplicity, celibacy and nonviolence are also austerities of the body.

15. Austerity in relation to the tongue consists of saying what is dear and truthful, not agitating others, and engaging in the study of the *Vedas*.

PURPORT

One should not speak in such a way as to cause agitation in the minds of others. Of course, when a teacher speaks, he can speak the truth for the instruction of his students, but even such a teacher should not speak to others who are not his students if he will agitate their minds. This is the practice of penance as far as talking is concerned. Besides that, one should not talk nonsense. The process of speaking in spiritual circles is to say something which is upheld by the scriptures. One should at once quote from the scriptural authority to back up what he is saying. At the same time, such talk should be very pleasurable to the ear. By such discussions, one may derive the highest benefit and elevate human society. There is a limitless stock of Vedic literature, and one should study this. That is called penance pertaining to the utilization of the voice.

16. Austerity in relation to the mind consists of satisfaction, simplicity, gravity, purity and control.

PURPORT

To make the mind austere is to detach it from sense gratification. It should be so trained that it can be always thinking of doing good for others. The best training for the mind is gravity of thought. One should not deviate from Kṛṣṇa consciousness and must always deviate from sense gratification. To transform one's nature into purity is to become Kṛṣṇa conscious. Satisfaction of the mind can be obtained only by taking the mind away from thoughts of sense enjoyment. The more we think of sense enjoyment, the more we lose the satisfaction of the mind. In the present age we unnecessarily engage the mind in so many different ways for sense gratification, and so there is no possibility of the mind's being satisfied. The best course is to divert the mind to the Vedic literature. The Vedic literature is full of satisfying stories, as in the *Purāṇas* and *Mahābhārata*. One can take advantage of this knowledge and thus become purified. The mind should be devoid of duplicity and should think of the welfare of all. Silence means that one is always thinking of self-realization. The person in Kṛṣṇa consciousness is to be understood as observing perfect silence in this sense. All these qualities together constitute austerity in mental activities.

17. The penance a man performs without expectation of material benefit and only for the sake of the Supreme is called penance in goodness.

18. Penance performed out of pride and to gain respect, honor and worship is in the mode of passion. It is neither stable nor permanent.

19. Penance performed out of foolishness, with self-torture or through the frustration of others, is said to be in the mode of darkness.

20. Charity given to a worthy person, in the proper place and time and as a matter of duty, without consideration of the benefit one might derive for oneself, is said to be in the mode of goodness.

21. But charity performed with the expectation of some return, with a desire for fruitive results, or in a grudging mood, is said to be charity in the mode of passion.

PURPORT

Charity is sometimes performed for elevation to the heavenly kingdom and sometimes with great trouble and with repentance afterward—"Why have I spent so much in this way?" Or charity is sometimes made under some obligation, under the request of a superior. These kinds of charity are said to be made in the mode of passion. There are many charitable foundations which offer their gifts to institutions where sense gratification goes on. Such charities are not recommended in the Vedic scripture. Only charity in the mode of goodness is recommended.

22. Charity given in an unpurified place, at an unpurified time, to unsuitable persons, without proper attention and without respect is said to be in the mode of darkness.

PURPORT

Contributions for indulgence in intoxication and gambling are not encouraged here. That sort of contribution is in the mode of ignorance. Such charity is not beneficial; rather, it encourages sinful persons. Similarly, if a person gives charity to a suitable person without respect and without attention, that sort of charity is also said to be in the mode of darkness.

23. From the beginning of the creation, the three words *oṁ tat sat* were used to indicate the Supreme Absolute Truth. Therefore, these three symbolic representations were used by *brāhmaṇas* while chanting the hymns of the *Vedas* and during sacrifices for the satisfaction of the Supreme.

PURPORT

Now it has been explained that penance, sacrifice, charity and eating are divided into three categories: the modes of goodness, passion and ignorance. But whether first class, second class, or third class, all of them are conditioned, contaminated by the material nature. When they are aimed at the Supreme—*oṁ tat sat,* or the Supreme Personality of Godhead, the eternal—such performances of charity and sacrifice become means for spiritual elevation. In the scriptural injunctions, such an objective is indicated. These three words, *oṁ tat sat,* particularly indicate the Absolute Truth, the Supreme Personality of Godhead. In the Vedic hymns, the word *om* is always found, and anyone who acts without the regulation of the scripture will not be aimed at the Absolute Truth. He will get some temporary result, but not the ultimate end of life. Therefore, the conclusion is that the performance of charity, sacrifice and penance must be done in the mode of goodness. Performed in the mode of passion or ignorance, they are certainly inferior in quality.

24. Thus the transcendentalists undertake sacrifices, charities and penances, beginning always with *om,* to attain the Supreme.

25. One should perform sacrifice, penance and charity with the word *tat.* The purpose of such transcendental activities is to get free from material entanglement.

26-27. The Absolute Truth, the objective of devotional sacrifice, is indicated by the word *sat.* These works of sacrifice, of penance and of charity, true to the absolute nature, are meant to please the Supreme Person, O son of Pṛthā.

28. Sacrifices, charities and penances performed without faith in the Supreme are nonpermanent. O son of Pṛthā, they are useless both in this life and in the next.

PURPORT

Anything done without a transcendental objective—whether it be sacrifice, charity or penance—is useless. Therefore in this verse it is declared that such activities are abominable. Everything should be done for the Supreme, in Kṛṣṇa consciousness. Without such faith and without proper guidance, there can never be any fruit. In all the Vedic scriptures, this faith in the Supreme is advised. In the pursuit of all Vedic instructions, the ultimate goal is to understand Kṛṣṇa. No one can obtain success without following this principle. Therefore, the best course is to work from the very beginning in Kṛṣṇa consciousness, under the guidance of a bona fide spiritual master. That is the way to make everything successful. In the conditional state, people are attracted to worshiping demigods, ghosts or Yakṣas like Kuvera. The mode of goodness is better than the modes of passion and ignorance, but one who takes directly to Kṛṣṇa consciousness is transcendental to all these three modes of material nature. Although there is a process of gradual elevation, if one, by the association of pure devotees, takes directly to Kṛṣṇa consciousness, that is the best way. That is recommended in this chapter. To achieve success in this way, one must first find the proper spiritual master and be trained under his direction. Then one can achieve faith in the Supreme. When that faith becomes mature, in course of time it is called love of God. This is the ultimate goal of the living entities. One should, therefore, take to Kṛṣṇa consciousness directly. That is the objective of this Seventeenth Chapter.

Thus end the Bhaktivedanta purports to the Seventeenth Chapter of the *Śrīmad Bhagavad-gītā* in the matter of the Divisions of Faith.

CHAPTER EIGHTEEN

Conclusion—
The Perfection of Renunciation

1. Arjuna said: O mighty-armed one, I wish to understand the purpose of renunciation and of the renounced order of life, O killer of the Keśī demon, master of the senses.

PURPORT

Practically speaking, the whole *Bhagavad-gītā* is finished in seventeen chapters. The Eighteenth Chapter is supplementary; it is meant to summarize the topics discussed before. In every chapter of the *Bhagavad-gītā*, it has been stressed that devotional service unto the Supreme Personality of Godhead is the ultimate goal of life. This same point will be summarized in the Eighteenth Chapter as the most confidential part of knowledge. In the first six chapters of the *Gītā*, stress was given to devotional service, for it was said that of all *yogīs* or transcendentalists, one who always thinks of Kṛṣṇa within himself is first class. In the next six chapters, pure devotional service and its nature and activity were variously discussed. In the third six chapters, knowledge, renunciation, the material nature and the transcendental nature, and devotional service were described.

Two words used in this verse to address the Supreme Lord—Hṛṣīkeśa and Keśiniṣūdana—are significant. Hṛṣīkeśa is Kṛṣṇa, the master of all senses, who can always help us to have equilibrium of the mind. Arjuna is expecting Him to summarize everything in such a way that he may remain equipoised. At the same time, he has some doubts, and doubts are always compared to demons. He therefore addresses Kṛṣṇa as Keśiniṣūdana. Keśī was a most formidable demon who was killed by the Lord. Therefore Arjuna is expecting Kṛṣṇa to kill the demon of doubt.

2. The Supreme Personality of Godhead said: To give up the results of all activities is called renunciation by the wise. And that state is called the renounced order of life by great learned men.

3. There are learned men who say that all kinds of fruitive activities should be given up, whereas other sages say that sacrifice, charity, and penance should never be given up.

4. O best of the Bhāratas, hear from Me now about renunciation. O tiger among men, there are three kinds of renunciation declared in the scriptures.

PURPORT

Although there are differences of opinion in the matter of renunciation, here the Supreme Personality of Godhead, Śrī Kṛṣṇa, gives His judgment, which should be taken as final. After all, the *Vedas* are different laws given by the Lord. Now, here, the Lord is personally present. His word should be taken as final.

5. Sacrifice, charity and penance are never to be given up; they must be performed by all intelligent men. They are purifying even for the great souls.

6. All these activities should be performed without any expectation of result. They should be performed as a matter of duty, O son of Pṛthā. That is My final opinion.

PURPORT

Although all sacrifices are purifying, one should not expect any result by such performances. In other words, all sacrifices meant for material advancement in life should be given up, but sacrifices that purify one's existence and elevate one to the spiritual plane should not be stopped. Everything that leads to Kṛṣṇa consciousness must be done. In the *Śrīmad-Bhāgavatam* it is said that any activity which leads to devotional service to the Lord should be accepted. That is the highest criterion of religion. A devotee of the Lord should accept any kind of work, sacrifice or charity that will help him in the discharge of devotional service to the Lord.

7. Prescribed duties should never be renounced. If, by illusion, one gives up his prescribed duties, such renunciation is said to be in the mode of ignorance.

8. Anyone who gives up prescribed duties as troublesome, or out of fear, is said to be in the mode of passion. Such action never leads to the elevation of renunciation.

PURPORT

One who is in Kṛṣṇa consciousness should not give up earning money out of fear that he is performing fruitive activities. If the money earned by his activity is engaged in Kṛṣṇa consciousness, or if by rising early in the morning his transcendental Kṛṣṇa consciousness is benefited, such activities should not be given up out of fear or because they are considered troublesome. Such renunciation is in the mode of passion. The result of passionate work is always miserable. Even if a person renounces work in that spirit, he never gets the result of renunciation.

9. O Arjuna, if one does everything as a matter of duty and gives up attachment to the result of his work, his renunciation is said to be in the mode of goodness.

PURPORT

Prescribed duties must be performed with this mentality. Everyone should act without attachment for the result and should not be associated with the modes of work. A man working in Kṛṣṇa consciousness in a factory does not associate himself with the work of the factory, nor with the workers of the factory. He simply works for Kṛṣṇa. And when he gives up the result for Kṛṣṇa, his renunciation is said to be transcendental, or in the mode of goodness.

10. Those who do not hate any inauspicious work, who are not attached to auspicious work and who are situated in the mode of goodness have no doubts about work.

11. It is not possible for an embodied soul to give up all activities. But he who renounces the results of activity is actually renounced.

12. One who does not give up the fruits of his work achieves three kinds of results after death: auspicious, inauspicious and mixed. But those who are in the renounced order of life have no such results to suffer or enjoy.

13. O mighty-armed one, according to Vedānta, there are five causes in the accomplishment of any kind of work. I shall now describe these to you.

14. The place of action, the doer, the senses, the endeavor and ultimately the Supersoul—these are the five factors of action.

PURPORT

The instruments of our work are our senses. By those senses we act, or the soul acts, in various ways, and for each and every action there is a different endeavor. But all one's activities depend on the Supersoul, who is seated within the heart as a friend. Under these circumstances, he who is acting in Kṛṣṇa consciousness, under the direction of the Supersoul situated within the heart, naturally is not bound by any activity he performs. Those in complete Kṛṣṇa consciousness have no responsibility for their actions. Everything is dependent on the supreme will, the Supersoul, the Supreme Personality of Godhead.

15. Whether a man acts with his body, mind or words, all his actions, right or wrong, are constituted of these five elements.

16. Therefore one who thinks himself the only doer, not considering the five factors, is certainly not very intelligent and cannot see things as they are.

PURPORT

A foolish person cannot understand that the Supersoul, sitting as a friend within him, is conducting his actions. Although the material causes are the place, the worker, the endeavor and the instruments, the final cause is the Supreme, the Personality of Godhead. Therefore, one should see not only these four material causes, but the supreme efficient cause as well. One who does not see the Supreme thinks of himself as supreme. He is not intelligent.

17. One who is not conducted by false ego and whose intelligence is not entangled, even though killing in this world, is not killing. Nor is he bound by his actions.

18. The stimuli to action are three: knowledge, the object of knowledge, and the knower. In the accomplishment of work, there are three factors—the senses, the work and the doer.

19. In terms of the modes of material nature, there are different kinds of knowledge, work and workers, which you may now hear of from Me.

PURPORT

In the Fourteenth Chapter of *Bhagavad-gītā,* the three divisions of the modes of material nature were described. In that chapter it was said that the mode of goodness is illuminating, the mode of passion materialistic, and the mode of darkness conducive to laziness and indolence. All the modes of material nature are binding; they are not sources of liberation. Even in the mode of goodness one is conditioned. In the Seventeenth Chapter, the different types of worship by different types of men in different modes of material nature were described. Now the Lord wishes to speak about the different types of knowledge, workers, and work itself, according to the material modes.

20. The knowledge of one who sees in every living entity one undivided spiritual nature, which is divided into innumerable forms, should be understood to be in the mode of goodness.

21. The knowledge by which one sees that in every different body there is a different type of living entity is knowledge in the mode of passion.

PURPORT

The concept that the material body is the living entity and that with the destruction of the body the consciousness is also destroyed is called knowledge in the mode of passion. According to that knowledge, bodies are different because of the development of different types of consciousness, otherwise there is no separate soul that manifests consciousness. The body is itself the soul, and there is no separate soul beyond this body. According to such knowledge, consciousness is temporary. Or else there are no individual souls, but there is one all-pervading soul, which is full of knowledge, and this body is a manifestation of temporary ignorance. Or beyond this body there is no special individual or Supreme Soul. All such ideas are products of the mode of passion.

22. That sort of knowledge which is attached to one kind of work as all in all, without knowledge of the truth, and which is very meager, is said to be in the mode of darkness.

PURPORT

The knowledge of the common man is always in the mode of darkness because every living entity in conditional life is born into the mode of darkness, without proper knowledge. Therefore, if one does not develop knowledge through the authorities or scriptural injunctions, his knowledge is focused upon the maintenance of the body. He has no concern about acting in terms of the directions of scripture. For him God is money, and knowledge means the satisfaction of the bodily demands. Such knowledge has no connection with the Absolute Truth. It is more or less like the knowledge of ordinary animals, which deals only with eating, sleeping, defending and mating. Such knowledge is described here as a product of the mode of darkness. In other words, knowledge concerning the spirit soul beyond this body is called knowledge in the mode of goodness, knowledge producing many theories and doctrines through mundane logic and mental speculation is the product of the mode of passion, and knowledge concerned only with keeping the body comfortable is said to be in the mode of ignorance.

23. Work which is regulated and which is performed without attachment, love or hatred and with no desire for fruitive results is said to be in the mode of goodness.

24. Work performed with a desire for its fruits, with great labor and under a false conception of the ego is said to be in the mode of passion.

25. Work performed in illusion, without consideration of future bondage and without dependence on scriptural injunctions, work which is violent and distressing to others, is said to be in the mode of ignorance.

26. The worker who performs his duty without association with the modes of material nature, without false ego, with great enthusiasm, and without wavering in success or failure is said to be in the mode of goodness.

27. The worker who is too attached to the work and to the result of the work, who wants to enjoy the result, who is always envious, unclean and subjected to joy and sorrow, is said to be in the mode of passion.

28. The worker who is always engaged in work against the injunction of the scriptures, who is materialistic, obstinate, cheating and expert in insulting others, who is lazy, always morose and procrastinating, is said to be in the mode of ignorance.

29. O winner of wealth, Arjuna, I shall now speak to you in detail about the differences in intelligence and determination according to the different modes of material nature. Please hear of this from Me.

30. O son of Pṛthā, that understanding by which one can recognize actions that should be done and actions that should not be done, what is fearful and what is not fearful, what is binding and what is liberating, is known to be in the mode of goodness.

31. O son of Pṛthā, that imperfect understanding which cannot distinguish between religion and irreligion and which therefore mistakes action to be done with action not to be done is said to be in the mode of passion.

32. The understanding which considers irreligion to be religion and religion to be irreligion, under the spell of illusion and darkness, striving always in the wrong direction, is said to be in the mode of ignorance.

33. O son of Pṛthā, that determination which is unbreakable, which is sustained with steadfastness by *yoga* practice, and which thus controls the mind, life, and the acts of the senses is in the mode of goodness.

34. Determination sustained only for the fruitive results in religion, economic development and sense gratification is in the mode of passion.

35. That determination which cannot go beyond dreaming, fearfulness, lamentation, moroseness and illusion—such unintelligent determination is in the mode of darkness.

36. O best of the Bhāratas, now please hear from Me about the three kinds of happiness which a conditioned soul enjoys, and by which he sometimes comes to the end of all distress.

PURPORT

A conditioned soul is engaged in enjoying material happiness again and again. Thus he is chewing what has already been chewed, but sometimes in the course of such enjoyment he becomes relieved from material entanglement by association with a great soul. In other words, a conditioned soul is always engaged in some type of sense gratification, but when he understands by good association that it is only a repetition of the same thing and awakens to his real Kṛṣṇa consciousness, he is sometimes relieved from the repetition of such so-called happiness.

37. That which in the beginning may be just like poison but at the end is like nectar, and which awakens one to self-realization, is said to be happiness in the mode of goodness.

PURPORT

In the pursuit of self-realization, one has to follow many rules and regulations to control the mind and the senses and to concentrate the mind on the self. All these procedures are very difficult, bitter like poison, but if one is successful in following those regulations and comes to the transcendental position, he enjoys life as though always drinking nectar.

38. Happiness derived from the contact of the senses with their objects appears like nectar in the beginning, but at the end it is just like poison. Such happiness is said to be in the mode of passion.

39. That happiness which in the beginning and the end is blind to the process of self-realization and is based on sleep, laziness and illusion is said to be in the mode of darkness.

40. There is nothing existing, either here or among the demigods in the higher planetary systems, which is free from the three modes of material nature.

41. *Brāhmaṇas*, *kṣatriyas*, *vaiśyas* and *śūdras* are distinguished by their qualities of work, O chastiser of the enemy, in accordance with the modes of nature.

42. Peacefulness, self-control, austerity, purity, tolerance, honesty, wisdom, knowledge and religiousness—these are the qualities by which the *brāhmaṇas* work.

43. Heroism, power, determination, resourcefulness, courage in battle, generosity and leadership are the qualities of work for the *kṣatriyas*.

44. Farming, cow protection and business are the qualities of work for the *vaiśyas,* and for the *śūdras* there is labor and service to others.

45. By following his qualities of work, every man can become perfect. Now please hear from Me how this can be done.

46. By worship of the Lord, who is the source of all beings and who is all-pervading, a man can become perfect while doing his work.

PURPORT

Everyone should think that he is engaged in a particular type of occupation by Hṛṣīkeśa, the master of the senses. And by the result of the work in which one is engaged, the Supreme Personality of Godhead, Śrī Kṛṣṇa, should be worshiped. If one thinks always in this way, in full Kṛṣṇa consciousness, then by the grace of the Lord he becomes fully aware of everything.

47. It is better to be engaged in one's own occupation, even if one performs it imperfectly, than to accept another's occupation and perform it perfectly. Prescribed duties, according to one's nature, are never affected by sinful reactions.

PURPORT

One's own occupational duty means the prescribed duties mentioned in *Bhagavad-gītā,* as we have already discussed in the previous verses. The duties of a *brāhmaṇa, kṣatriya, vaiśya* and *śūdra* are prescribed according to the particular modes of nature. One should not imitate another's duty. A man who is by nature attracted to the work done by *śūdras* should not artificially claim to be a *brāhmaṇa,* although he may be born into a *brāhmaṇa* family. In this way one should work according to his own nature; no such work is abominable, if performed for the purpose of serving the Supreme Lord. The occupational duty of a *brāhmaṇa* is certainly in the mode of goodness, but if a person is not by nature in the mode of goodness, he should not imitate the occupational duty of a *brāhmaṇa.* In the occupational duty of a *kṣatriya,* or administrator, there are so many abominable things; a *kṣatriya* has to be violent to kill his enemies or apprehend culprits, and sometimes a *kṣatriya* has to tell lies for the sake of diplomacy. Such violence and diplomacy accompany political affairs. But a *kṣatriya* is not supposed to give up his occupational duty and try to perform the duties of a *brāhmaṇa.*

One should act to satisfy the Supreme Lord. For example, Arjuna was a *kṣatriya.* He was hesitating to fight the other party. But if such fighting is performed for the sake of Kṛṣṇa, the Supreme Personality of Godhead, there need be no fear of degradation. In the business field also, sometimes a merchant has to tell so many lies to make a profit. If he does not do so, there can be no profit. Sometimes a merchant promises, "Oh, my dear customer, for you I am making no profit," but one should know that without profit the merchant cannot exist. Therefore it should be taken as a simple lie if a merchant says that he is not making a profit. But the merchant should not think that because he is engaged in an occupation where the telling of lies is compulsory, he should give up his profession and pursue the profession of a *brāhmaṇa.* That is not recommended.

Whether one is a *kṣatriya,* a *vaiśya* or a *śūdra* doesn't matter, if he serves, by the result of his work, the Supreme Personality of Godhead. Even *brāhmaṇas,* who perform different types of sacrifice, also sometimes kill animals because sometimes animals are sacrificed in such ceremonies. Similarly, if a *kṣatriya* engaged in his own occupation kills an enemy, there is no fault on his part. In the Third Chapter these points have been clearly and elaborately explained; every man should work for the purpose of *yajña,* or for Viṣṇu, the Supreme Personality of Godhead. Anything done for personal sense gratification is a cause of bondage. The conclusion is that everyone should be engaged according to the particular modes of nature he has acquired, and he should decide to work only for the sake of serving the supreme cause of the Supreme Lord.

48. Every endeavor is covered with some sort of fault, just as fire is covered by smoke. Therefore one should not give up the work which is born of his nature, O son of Kuntī, even if such work is full of fault.

49. One can obtain the result of renunciation simply by self-control and by becoming unattached to material things and disregarding material enjoyments. That is the highest perfectional stage of renunciation.

PURPORT

Real renunciation means that one should always think that since he is part and parcel of the Supreme Lord, he has no right to enjoy the results of his work. Because he is part and parcel of the Supreme Lord, the results of his work must be enjoyed by the Supreme Lord. This is actually Kṛṣṇa consciousness. The person acting in Kṛṣṇa consciousness is really a *sannyāsī,* one in the renounced order of life.

50. O son of Kuntī, learn from Me how one can attain to the supreme perfectional stage, Brahman, by acting in the way I shall now summarize.

51-53. Being purified by his intelligence and controlling the mind with determination, giving up the objects of sense gratification, being freed from attachment and hatred, one who lives in a secluded place, who eats a small quantity of food, who controls the body and the speaking power, who is always in trance, detached and free from false ego, false strength, false pride, lust, anger and acceptance of material things—such a person is certainly elevated to the position of self-realization.

54. One who is thus transcendentally situated at once realizes the Supreme Brahman and becomes fully joyful. He never laments nor desires to have anything; he is equally disposed toward every living entity. In that state he achieves pure devotional service unto Me.

PURPORT

To the impersonalist, achieving the *brahma-bhūta* stage, becoming one with the Absolute, is the last word. But for the personalist, or pure devotee, one has to go still further and become engaged in pure devotional service. This means that one who is engaged in pure devotional service to the Supreme Lord is already in the state of liberation called *brahma-bhūta,* oneness with the Absolute. Without being one with the Supreme, the Absolute, one cannot render service to Him. In the absolute conception of life there is no difference between the served and the servitor; but the distinction is there, in a higher spiritual sense. In the material concept of life, when working for sense gratification, one perceives misery, but in the absolute world, when one is engaged in pure devotional service, there is no such thing as trouble. Therefore, the devotee in Kṛṣṇa consciousness has nothing to lament over and nothing to desire. Since God, the Supreme Lord, is full, a living entity who is engaged in God's service, in Kṛṣṇa consciousness, becomes full in himself.

55. One can understand the Supreme Personality as He is only by devotional service. And when one is in full consciousness of the Supreme Lord by such devotion, he can enter into the kingdom of God.

PURPORT

The Supreme Personality of Godhead, Kṛṣṇa, or His plenary portions, cannot be understood by mental speculation nor by nondevotees. If one wants to understand the Supreme Personality of Godhead, he has to take to pure devotional service under the guidance of a pure devotee. Otherwise, the truth of the Supreme Personality of Godhead will always be hidden from him. Neither erudite scholarship nor mental speculation can reveal the Supreme Lord. Only one who is actually engaged in Kṛṣṇa consciousness and devotional service can understand what Kṛṣṇa is. University degrees are not helpful. One who is fully conversant with the science of Kṛṣṇa becomes eligible to enter into the spiritual kingdom, the abode of Kṛṣṇa. Becoming Brahman does not mean that one loses his identity. Devotional service is there, and as long as devotional service exists, there must be God, the devotee and the process of devotional service. Such knowledge is never vanquished, even after liberation.

56. Though engaged in all kinds of activities, the pure devotee, by My mercy, reaches the spiritual kingdom in the end, without pain.

57. Just depend upon Me for the results of all activities, and work always under My protection. In such devotional service, be fully conscious of Me.

PURPORT

That one should act in Kṛṣṇa consciousness means that he should not act as the master of the world. Just like a servant, one should act fully under the direction of the Supreme Lord. A servant has no individual independence. He acts only on the order of the master. A servant acting on behalf of the supreme master has no affection for profit and loss. He simply discharges his duty faithfully, in terms of the order of the Lord. Now, one may argue that Arjuna was acting under the personal direction of Kṛṣṇa, but when Kṛṣṇa is not present, how should one act? If one acts according to the direction of Kṛṣṇa in this book, as well as under the guidance of the representative of Kṛṣṇa, then the result will be the same. The Sanskrit word *mat-paraḥ* is very important in this verse. It means that one has no goal in life save and except to act in Kṛṣṇa consciousness, just to satisfy Kṛṣṇa. And while acting in such a way, one should think of Kṛṣṇa only: "I have been appointed to discharge this particular duty by Kṛṣṇa." While acting in such a way, one naturally has to think of Kṛṣṇa. This is perfect Kṛṣṇa consciousness. One should note, however, that after doing something whimsically, one should not offer the result to the Supreme Lord. That sort of duty is not in the devotional service of Kṛṣṇa consciousness. One should act according to the order of Kṛṣṇa. This is a very important point. That order of Kṛṣṇa comes through disciplic succession from the bona fide spiritual master. Therefore, the spiritual master's order should be taken as the prime duty of life. If one gets a bona fide spiritual master and acts according to his direction, his perfection of life in Kṛṣṇa consciousness is guaranteed.

58. One who becomes conscious of Me passes over all the obstacles of conditional life. However, if one does not work in such consciousness but acts through false ego, not hearing Me, he is lost.

PURPORT

A person in full Kṛṣṇa consciousness has no anxieties in executing the duties of his existence. The foolish cannot understand this great freedom from anxiety. For one who acts in Kṛṣṇa consciousness, Lord Kṛṣṇa becomes the most intimate friend. He always looks after his friend's comfort, and He gives Himself to His friend, who is so devotedly engaged, working twenty-four hours a day to please the Lord. Therefore, no one should be carried away by the false ego of the bodily concept of life. One should not falsely think himself independent of the laws of material nature or free to act. He is already under the strict material laws. But as soon as he acts in Kṛṣṇa consciousness, he is liberated, free from the material perplexities. One should note very carefully that anyone who is not active in Kṛṣṇa consciousness is losing himself in the material whirlpool, in the ocean of birth and death. No conditioned soul actually knows what is to be done and what is not to be done, but a person who acts in Kṛṣṇa consciousness is free to act because everything is prompted by Kṛṣṇa from within and confirmed by the spiritual master.

59. If you do not act according to My direction and do not fight, then you will be falsely directed. By your nature, you will have to be engaged in warfare.

PURPORT

Arjuna was a military man, born with the nature of a *kṣatriya.* Therefore his natural duty was to fight. But because of false ego he was thinking that there would be a sinful reaction from killing his teacher, grandfather and friends. He was considering himself the master of the action, as if he was directing the good and bad results of such work. He forgot that the Supreme Personality of Godhead was present there, instructing him to fight. That is the forgetfulness of the conditioned soul. The Supreme Personality gives directions as to what is good and what is bad, and one simply has to act in Kṛṣṇa consciousness to attain the perfection of life. No one can ascertain his destiny as completely as the Supreme Lord can, and therefore the best thing to do is to take direction from the Supreme Lord and act. No one should neglect the order of the Supreme personality of Godhead or the order of the spiritual master, who is the representative of God. One should act unhesitatingly to execute the order of the Supreme Personality of Godhead. That will keep him safe under all circumstances.

60. Under illusion you are now declining to act according to My direction. But, compelled by your own nature, you will act all the same, O son of Kuntī.

PURPORT

If one refuses to act under the direction of the Supreme Lord, then he will be compelled to act by the modes in which he is situated. Everyone is under the spell of a particular combination of the modes of nature and is acting in that way. But one who voluntarily engages himself under the direction of the Supreme Lord becomes glorious.

61. The Supreme Lord is situated in everyone's heart, O Arjuna, and is directing the wanderings of all living entities, who are seated as on a machine, made of the material energy.

62. O scion of Bharata, surrender unto Him in all respects, and by His mercy you can have transcendental peace and attain the eternal abode.

63. Thus I have explained to you the most confidential of all knowledge. Deliberate on this fully and then do what you wish to do.

PURPORT

God does not interfere with the little independence of the living entity. In the *Bhagavad-gītā*, the Lord has explained in all respects how one can elevate his living condition. The best advice imparted to Arjuna is to surrender unto the Supersoul sitting in everyone's heart. By right discrimination, one should agree to act according to the order of the Supersoul. That will help one be situated constantly in Kṛṣṇa consciousness, the highest perfectional stage of human life. Arjuna is being directly ordered by the Personality of Godhead to fight. Therefore he has no alternative than to fight. To surrender to the Supreme Personality of Godhead is in the best interest of the living entities. It is not for the interest of the Supreme. Before surrendering, one is free to deliberate on this subject as far as intelligence goes; that is the best way to accept the instruction of the Supreme Person. Such instruction comes also through the spiritual master, the bona fide representative of Kṛṣṇa.

64. Because you are My very dear friend, I am speaking to you the most confidential part of knowledge. Hear this from Me, for it is for your benefit.

65. Always think of Me, become My devotee, worship Me, and offer your homage unto Me. Thus you will come to Me without fail. I promise you this because you are My very dear friend.

PURPORT

The most confidential part of knowledge is that one should become a pure devotee of Kṛṣṇa and always think of Him and act for Him. One should not become an official meditator. One's life should be so molded that one will always have the chance to think of Kṛṣṇa. One should always act in such a way that all his daily activities are in connection with Kṛṣṇa. He should arrange his life in such a way that throughout the twenty-four hours of the day he cannot but think of Kṛṣṇa. The Lord's promise is that anyone who is in such pure Kṛṣṇa consciousness will certainly go back to the abode of Kṛṣṇa, where he will be engaged in the association of Kṛṣṇa face to face. This most confidential part of knowledge is spoken to Arjuna because he is the dear friend of Kṛṣṇa. Everyone who follows the path of Arjuna can also become a dear friend to Kṛṣṇa and obtain the same perfection as Arjuna.

66. Give up all varieties of religion and just surrender unto Me. I shall protect you from all sinful reactions. Therefore you have nothing to fear.

PURPORT

It has been said that only one who has become free from all sinful reactions can take to the worship of Lord Kṛṣṇa. Therefore one may think that unless he is free from all sinful reactions he cannot take to the surrendering process. In answer to such doubts it is here said that even if one is not free from all sinful reactions, simply by the process of surrendering to Śrī Kṛṣṇa he automatically becomes free from them. There is no need of strenuous effort to free oneself from sinful reactions. One should unhesitatingly accept Kṛṣṇa as the supreme savior of all living entities. With faith and love, one should surrender unto Him. Devotional service to Kṛṣṇa in full consciousness is the most confidential part of knowledge. This is the essence of the whole study of the *Bhagavad-gītā*.

67. This confidential knowledge may not be explained to those who are not austere, or devoted, or engaged in devotional service, nor to one who is envious of Me.

68. For anyone who explains this supreme secret to the devotees, devotional service is guaranteed, and at the end he will come back to Me.

69. There is no servant in this world more dear to Me than he, nor will there ever be one more dear.

70. And I declare that he who studies this sacred conversation worships Me by his intelligence.

71. And one who listens with faith and without envy becomes free from sinful reactions and attains to the planets where the pious dwell.

PURPORT

In the sixty-seventh verse of this chapter, the Lord explicitly forbade the *Gītā's* being spoken to those who are envious of Him. In other words, the *Bhagavad-gītā* is for devotees only, but it so happens that sometimes a devotee of the Lord will hold open class, and in that class all the students are not expected to be devotees. Why do such persons hold open class? It is explained here that although everyone is not a devotee, still there are many men who are not envious of Kṛṣṇa. They have faith in Him as the Supreme Personality of Godhead, and if such persons hear from a bona fide devotee about the Lord, the result is that they become at once free from all sinful reactions and after that attain to the planetary systems where all righteous persons are situated.

72. O conqueror of wealth, Arjuna, have you heard this with your mind at perfect attention? And are your ignorance and illusion now dispelled?

73. Arjuna said: My dear Kṛṣṇa, O infallible one, my illusion is now gone. I have regained my memory by Your mercy, and now I am steady and free from doubt and am prepared to act according to Your instructions.

74. Sañjaya said: Thus have I heard the conversation of two great souls, Kṛṣṇa and Arjuna. And so wonderful is that message that my hair is standing on end.

75. By the mercy of Vyāsa, I have heard these most confidential talks directly from the master of all mysticism, Kṛṣṇa, who was speaking personally to Arjuna.

PURPORT

Vyāsa was the spiritual master of Sañjaya, and he admits that it was by his mercy that he could understand the Supreme Personality of Godhead.

This means that one has to understand Kṛṣṇa not directly but through the medium of the spiritual master. The spiritual master is the transparent medium, although it is true that the experience is still direct. This is the mystery of the disciplic succession. When the spiritual master is bona fide, then one can hear *Bhagavad-gītā* directly, as Arjuna heard it.

76. O King, in the repeated remembrance of that conversation between Kṛṣṇa and Arjuna I am taking pleasure, being thrilled at every moment.

PURPORT

The understanding of *Bhagavad-gītā* is so transcendental that anyone who becomes conversant with the topics of Arjuna and Kṛṣṇa becomes perfect in righteousness, and he cannot forget such talks. This is the transcendental position of spiritual life. In other words, one who hears the *Gītā* from the right source, directly from Kṛṣṇa, becomes fully Kṛṣṇa conscious. The result of his Kṛṣṇa consciousness is that he becomes enlightened more and more, and he enjoys life with a thrill, not only for some time but at every moment.

77. O King, as I remember the wonderful form of Lord Kṛṣṇa, I am struck with greater and greater wonder, and I rejoice again and again.

78. Wherever there is Kṛṣṇa, the master of all mystics, and wherever there is Arjuna, the supreme archer, there will also certainly be opulence, victory, extraordinary power, and morality. That is my opinion.

PURPORT

The *Bhagavad-gītā* began with the inquiry of King Dhṛtarāṣṭra. He was hopeful of the victory of his sons, assisted by great warriors like Bhīṣma, Droṇa and Karṇa. He was hopeful that the victory would be on his side. But after describing the scene in the battlefield, Sañjaya told the King, "You are thinking of victory, but my opinion is that where there is Kṛṣṇa and where there is Arjuna, there will also be everything auspicious." He directly confirmed that Dhṛtarāṣṭra could not expect victory for his side. Victory was sure for the side of Arjuna because Kṛṣṇa was there. Some may protest that Kṛṣṇa incited Arjuna to fight, which is immoral, but the reality is clearly stated: *Bhagavad-gītā* is the supreme instruction of morality. The instructions of *Bhagavad-gītā* constitute the supreme process of religion and the supreme process of morality. All other processes may be purifying and may lead to this process, but the last instruction of the *Gītā* is the last word of all morality and religion: surrender unto Kṛṣṇa. That is the verdict of the Eighteenth Chapter, the last chapter, of *Bhagavad-gītā.*

Thus end the Bhaktivedanta purports to the Eighteenth Chapter of the *Śrīmad Bhagavad-gītā* in the matter of its Conclusion and the Perfection of Renunciation.

The Author

His Divine Grace A. C. Bhaktivedanta Swami Prabhupāda appeared in this world in 1896 in Calcutta, India. He first met his spiritual master, Śrīla Bhaktisiddhānta Sarasvatī Gosvāmī, in Calcutta in 1922. Bhaktisiddhānta Sarasvatī, a prominent devotional scholar and the founder of sixty-four Gauḍīya Maṭhas (Vedic Institutes), liked this educated young man and convinced him to dedicate his life to teaching Vedic knowledge. Śrīla Prabhupāda became his student, and eleven years later (1933) at Allahabad he became his formally initiated disciple.

At their first meeting, in 1922, Śrīla Bhaktisiddhānta Sarasvatī Ṭhākura requested Śrīla Prabhupāda to broadcast Vedic knowledge through the English language. In the years that followed, Śrīla Prabhupāda wrote a commentary on the *Bhagavad-gītā,* assisted the Gauḍīya Maṭha in its work and, in 1944, without assistance, started an English fortnightly magazine, edited it, typed the manuscripts and checked the galley proofs. He even distributed the individual copies freely and struggled to maintain the publication. Once begun, the magazine never stopped; it is now being continued by his disciples in the West.

Recognizing Śrīla Prabhupāda's philosophical learning and devotion, the Gauḍīya Vaiṣṇava Society honored him in 1947 with the title "Bhaktivedanta." In 1950, at the age of fifty-four, Śrīla Prabhupāda retired from married life, and four years later he adopted the *vānaprastha* (retired) order to devote more time to his studies and writing. Śrīla Prabhupāda traveled to the holy city of Vṛndāvana, where he lived in very humble circumstances in the historic medieval temple of Rādhā-Dāmodara. There he engaged for several years in deep study and writing. He accepted the renounced order of life (*sannyāsa*) in 1959. At Rādhā-Dāmodara, Śrīla Prabhupāda began work on his life's masterpiece: a multivolume translation and commentary on the eighteen thousand verse *Śrīmad-Bhāgavatam* (*Bhāgavata Purāṇa*). He also wrote *Easy Journey to Other Planets.*

After publishing three volumes of *Bhāgavatam,* Śrīla Prabhupāda came to the United States, in 1965, to fulfill the mission of his spiritual master. Since that time, His Divine Grace has written over forty volumes of authoritative translations, commentaries and summary studies of the philosophical and religious classics of India.

In 1965, when he first arrived by freighter in New York City, Śrīla Prabhupāda was practically penniless. It was after almost a year of great difficulty that he established the International Society for Krishna Consciousness in July of 1966. Under his careful guidance, the Society has grown within a decade to a worldwide confederation of almost one hundred *āśramas*, schools, temples, institutes and farm communities.

In 1968, Śrīla Prabhupāda created New Vṛndāvana, an experimental Vedic community in the hills of West Virginia. Inspired by the success of New Vṛndāvana, now a thriving farm community of more than one thousand acres, his students have since founded several similar communities in the United States and abroad.

In 1972, His Divine Grace introduced the Vedic system of primary and secondary education in the West by founding the *Gurukula* school in Dallas, Texas. The school began with 3 children in 1972, and by the beginning of 1975 the enrollment had grown to 150.

Śrīla Prabhupāda has also inspired the construction of a large international center at Śrīdhāma Māyāpur in West Bengal, India, which is also the site for a planned Institute of Vedic Studies. A similar project is the magnificent Kṛṣṇa-Balarāma Temple and International Guest House in Vṛndāvana, India. These are centers where Westerners can live to gain firsthand experience of Vedic culture.

Śrīla Prabhupāda's most significant contribution, however, is his books. Highly respected by the academic community for their authoritativeness, depth and clarity, they are used as standard textbooks in numerous college courses. His writings have been translated into eleven languages. The Bhaktivedanta Book Trust, established in 1972 exclusively to publish the works of His Divine Grace, has thus become the world's largest publisher of books in the field of Indian religion and philosophy. Its latest project is the publishing of Śrīla Prabhupāda's most recent work: a seventeen-volume translation and commentary—completed by Śrīla Prabhupāda in only eighteen months—on the Bengali religious classic *Śrī Caitanya-caritāmṛta.*

In the past ten years, in spite of his advanced age, Śrīla Prabhupāda has circled the globe twelve times on lecture tours that have taken him to six continents. In spite of such a vigorous schedule, Śrīla Prabhupāda continues to write prolifically. His writings constitute a veritable library of Vedic philosophy, religion, literature and culture.

References

The statements of *Bhagavad-gītā As It Is* are all confirmed by standard Vedic authorities. The following authentic scriptures are quoted in this book on the pages listed.

Brahma-saṁhitā, 18, 50, 65, 70, 108, 111, 148, 152, 153, 154, 164, 170, 192

Bṛhan-nāradīya Purāṇa, 107

Caitanya-caritāmṛta (Kṛṣṇadāsa Kavirāja), xxii–xxiii

Garga Upaniṣad, 20, 153

Kaṭha Upaniṣad, 22, 208

Muṇḍaka Upaniṣad, 28

Nārada-pañcarātra, 112

Nirukti Dictionary, 34

Padma Purāṇa, 106

Śrīmad-Bhāgavatam, xiv, 15, 34, 46, 49, 55, 57, 74, 84, 89, 95, 118, 122, 125, 139, 141, 151, 160, 180, 187, 189, 226, 241, 247, 257

Sātvata-tantra, 124

Śvetāśvatara Upaniṣad, 22, 28

Vedānta-sūtra, xv, 98, 155, 242, 258

Viṣṇu Purāṇa, 25

Glossary

A

Ācārya—a spiritual master who teaches by example.
Acintya—inconceivable.
Acintya-bhedābheda-tattva—Lord Caitanya's doctrine of simultaneous oneness and difference of the Absolute Truth.
Advaita—nondual.
Ahaṁ brahmāsmi—realization that "I am not this body."
Ahiṁsā—nonviolence.
Ānanda—transcendental bliss.
Aṇu-ātmā—the minute spirit soul.
Arcanā—Deity worship.
Arcā-vigraha—the incarnation of the Lord in an apparently material form to facilitate personal service by the devotee.
Āryan—one whose life is based on spiritual values.
Āśrama—a spiritual order of life.
Aṣṭāṅga-yoga—(*aṣṭa*—eight; *aṅga*—parts) a mystic *yoga* system propounded by Patañjali.
Asura—a demon.
Ātmā—the self (the body, the soul, or the senses).
Avatāra—one who descends from the spiritual sky.

B

Bhagavān—(*bhaga*—opulence; *vān*—possessing) the Lord as the possessor of all opulences.
Bhakta—a devotee.
Bhakti—pure devotional service to Lord Kṛṣṇa.
Bhakti-yoga—the system of cultivation of *bhakti.*
Bhāva—the preliminary stage of love of God.
Brahma-bhūta—the state of complete freedom from material contamination.
Brahmacārī—a celibate student under the care of a bona fide spiritual master.
Brahma-jijñāsā—spiritual inquiry into one's real identity.

Brahmajyoti—(*brahma*—spiritual; *jyoti*—light) the impersonal effulgence emanating from the body of Kṛṣṇa.
Brahmaloka—the abode of Lord Brahmā, in the highest planetary system of the material universe.
Brahman—the all-pervading impersonal aspect of Kṛṣṇa.
Brāhmaṇa—the intelligent class of men, according to the system of social and spiritual orders.
Buddhi-yoga—(*buddhi*—intelligence; *yoga*—mystic elevation) devotional service.

D

Dharma—the essential quality of the living being to render service.
Dhīra—a sober man; one who has perfect material and spiritual knowledge.
Dvāpara-yuga—the third age of the cycle of a *mahā-yuga.*

G

Ganges—a sacred river that flows from the lotus feet of Lord Viṣṇu.
Gāyatrī—a transcendental vibration chanted by *brāhmaṇas.*
Godāsa—a servant of the senses.
Goloka Vṛndāvana—Kṛṣṇa's eternal abode in the spiritual sky.
Gosvāmī—one who controls the mind and senses.
Gṛhastha—one in the householder order of spiritual life.
Guṇa—a material quality or mode of nature.
Guru—a spiritual master.

I

Īśvara—a controller.

J

Jīva—the soul or atomic living entity.
Jñāna—theoretical knowledge.
Jñānī—one who is engaged in the cultivation of knowledge.

K

Kali-yuga—the age of quarrel; last age in the cycle of a *mahā-yuga.*
Kalpa—a day of Brahmā, (twelve hours), 4,320,000,000 earth years.
Karma—material action performed according to scriptural regulations.
Kīrtana—glorification of the Supreme Lord.
Kṛpaṇa—a miser.
Kṛṣṇaloka—Kṛṣṇa's eternal abode in the spiritual sky.
Kṣatriya—the administrative and protective occupation according to the system of four social and spiritual orders.

L

Līlā—pastime.

M

Mahā-mantra—the great chanting for deliverance: Hare Kṛṣṇa, Hare Kṛṣṇa, Kṛṣṇa Kṛṣṇa, Hare Hare/ Hare Rāma, Hare Rāma, Rāma Rāma, Hare Hare.
Mahātmā—a great soul, or devotee.
Mahat-tattva—the total material energy.
Māyā—(*mā*—not; *yā*—this) illusion; forgetfulness of one's relationship with Kṛṣṇa.
Māyāvādī—an impersonalist or voidist.
Mukti—liberation.
Muni—a sage or self-realized soul.

N

Nirvāṇa—the end of the process of materialistic life.

O

Oṁkāra—the impersonal sound representation of the Lord.
Oṁ tat sat—transcendental syllables chanted by *brāhmaṇas* during sacrifice.

P

Paramahaṁsa—the topmost class of devotees.
Paramātmā—the Supersoul or localized aspect of the Supreme Lord.
Paramparā—disciplic succession.
Prakṛti—(lit., that which is predominated), material nature.
Prasāda—food offered to Kṛṣṇa, the remnants of which are spiritual and can purify any living entity.
Prema—the highest perfectional stage of love of God.

R

Rasa—the mellow or relationship between the Lord and the living beings.

S

Sac-cid-ānanda-vigraha—Kṛṣṇa's form of eternity, knowledge and bliss.
Sādhu—a holy man, or devotee.
Samādhi—the state of trance when the mind is fixed on the Supreme.
Sanātana-dharma— the eternal religion of the living being, to render service to the Supreme Lord.
Sāṅkhya—analytical study of the body and the soul.
Saṅkīrtana—congregational chanting of the Lord's glories.
Sannyāsa—the renounced order of life.
Śāstra—revealed scripture.
Satya-yuga—the first of the four ages of a *mahā-yuga.*
Śravaṇa—the devotional process of hearing.
Śruti—scriptures received directly from God.
Śūdra—the laborer class of men according to the system of social and spiritual orders.
Surabhi—the cows in Kṛṣṇaloka, who supply unlimited milk.
Svāmī—one who can control his mind and senses.
Svarūpa—(*sva*—own; *rūpa*—form) the real form of the soul.

T

Tapasya—voluntary acceptance of some material inconvenience for progress in spiritual life.

Tattvavit—one who knows the complete Absolute Truth.
Tretā-yuga—the second age in the cycle of a *mahā-yuga.*

U

Upaniṣads—108 philosophical portions of the *Vedas.*

V

Vaikuṇṭha—(lit., without anxiety), the spiritual sky.
Vaiṣṇava—a devotee of the Supreme Lord Viṣṇu or Kṛṣṇa.
Vaiśya—the class of men engaged in business and farming according to the system of social and spiritual orders.
Vānaprastha—retired life.
Vikarma—work performed without the direction of the *Vedas.*

Y

Yajña—sacrifice.
Yoga—linking with the Supreme.

Personalities in Bhagavad-gītā As It Is

A

Acyuta—Kṛṣṇa, who is infallible.
Agni—the god of fire.
Arjuna—one of the five sons of Pāṇḍu; dearmost devotee and friend of Kṛṣṇa, and warrior-hero of *Gītā*.
Aśvatthāmā—son of Droṇācārya who killed five sons of Draupadī and threw the *brahmāstra*, attempting to kill Mahārāja Parīkṣit in the womb.

B

Bhīma—one of the five sons of Pāṇḍu.
Bhīṣma—a great devotee and senior family member of the Kuru dynasty.
Brahmā—the first created living being, chief among the demigods.

C

Caitanya Mahāprabhu—Kṛṣṇa Himself who appeared as an incarnation to propagate the *saṅkīrtana* movement.

D

Devakī—the mother of Lord Kṛṣṇa.
Devakī-nandana—Kṛṣṇa, the son of Devakī.
Dhṛṣṭadyumna—the son of Drupada who arranged the military phalanx of the Pāṇḍavas.
Dhṛtarāṣṭra—the blind father of the Kurus.
Draupadī—the daughter of King Drupada and wife of the Pāṇḍavas.
Droṇācārya—the commander in chief of the Kurus.
Drupada—a warrior for the Pāṇḍavas; father of Draupadī and Dhṛṣṭadyumna.
Duryodhana—the chief son of Dhṛtarāṣṭra.

G

Garbhodakaśāyī Viṣṇu—the Viṣṇu expansion of the Supreme Lord who enters into each universe.

Garuḍa—the gigantic bird carrier of Lord Viṣṇu.

Govinda—Kṛṣṇa, who gives pleasure to the senses and the cows.

H

Haridāsa Ṭhākura—a devotee of Lord Caitanya who was known as *nāmācārya* (teacher of chanting the holy name).

Hṛṣīkeśa—Kṛṣṇa, master of all senses.

I

Ikṣvāku—a son of Manu who received the science of *Bhagavad-gītā.*

Indra—the king of the heavenly planets.

J

Janaka—a self-realized king and father-in-law of Lord Rāmacandra.

K

Kaṁsa—Kṛṣṇa's uncle who was always trying to kill Him.

Kapila—an incarnation of Kṛṣṇa who appeared as the son of Devahūti and Kardama to propound the *Sāṅkhya* philosophy.

Kāraṇodakaśāyī Viṣṇu (Mahā-Viṣṇu)—the Viṣṇu expansion from whom all material universes emanate.

Karṇa—a son of Kuntī and half brother of Arjuna who fought against the Pāṇḍavas.

Kṛṣṇa—the original, two-armed form of the Supreme Lord, who is the origin of all expansions.

Kṣīrodakaśāyī Viṣṇu—the Viṣṇu expansion known as Supersoul who enters into the atoms and into the hearts of every living entity.

Kumāras—four young sons of Brahmā who became great authorities on devotional service.

Kuntī—*See:* Pṛthā.
Kurus—the one hundred sons of Dhṛtarāṣṭra.

L

Lakṣmī—the goddess of fortune.

M

Mādhava—Kṛṣṇa, the husband of the goddess of fortune.
Madhusūdana— Kṛṣṇa, the killer of the demon Madhu.
Mahā-Viṣṇu—*See:* Kāraṇodakaśāyī Viṣṇu.
Manu—the administrative demigod who is the father of mankind.
Mukunda—Kṛṣṇa, the giver of liberation.

N

Nakula—one of the five sons of Pāṇḍu and younger brother of Arjuna.
Nanda Mahārāja—Kṛṣṇa's foster father.
Nārada Muni—a great devotee who travels through space to preach the Lord's glories.
Nārāyaṇa—four-handed expansion of the Lord.
Nṛsiṁha—the half-man, half-lion incarnation of the Lord.

P

Pāñcajanya—the name of Kṛṣṇa's conchshell.
Pāṇḍavas—the five sons of King Pāṇḍu: Yudhiṣṭhira, Arjuna, Bhīma, Nakula and Sahadeva.
Pāṇḍu—Dhṛtarāṣṭra's younger brother who died at any early age; father of the five Pāṇḍavas.
Parāśara Muni—the father of Vyāsadeva.
Pārtha-sārathi—Kṛṣṇa, the charioteer of Arjuna.
Patañjali—a great authority on the *aṣṭāṅga-yoga* system and author of the *Yoga-sūtra.*
Pṛthā—the wife of Pāṇḍu, mother of the Pāṇḍavas and aunt of Lord Kṛṣṇa.

R

Rāmacandra—an incarnation of the Lord as a perfect *kṣatriya.*

Rāvaṇa—a powerful demon killed in battle by Rāmacandra.

Rūpa Gosvāmī—chief of the six great spiritual masters of Vṛndāvana who were authorized by Lord Caitanya to preach Kṛṣṇa consciousness philosophy.

S

Sahadeva—one of the five sons of Pāṇḍu and younger brother of Arjuna.

Sañjaya—the secretary of Dhṛtarāṣṭra.

Śaṅkarācārya—an incarnation of Lord Śiva who expounded impersonalism.

Sarasvatī—the goddess of learning.

Sītā—the wife of Lord Rāmacandra, an incarnation of Lakṣmī.

Śiva—the personality in charge of the mode of ignorance and the destruction of the material universe.

Śyāmasundara—Kṛṣṇa, in His original form, blackish and most beautiful.

T

Tulasī—a great devotee in the form of a plant, whose leaves are offered to the Lord's lotus feet.

V

Vasudeva—the father of Lord Kṛṣṇa.

Vāsudeva—Kṛṣṇa, the son of Vasudeva.

Vivasvān—the sun-god.

Vyāsadeva—incarnation of Viṣṇu who compiled the *Vedas, Purāṇas, Mahābhārata, Vedānta-sūtra,* etc.

Y

Yajñeśvara—Kṛṣṇa, Lord of sacrifice.

Yāmunācārya—a great spiritual master in the Śrī-sampradāya, a Vaiṣṇava disciplic succession.

Yaśodā—Kṛṣṇa's foster mother.
Yaśodā-nandana—Kṛṣṇa, the son of Yaśodā.
Yogeśvara—name of Kṛṣṇa meaning the master of all mystic power.
Yudhiṣṭhira Mahārāja—the eldest of the five sons of Pāṇḍu.

Sanskrit Pronunciation Guide

Vowels

अ a आ ā इ i ई ī उ u ऊ ū ऋ ṛ ॠ ṝ

ऌ ḷ ए e ऐ ai ओ o औ au

ं ṁ *(anusvāra)* ः ḥ *(visarga)*

Consonants

Gutturals:	क ka	ख kha	ग ga	घ gha	ङ ṅa
Palatals:	च ca	छ cha	ज ja	झ jha	ञ ña
Cerebrals:	ट ṭa	ठ ṭha	ड ḍa	ढ ḍha	ण ṇa
Dentals:	त ta	थ tha	द da	ध dha	न na
Labials:	प pa	फ pha	ब ba	भ bha	म ma
Semivowels:	य ya	र ra	ल la	व va	
Sibilants:	श śa	ष ṣa	स sa		
Aspirate:	ह ha	ऽ = ' *(avagraha)* - the apostrophe			

The vowels above should be pronounced as follows:

a – like the *a* in org*a*n or the *u* in b*u*t.
ā – like the *ā* in f*a*r but held twice as long as *a*.
i – like the *i* in p*i*n.
ī – like the *ī* in p*i*que but held twice as long as *i*.
u – like the *u* in p*u*sh.
ū – like the *ū* in r*u*le but held twice as long as *u*.

ṛ – like the *ri* in *Ri*ta (but more like French *ru*).
ṝ – same as *ṛi* but held twice as long.
ḷ – like *lree (lruu)*.
e – like the *e* in they.
ai – like the *ai* in *ai*sle.
o – like the *o* in g*o*.
au – like the *ow* in h*ow*.
ṁ *(anusvāra)* – a resonant nasal like the *n* in the French word *bon*.
ḥ *(visarga)* – a final *h*-sound: *aḥ* is pronounced like *aha; iḥ* like *ihi*.

The consonants are pronounced as follows:

k – as in *k*ite
kh – as in Ec*kh*art
g – as in *g*ive
gh – as in di*g-h*ard
ṅ – as in si*ng*
c – as in *ch*air
ch – as in staun*ch-h*eart
j – as in *j*oy
jh – as in he*dgeh*og
ñ – as in ca*ny*on
ṭ – as in *t*ub
ṭh – as in ligh*t-h*eart
ṇ – as r*n*a (prepare to say the *r* and say *na*).
ḍha- as in re*d-h*ot
ḍ – as in *d*ove

Cerebrals are pronounced with tongue to roof of mouth, but the following dentals are pronounced with tongue against teeth:

t – as in *t*ub but with tongue against teeth.
th – as in ligh*t-h*eart but tongue against teeth.
d – as in *d*ove but tongue against teeth.
dh – as in re*d-h*ot but with tongue against teeth.
n – as in *n*ut but with tongue in between teeth.
p – as in *p*ine
ph – as in u*p-h*ill (not *f*)
b – as in *b*ird
bh – as in ru*b-h*ard
m – as in *m*other
y – as in *y*es
r – as in *r*un
l – as in *l*ight
v – as in *v*ine.
s – as in *s*un
ś (palatal) – as in the *s* in the German word *sprechen*
ṣ (cerebral) – as the *sh* in *sh*ine
h – as in *h*ome

There is no strong accentuation of syllables in Sanskrit, only a flowing of short and long (twice as long as the short) syllables.

General Index

Numerals in bold type indicate references to the verses of *Bhagavad-gītā As It Is*. Numerals in regular type are references to its purports.

Absolute Truth
- anxiety due to lack of knowledge of, 95
- as objective of devotional service, **252**
- constituents of, xv
- impersonal conception of recommended to point of surrender, 203
- Kṛṣṇa as, 121, 161
- lies beyond man's reasoning powers, 168, 215
- *oṁ tat sat* used to indicate, **251**
- one in knowledge of doesn't engage in sense gratification, **56**
- realized in food, 208
- search for as constituent of knowledge, **209**
- three features of, 57, 141
- ultimate realization of, 225
- understood by surrendered soul, 190
- *See also:* Kṛṣṇa; Supreme Lord

Ācāryas
- *See:* Disciplic succession; Pure devotees; Spiritual master

Activities
- arise from *Vedas*, **50**
- body as field of, 205
- cease on attainment of *yoga*, **104**
- complete success required in material 33–34
- conditioned souls can't give up all, **258**
- constituents of field of, **208**
- determined by three modes, xvii
- everything as combination of knower of field and field of, **215**
- five factors of, **258–259**
- impersonalists maintain desire for, 73
- in knowledge advance one's knowledge, 90
- in mode of goodness lead to liberation, 235
- knowledge nullifies reactions to material, **84**
- Kṛṣṇa conscious person is not affected by sensual, 40
- leading to devotional service should be done, 257
- Lord engages in spiritual, 154
- material, as source of perplexity, 20
- meant to be dovetailed in devotional service, 57
- nature as cause of material, **214**
- not created by embodied spirit, **96**
- nothing beyond modes in all, **224**
- of empowered servants can't be imitated, 55
- of living entities during Brahmā's day, 147
- of Lord determine His names, 6
- one should depend on Kṛṣṇa in all, **267**
- one who understands Kṛṣṇa's is delivered, **69–71**
- only devotees can understand field of, **213**
- performed for satisfaction of Viṣṇu, 47–48, **199**
- purification of impious, 53
- purified by sacrifice, 49
- renunciation as giving up results of, **256**
- retirement from, 75
- soul thinks himself doer of, **56**
- taking birth according to one's past, 31, 220
- two divisions of spiritual, 86
- *See also:* Fruitive activities; *Karma*

Ādityas
- as devotees, 173
- Kṛṣṇa as Viṣṇu of the, **169**
- shown in universal form, **179**

Advaitam acyutam anādim ananta-rūpam
- quoted, 70

Affection
- Arjuna's family, 12
- *bhakti-yoga* severs knot of, 122
- family members as objects of, 212

Age of Kali
- *See:* Kali-yuga

Matter
as inferior to senses, **61**
attachment to Kṛṣṇa same as detachment from, 92
belongs to inferior nature, xii
consciousness not generated by, xiv
defined, 79
forgetfulness caused by influence of, 125
in mode of ignorance, xxii
spirit and, difference between, 25
Supersoul beyond darkness of, **213**
Māyā
as cause of suffering, 102
compared to cloud, 138
newborn child influenced by, 132
Māyādevī
Haridāsa allured by incarnation of, 39
Māyāvādīs
Lord doesn't support theory of, 23–24
studies of, 92–93
See also: Impersonalists
Meat-eating
as tendency of human society, 81
Meditation
as means of understanding Supersoul, **215**
as superior to knowledge, **201**
difficulty of impersonal, 196, 198
of Śiva broken by Pārvatī, 39
of transcendentalist, **107, 109**
on Supersoul, **111**–112
on void, 144
requirements for, 107
sincere street sweeping better than charlatan, 47
Memory
comes from Lord in heart, **232**
difference between Kṛṣṇa's and Arjuna's, **64–66**
sanctified by purification of existence, 49
Mental speculation
Absolute Truth not understood by, 168
answer to question of, 102
Kṛṣṇa not understood by, 164, **190**
muni engages in, 37
no progress in spiritual life by, **84**
philosophy without religion as, **45**
Mental speculation
Supreme Lord not understood by, 267
useless for Māyāvādīs, 93
Mercy
accepting material reaction as, 57
Arjuna regained his memory by Kṛṣṇa's, **272**
attaining God's, **40**
demons have little chance of getting Kṛṣṇa's, 241
dependence on Lord's, 73
Kṛṣṇa descends out of His, 164
Kṛṣṇa's appearance in original form as, 67–68
of Lord on pure devotee, **168**
peace achieved by Kṛṣṇa's, **270**
Meru Mountain
Kṛṣṇa as, **170**
Mind
as central point of *yoga,* 105
as constituent of field of activities, **208**
as friend or enemy, **105**
as higher than senses, **61**
as separated energy, **124**
as sitting place of lust, **61**
austerity in relation to, **250**
cleansing mirror of, 60
concentration of, on Kṛṣṇa, **121, 199**
conditioned souls struggle with, **230**
controlled due to pure consciousness, 93
devotee controls his, **266**
does not degrade one who sees Supersoul in all, **216**
equanimity of, **99**
equilibrium of, as constituent of knowledge, **209**
fixed in trance of self-realization, **37**
fixed on heart, **145**
fixed on senses, **40**
in *samādhi,* 79, **109**
Kṛṣṇa as nondifferent from His, 161
man of understanding acts with controlled, **77**
Manus born from Kṛṣṇa's, **166**
no peace without controlled, **40**
of Arjuna disturbed by universal form, **187**

Suffering
māyā as cause of, 102
one should inquire about, xi
Sughoṣa
blown by Nakula, **7**
Sun
as effulgence of Lord, 170
as eye of Lord, 153, **182**
Brahmā compared to, xv
controlled by *īśvara*, 55
death during passage of, **149**
effulgence of universal form compared to rising suns, **181**
eligibility for entering, 11
knowledge compared to, **98–99**
Kṛṣṇa as light of, **126**
Kṛṣṇa's appearance like rising, 67
living entity compared to, **216**–217
movement of, 153
not needed in eternal sky, xix, **229**
of lights Kṛṣṇa is, **169**
splendor of due to Kṛṣṇa, **231**
worship of, 136
Supersoul
Arjuna's mind understood by, 9
as controller, xiii
as friend in heart, 259
as infallible, 208
as one of five factors of action, **258**
as supreme proprietor, **214**
characteristics of, 213
dwells in heart of living being, **143**
exists everywhere, **212**
knows everything about all bodies, 206
Kṛṣṇa as source of, 18
Kṛṣṇa enters all things as, 176
Kṛṣṇa in everyone's heart as, xx, **135**, 136
Kṛṣṇa partially realized as, 73
meditation on, **111**–112
parched by demons, **247**
perceived by meditation, knowledge and nonfruitive work, **215**
reached by conqueror of mind, **106**
sinful action not impelled by, 60
transmigration made possible by, 28
See also: Paramātmā
Supreme Lord
as central figure in existence, xv
as controller of all living entities, 96
as predominator, 101
as seed-giving father, 220
association with, 82
as supreme proprietor of all bodies, 207
as soul of all souls, 58
attained by working without attachment, **52**–53
can't be covered by *māyā*, 138
can't be understood by nondevotees, 137
devotees, in love, may forget that Kṛṣṇa is, 180
doesn't have material senses, 213
forgotten when one is entangled with modes, 128
full in six opulences, 226
Gītā directly spoken by, 1
has no prescribed duties, **54**
hearing about, 151
how to think of, **144**
injunction of, as eternally true, 58
living entity never equals, 65–66
manifestations vanquished by, 184
materialist calculation of, 190
Nārada and Vyāsa accept Kṛṣṇa as, xi
not perceivable through gross senses, 152
one can't avoid service to, 117–118
one in ignorance doesn't accept Kṛṣṇa as, 71
Paramātmā and Brahman are within, 225
pious men approach, 206
prosperity of world depends upon, 51
religious principles as direct orders of, 68
remembering, at death, 142
responsible for living entities, 54
Śaṅkarācārya accepts Kṛṣṇa as, 123
transcendental to modes, **224**
Vedas manifested from breathing of, 50
See also: Absolute Truth; God; Kṛṣṇa
Supreme Personality of Godhead
See: Supreme Lord, *all entries*